The Way That Leads Among the Lost
Life, Death, and Hope in Mexico City's Anexos
Angela Garcia

A powerful journey into Mexico City's and California's anexos, the informal addiction treatment centers where mothers send their children to escape the violence of the drug war.

The Way That Leads Among the Lost reveals a hidden place where care and violence are impossible to separate: the anexos of Mexico City. The prizewinning anthropologist Angela Garcia takes us deep into the world of these small rooms, informal treatment centers for addiction and mental illness, that are spread across Mexico City's tenements and reach into the United States. For many Mexican families desperate to keep their loved ones safe, these rooms offer an alternative to what lies beyond them—the intensifying violence surrounding the drug war.

This is the first book ever written on the anexos. Garcia, who spent a decade conducting fieldwork in Mexico City, wrestles with the question of why mothers turn to them as a site of refuge even as they reproduce violence. Woven into these portraits is Garcia's own powerful story of family, homelessness, and drugs—a blend of ethnography and memoir converging on a set of fundamental questions about the many forms and meanings that violence, love, care, family, and hope may take. Infused with profound ethnographic richness and moral urgency, *The Way That Leads Among the Lost* is a stunning work of narrative nonfiction, a book that will leave a deep mark on readers.

Angela Garcia is a professor of anthropology at Stanford University. Her first book, *The Pastoral Clinic: Addiction and Dispossession Along the Rio Grande*, received the Victor Turner Prize in Ethnographic Writing and the PEN Center USA Exceptional First Book Award. She has worked as a baker, a hotel maid, a corset model, a dishwasher, a phone banker, a record store clerk, an HIV activist, and a waitress, among other jobs. Garcia was born in New Mexico and now lives in San Francisco, California, with her two children.

Farrar, Straus and Giroux | 4/30/2024
9780374605780 | $30.00 / $40.00 Can.
Hardcover with dust jacket | 272 pages
Recommended Reading, Index | Carton Qty:
20 | 9 in H | 6 in W

Brit., trans., 1st ser., audio: FSG
Dram.: Janklow & Nesbit Associates

THE WAY
THAT LEADS
AMONG
THE LOST

THE WAY
THAT LEADS
AMONG
THE LOST

LIFE, DEATH, AND HOPE IN
MEXICO CITY'S ANEXOS

ANGELA GARCIA

FARRAR, STRAUS AND GIROUX
NEW YORK

Farrar, Straus and Giroux
120 Broadway, New York 10271

Printed in the United States of America
First edition, 2024

Perm acks tk?

Library of Congress Cataloging-in-Publication Data
ISBN: 978-0-374-60578-0

Our books may be purchased in bulk for promotional, educational, or
business use. Please contact your local bookseller or the Macmillan Corporate
and Premium Sales Department at 1-800-221-7945, extension 5442, or by
email at MacmillanSpecialMarkets@macmillan.com.

www.fsgbooks.com
www.twitter.com/fsgbooks • www.facebook.com/fsgbooks

1 3 5 7 9 10 8 6 4 2

The names and identifying characteristics of some persons described in this
book have been changed, as have places and other details
of events depicted in the book.

For my mother

Vivos estamos. Los que no nos hemos ido. Vivos. Aquí.

—SARA URIBE, *Antígona González*

CONTENTS

PROLOGUE 3

1. SERENITY 7

2. THE LITTLE ROOM 44

3. HEAVEN 78

4. MOTHER OF SORROWS 109

5. THE LOWER DEPTHS 139

6. THE EXPERIENCE 170

7. THE GRAY ZONE 199

EPILOGUE 223

Recommended Reading 229

Acknowledgments 243

Index 245

THE WAY

THAT LEADS

AMONG

THE LOST

PROLOGUE

At six o'clock in the morning on July 19, 2014, Hortencia opened the door of the apartment she shared with her teenage son, Daniel. They lived on the second floor of a century-old tenement in Mexico City's historic center. The three-story building was composed of small two-room units that faced an open-air courtyard on the ground floor. Hortencia could hear her neighbors in the courtyard preparing food and setting up shop for another day's work.

Two men stood at the threshold of her door. She'd never seen them before and didn't know their names, but she knew they were the "servers" that she'd called to deliver Daniel to an *anexo*, an annex, the name for a clandestine, low-cost drug recovery center. Anexos are controversial for their illegality and use of violence, but for many Mexican mothers, they are the only way to ensure a child's safety from the danger that surrounds the narco war. The anexo Hortencia called upon had been recommended by a neighbor, a mother with a son very much like her own: aimless, worryingly depressed, using drugs and selling them, too. *Descontrolado*, out of control, was how Hortencia described Daniel to me. At her wit's end and afraid for his life, Hortencia took the number her neighbor gave her, and the pick-up was quickly arranged.

The men pushed past Hortencia and headed straight for Daniel, who was passed out on a recliner in front of the television. Hortencia closed the door and rushed to her son's side, unsure if she should help the men wrestle Daniel awake or protect him from them.

"They told me to get out of the way," she recalled as we sat together in her cramped but orderly home. It was just a few weeks after the house call. The harrowing story Hortencia told me would take years for me to fully understand. I asked very few questions and listened quietly while Hortencia spoke.

"I sat right here," she said, tapping the sofa that was also Daniel's bed. One of the servers had ordered her to turn up the volume on the television. Hortencia reenacted the scene, pointing the remote control to turn the television on. A talk show lit up the screen, brightening the room. She increased the volume to its maximum level, just as she was ordered to do that night. Dialogue blared indecipherably and filled the room with confusion. Hortencia turned off the TV and fixed her eyes on the empty recliner.

The servers worked in brusque, well-practiced movements. One yanked Daniel out of the chair and tossed him to the floor; the other kicked him. As she recalled that morning, Hortencia took deep breaths and swept aside the dark bangs that kept falling in front of her eyes, like curtains repeatedly opening and closing on a difficult scene. She described one of the men hovering inches from Daniel's face, spewing insults at him. "I could hear the terrible, terrible things he said. Even with the TV on I heard everything. The other one? He kicked and kicked my son."

Hortencia pleaded with the men to stop hurting Daniel, but they kept on. "I told them I made a mistake; I didn't ask for this. I told them to let go of Daniel and I'd still pay the fee." Unable to take it anymore, Hortencia leaped off the sofa and grabbed the arm of one of the men. He turned to her and told her to back off. *"You want this to work, señora? You want him to live? That's what he said."* Hortencia realized then that she had subjected Daniel and herself to a violence she could not undo.

Hortencia sat back down and forced herself to watch what happened next, "in case I needed to make a report." But she didn't know whom she would submit a report to. She knew of no trusted authorities or organizations that might help. Not the police—everyone knew they were corrupt and dangerous. In fact, the servers who were degrading and beating Daniel were the only ones she knew willing to help.

"There was nothing I could do but watch," Hortencia repeated. "In case I needed to make a report."

One of the servers pulled Daniel to his feet and secured him in a head-lock. The other zip-tied Daniel's hands behind his back, slipped a hood over his head, and dragged him out the front door. "It was boom, boom, boom. And then they were gone."

Hortencia led me outside to the porch she shared with her neighbors and acted out what she'd done that morning. We looked to the end of the outdoor corridor—the concrete building wall on one side, a wall of made of neighbors' hanging plants on the other. She'd watched the men drag Daniel past her neighbors' doors—some closed, some open—and disappear down the dark stairwell that connected the building's three levels. "I knew they'd have to cross the courtyard to get out," she said. She turned toward the plants hanging from the ceiling—ferns, petunias, long-trailing succulents—and showed me how she'd separated their tangled fronds to create a small window onto the courtyard. Daniel momentarily reappeared, bound, hooded, and stumbling. "My eyes followed him," Hortencia said. The servers pushed Daniel into the vestibule that led to the street. At that point, Hortencia could no longer see him.

We went back into the apartment and sat on the sofa.

"Did the neighbors in the courtyard see what was happening?"

"Of course."

"Did they respond in any way?"

She shook her head. "What could they do? They've seen this before. They knew what was happening."

We both fell quiet. A few moments passed before I asked Hortencia what she did after losing sight of her son.

"I came back inside. I sat right here. I cried for a while. And then I went to work."

| 1 |

SERENITY

I didn't go to Mexico to study the drug war. As an anthropologist, I had already spent years among families struggling with addiction problems in the United States. Families like my own. Mexico was my destination for vacations and roots trips, for sharpening Spanish language skills and for romantic rendezvous. It's where I took a culinary class to learn the art of making mole, and where I first encountered the erotic poetry of Sor Juana Inés de la Cruz. I celebrated my honeymoon there, at an all-inclusive eco-resort located on a secret cove near Puerto Vallarta, accessible only by boat.

I selected that resort because of its remoteness. I had wanted to start life afresh, on a landscape so different from the New Mexican desert where I was raised. At the resort, I spent my mornings journaling in a hammock, surrounded by nesting parrots. And in the afternoons, I lounged on a towel-covered recliner while my new husband, Benjamin, sat beside me on his. Mountains behind us, we faced the Pacific, our heads buried in books.

I read Malcolm Lowry's *Under the Volcano*, a 1947 novel set in a small Mexican town called Quauhnahuac, recognizable today as Cuernavaca, where Lowry lived during the disintegration of his first marriage. Two volcanic mountains—Popocatépetl and Itzaccíhuatl—frame Quauhnahuac and its ruinous landscape. The towering volcanoes convey a sense of doom. In a letter to his publisher, Lowry described them as "getting closer throughout . . . a symbol of the approaching war."

The entire novel unfolds over one day, November 2, 1939, the Day of the Dead, and follows the dissolution of British ex-consul Geoffrey Firmin. In the backdrop of the story is the rise of fascism in Europe, the Spanish Civil War, and the turbulence of post-revolution Mexico. In one scene, the consul voices a sense of resignation. "Read history," he says.

> Go back a thousand years. What is the use of interfering with its worthless stupid course? Like a *barranca*, a ravine, choked up with refuse, that winds through the ages, and peters out in a—What in God's name has all the heroic resistance put up by poor little defenceless peoples all rendered defenceless in the first place for some well-calculated and criminal reason [. . .] Countries, civilisations, empires, great hordes, perish for no reason at all, and their soul and meaning with them.

Despite his anguish, Lowry's consul longs for some sort of personal redemption. But at the end of the book, he meets a violent death, his body plunging to the bottom of the *barranca*, a pariah dog thrown in after him.

I read *Under the Volcano* while Benjamin read a first edition of D. H. Lawrence's *The Plumed Serpent*, the twisted plot of which is also set in a small Mexican town. We read each other passages—laughing at Lawrence's awful sex scenes, wowed by Lowry's lyricism. And at night we drunkenly fucked and fought and threatened divorce. Benjamin was afraid of the scorpions that dropped from the thatched roof of our cabana, I of drowning in the Pacific.

Under the Volcano made a lasting impression on me, not only because of Lowry's dizzying prose but also for his portrait of the Mexican landscape. The land itself reflects the cruelty and tragedy of the time in which the novel was written, and the characters' inner lives are presented in vivid detail. In one passage, the volcanoes, "clear and magnificent," are juxtaposed with "a thin blue scarf of illegal smoke, someone burning wood for carbon." A local cinema's flickering lights announce "*No se puede vivir sin amar.*" You can't live without loving.

Fourteen years after my honeymoon, and after the demise of my marriage, I bought a copy of *Bajo el volcán* at a street-corner kiosk in Mexico City. The merchant placed it in a thin pink plastic bag and handed it to me with a serious look. He called it the greatest work about Mexico—more honest than Paz, more beautiful than Pacheco; a story about war. He told me to read it with great care.

Mexico City sits in the center of a valley seven thousand feet above sea level and is surrounded by mountains and volcanoes. Every year, one of the volcanoes erupts with fire, smoke, and ash. Popocatépetl, *smoking mountain* in the Nahuatl language, is Mexico's largest active volcano and rises forty-five miles southeast of the capital. On clear days, El Popo can be seen from the city, and on days when it's active and the wind is blowing toward Mexico City, ash descends on buildings and streets. The base of the volcano and Mexico City's surrounding mountains have become clogged with poor towns, their neighborhoods crammed with self-built houses. The *pueblos* continually expand into these high-risk areas, where residents are vulnerable to natural disasters of all kinds—earthquakes, floods, volcanic eruptions. More recently, they have become vulnerable to unthinkable acts of criminal violence.

Two thousand years ago, the Xitle volcano erupted and molten lava poured into what is now Mexico City's valley. The eruption buried Cuicuilco, one of the oldest cities in Mesoamerica. The only major remnant of the settlement is its partially excavated pyramid, a massive circular ruin. The deep lava field that covered the ancient city is now known as El Pedregal de San Ángel. For centuries the Pedregal was called *malpaís*: the badland.

In 1942, the Pedregal was chosen as the site for Ciudad Universitaria, University City in English, home to the prestigious National Autonomous University of Mexico. University City was a massive urban project, a utopian vision of what Mexico could be. Designed by the architects Mario Pani and Enrique del Moral, the campus combined modern functionalism with pre-Hispanic urbanism and included the use of volcanic stone.

In its scale and ambition, the new home for the university crystallized the transformative political agenda of the time. With murals by David Alfaro Siqueiros and Juan O'Gorman, University City was meant to lead Mexico away from its repressive past and into a new, progressive future. According to project manager Carlos Lazo Barreiro, University City was "where the ultimate goals of the Revolution would be attained."

I went to Mexico City in 2011 with Benjamin and our four-year-old twin daughters to study the Pedregal and a massive development plan called *Ciudad Salud*, Health City, which would be built there. Mexico has some of the most persistent wealth and health inequalities in the world, and Health City was supposed to narrow these gaps. I never believed that Health City would solve these problems, but studying the project was a way for me to engage my longstanding interest in architecture and health, and to safeguard myself from the pain that accompanied studying addiction and the impact of the war on drugs in New Mexico.

I was born and raised in New Mexico and returned there as a graduate student to study its heroin epidemic, one of the worst in the United States. Most of my anthropological research there took place in a drug recovery clinic, where I worked alone during the graveyard shift, tending to the needs of detoxing patients. The clinic was a rehabbed adobe house that had been abandoned for years, and the people who were court-appointed to it were young and poor, many related to each other by bonds of blood and friendship. Drugs and the pain of caring for someone using them were not new to me. I grew up in a family that suffered from addiction problems. During my three years of research, several of the people I knew and cared for were incarcerated or had overdosed and died. I fell into a deep depression. By the time I finished my book, I was done with New Mexico, done with drugs, and done caring for people addicted to them.

Health City was my antidote to New Mexico. The high-tech development would be built on a lava-covered landscape near University City. And like University City, it promised to uphold ideals of progress and equality. The entire project was infused with optimistic ideas about architecture's capacity to improve people's health and lives. But the backdrop of the project wasn't just the volcanic landscape. It was Mexico's national disaster.

———

In December 2006, four years before the unveiling of Health City, Mexico's newly elected president Felipe Calderón declared "war" against drug cartels and deployed the military where intensive cartel activity was taking place. While the fight against drug traffickers and dealers was not an invention of the Calderón administration, it was Calderón who ushered in the military's current role in Mexican anti-crime strategy. With money, arms, and aid from the United States, his administration broadcast a message that military force would be used against leaders of drug trafficking organizations. The resulting violence was unprecedented. By the end of Calderón's six-year administration, there were more than 121,600 murders recorded by the National Institute of Statistics and Geography and 30,000 disappearances registered by the Secretariat of the Interior. Contrary to what the government repeatedly maintained—that the victims were "criminals"—many victims were civilians caught in the crossfire. The rhetoric of "collateral damage," often used by Calderón, reduced official culpability while depriving the dead and disappeared of their humanity.

Calderón's "kingpin" strategy—fighting cartels with high-profile arrests and by assassinating leaders—led to the fragmentation and expansion of criminal organizations. These organizations and smaller gangs started to sell drugs to a growing domestic drug market, not just to the United States. They also diversified into other criminal activities, including extortion, kidnapping, human trafficking, and resource extraction, to name a few. Journalists observed that the intensifying climate of violence and impunity allowed the torture and assassinations not only of suspected criminals, but also of political opponents. These crimes were swept into a war that continues to provide cover for acts of violence against Mexico's "disposable" populations—migrants in transit to the United States, indigenous communities, and the poor and marginalized. It is well documented that these crimes are committed by both state agents and criminal organizations, acting independently and in collusion.

The violence in Mexico is fueled by the estimated 200,000 firearms that enter the country illegally from the United States every year. Mexico has some of the most restrictive gun laws in the world, with only two gun stores in the entire country. But there are over 6,700 gun stores in the US Southwest alone, most within a few hours' drive from the border. Between 70 and 90 percent of guns recovered at crime scenes in Mexico can be traced to the United States. In 2021, the Mexican government filed a federal lawsuit against ten US gun manufacturers, an unprecedented move that seeks to expand responsibility for gun violence. The lawsuit alleges US arms companies "design, market, distribute, and sell guns in ways they know routinely arm the drug cartels in Mexico." Mexico wants financial compensation and an end to the harms caused by trafficked guns.

The trade in guns is linked to Americans' demand for drugs. In the 1980s, Americans wanted cocaine; in the 90s, marijuana. Today, it's opioids. Mexico supplies the US with black tar heroin and black-market prescription opioids, including the synthetic opioid fentanyl, which is fifty times stronger than heroin. The consequences have been devastating. In 2021, more than 107,000 Americans died from drug overdoses, the vast majority caused by opioids. I witnessed the damage caused by opiod addiction in the United States: multiple relatives within one household addicted to heroin, young children schooled in overdose prevention, teenagers dying on their way to the ER, prisons overcrowded with heroin-addicted nonviolent offenders. Despite government antidrug strategies, the availability of drugs, and people's addiction to them, continues unabated.

Mexico is, as the author Cristina Rivera Garza puts it, a wounded country, a country in pain. Citizens refer not to the "war on drugs" or even the "war on narcos" but to *la violencia*, the violence. By 2022, the violence in Mexico resulted in over 340,000 officially recorded deaths. At least 100,000 people have disappeared, and hundreds of thousands of people have been displaced, orphaned, and exiled. There are 40,000 unidentified bodies and more than 4,000 clandestine graves.

The contradictions between Health City's rhetoric of improving lives and the growing reality of violence filled me with doubt. I questioned whether studying a utopian project during a profound social and political crisis had value. During the day, I studied Health City's master plan, and, in the evening, I watched the news and learned of another massacre, mass kidnapping, or assassination. More and more, Health City came to seem like nothing more than a propogandist spectacle for a future that would never exist.

————

In 2011, my first summer of field research, I started dreaming about Pompeii, the ancient Roman city that stood in the shadow of Mount Vesuvius. Almost two thousand years ago, the volcano erupted, smothering the city. In my dreams, Pompeii transformed into Cuicuilco and I saw its people unable to outrun the volcano's fiery waves, forever confined beneath the lava's ossified swirls and folds. I walked the rocky landscape, discovering people under the ash, their bodies locked in the very positions discovered during excavations of Pompeii: a mother and daughter killed side by side; an entire family huddled together; a young woman on her back with her left arm raised, reaching for help.

But the Pedegral wasn't Pompeii. During my walks in the lava field, I took note of the bright green lichen that blanketed the dark stone and the delicate white flowers that grew in the rocky crevices. Sometimes I brought colored pencils to sketch the porous rock and the colorful life that sprang from it. The natural surroundings contrasted with the high-tech vision of Health City to such a degree that it was hard to conjure their coexistence.

Exclusive neighborhoods framed the lava field's periphery. I strolled the streets, trying to be inconspicuous as I gawked at the modernist houses designed by Luis Barragán and his acolytes. Austere, cubist structures configured to incorporate lava outcroppings and painted in palettes that matched the colors of stone. Today, some of Mexico's richest families live in the Pedregal estates. Another half million people live on top of the rock, most of them in poor, densely packed, and unplanned neighborhoods.

To my surprise, some of Health City's architects and urban planners whom I talked to had never visited the Pedregal. Instead they worked from chic offices in London and Mexico City and relied on computer programs to reimagine and transform the volcanic landscape. "Aren't you bothered by the lack of direct contact with the site?" I asked a planner who was working on the project. He answered without hesitation and insisted that maintaining distance from the site enabled design without nostalgia.

By the fall of 2011, the construction of Health City had come to a halt. There were mounting disputes about who owned the rocky land upon which it was to be built. A codex dated to 1532 named 1,799 co-owners. Other documents soon emerged that named dispossessed agrarian communities, real estate conglomerates, and private individuals as the rightful owners. Accusations of fraud ensued, as did demands for rent. The futuristic City of Health was mired in the past.

I still occupied my time with studying the Pedregal—everything from its vegetation to the architectural efforts to overcome the challenges the volcanic rock presented. My study provided a refuge from the violence that gripped Mexico, as well as the difficulties in my own life. My lingering depression, fraying marriage, and restless daughters were the surrounds of my life. The girls wanted to go home to Los Angeles, where they had a dog and a yard and could play unattended. Benjamin wanted to stay in Mexico City, where he had lived in his twenties and thirties among artists and musicians and with whom he still wanted to spend every evening. And I wanted to be alone on a surreal landscape of black rock, insulated from pain.

———

One afternoon, after another visit to the lava field, I called Manuel, a seasoned driver I sometimes hired for my excursions. Before Uber had taken over the city, Mexican friends urged me to hire a private driver, saying it was necessary to protect myself from being held up while stuck in the city's relentless traffic. Manuel picked me up near the Health City site and started off toward my apartment in Colonia Roma, an artsy, tree-lined neighborhood filled with art deco mansions, hip restaurants, and boutiques. It was the rainy season and another thunderstorm was brewing in the low gray sky. Tired and grimy, I was relieved to settle into the back seat of Manuel's roomy sedan. I gazed out the window, staring at the bumper-to-bumper traffic. Eventually I closed my eyes.

"What are you investigating?" Manuel asked. Manuel was a quiet man who avoided chitchat, so I was surprised by his question. I gathered my thoughts and told him about my research on Health City. He said he'd never heard of the place. "City of Knowledge? Biometropolis?" I asked, using the project's other names. He shook his head no.

I told him the basics. Cutting-edge research and health care facilities, fancy apartments, and an ecological reserve. The master plan was complete, and the construction would begin soon, but legal problems were stalling things.

I waited for Manuel to offer comment, but he had nothing more to say. I didn't want to leave our conversation there, partly because it all seemed so ridiculous, studying a place that wasn't a place. So I told him I also studied families with drug addiction problems. He glanced at me in the rear-view mirror, which I interpreted as an invitation to say more. I described my earlier research, which I admitted was much more than research because it took me back home. I didn't tell him that home was a difficult place for me to be.

As I spoke about New Mexico's heroin epidemic, I noticed that the traffic was thinning. We turned off Insurgentes, Mexico City's longest avenue, and into an area unknown to me. In the distance, I could see buildings giving way to ramshackle houses. Paved linear streets transformed into a web of narrow roads. There were no street signs, and the buildings were unnumbered.

A few minutes passed before Manuel stopped driving. We sat in his car with its engine still running. Heart pounding, I waited for the car door to fly open and for narcos to drag me out and stuff me into the trunk of another car. No doubt my fear was inspired by ubiquitous images of narco violence circulated by the media-entertainment industry on both sides of the US-Mexico border. For decades, cultural productions of the drug war and narcoculture have invariably cast Mexico as lawless and chaotic, with little context about how the United States fuels the violence. But instead of disappearing me, Manuel opened my eyes to a world that would have otherwise been hidden from my view.

He pointed to a small building behind a metal gate and said the young-est of his three daughters was there. He called the place an *anexo*. At the time, I didn't know what he was talking about. *Una granja*, a farm, he said, using its alternative name. I shook my head no, I still wasn't familiar. Manuel explained that anexos, or farms as they're sometimes called, are places for people with drug and alcohol problems. They are committed there by their families and stay until they are better. But sometimes they come out even worse.

It was his daughter Lili's third time in an anexo. Manuel and his wife couldn't deal with her on-and-off drug use anymore, but they didn't want to lose her either. "We don't want her to disappear," he said.

That summer there had been constant reports of murders of young women around Lili's age of seventeen. Most of these crimes took place in Ecatepec, a sprawling municipality northeast of Mexico City. Ecatepec has the highest rate of femicide in the country. Across Mexico, rates of femicide have increased 137 percent since 2018, four times the rate of in-crease in general homicide.

Ecatepec's population largely consists of people who migrated closer to the nation's capital in search of a better life and more economic op-portunities. Many turned to work in maquiladoras, export-processing factories owned by foreign countries. First established in 1965 on Mex-ico's northern border, maquiladoras employ low-paid Mexican workers, often women, to assemble US-produced parts into finished goods for sale on the US market. Their output and growth accelerated rapidly with the implementation of the North American Free Trade Agreement in 1994. Scholars have linked Mexico's maquiladoras with femicide. Gender-based violence can be highly visible in Ecatepec, where women's bodies are rou-tinely found in streets and empty lots. Others disappear entirely.

Manuel admitted that the anexos he previously committed Lili to were too hard on her. After a few months inside she came home skinny and bruised. She'd mope around the house for a couple of weeks then start

using again, staying out for days, sometimes longer. Manuel said he'd lock
her away forever if that's what it took to keep her safe. In the end, he'd
committed Lili to this anexo for six months at a cost of about forty dollars
a month—more expensive than the previous anexos, but manageable if he
and his wife worked a few more hours a week. Manuel looked at me in the
rearview mirror. "What else can we do?"

I looked at the metal gate and noticed a small hand-painted sign in
the upper right corner. LA CLÍNICA DE LAS EMOCIONES. Coming into view
on the street outside was a woman dressed in a gray work uniform. She
yanked a scrawny teenager by the ear and the girl pulled against her grip,
trying to free herself. The woman frantically pounded on the gate with
her free hand. *We're here! We're here! Open! Open!* The gate opened just
enough for the woman to slip inside, pulling the girl in behind her.

Manuel started to drive away. When we arrived at my apartment, he
turned to me and said, "Health City will never happen. But anexos are
everywhere."

A few days after my drive with Manuel, I was back in the lava field. But
Health City was far from my mind. I thought only about Lili—young,
poor, addicted to drugs. Social scientists call girls like her "high-risk." But
Lili wasn't high-risk; she was endangered. That's why Manuel had walled
her off.

It was midmorning and the reserve was already filling up with people
carrying walking sticks. I wanted to be apart from the crowd but didn't
know which way to go. A rectangular-shaped rock stood in the distance,
and I headed toward it. Lizards darted everywhere, stopping and staring
at me as I approached. When I came too close, they quickly scrambled off
to safety.

I sat on the rock's porous plateau and stared at my hands, which
were speckled with the imprint of rough basalt, and I thought about the
Clinic of Emotions. Was it like the detox clinic in New Mexico? Who was
locked inside? What did Manuel mean when he said he didn't want Lili
to disappear?

In the following weeks, I started to read about anexos. To my surprise, I couldn't find one scholarly article or government report on them. I did come across dozens of newspaper articles. They either described anexos as clandestine and hellish, teeming with people deprived of their liberty and subjected to horrific violence, or as hideouts for gang members and narcos. One televised nightly news segment on anexos opened onto a dramatic scene of police pulling women out of a run-down building. The reporter called the women *esclavas*, slaves. I dismissed these stories as yellow journalism.

A few months before Health City's master plan was revealed in 2010, hit men attacked an anexo in Ciudad Juárez and killed seventeen people. Thirteen days later there was an attack at another anexo that killed ten people. The Mexican government called anexos *asilos*, asylums, for drug dealers. They said the victims of these massacres were gang members and so there was no investigation.

I was deeply unsettled by these events. I kept thinking about the Clinic of Emotions. Manuel said anexos like it were everywhere. I started looking for anexos in my own neighborhood—peering past metal gates topped with spirals of barbed wire, wondering if the shuttered building two doors down from my apartment held a secret. But I didn't really know what I was looking for.

I reached out to academics and government officials for help. Most of them ignored my inquiries or brushed me off. Members of various civil society organizations dedicated to drug policy gave me leads, as did a social epidemiologist who was eager to talk with me. I met Beatriz at her office in a research institute not far from the Health City site. Her office was a mess, with teetering columns of books, journals, and papers scattered on the floor, unwashed coffee cups and a pack of cigarettes on her desk.

"I'm sorry if this conversation disappoints you," Beatriz said in a raspy voice. "I don't study anexos. I can't." She explained that research conducted within public institutions needed to be relevant to Mexican society, and "relevant" topics concerned populations deemed worthy of public investment. "Do you know what people call anexos? Garbage cans for trash."

Beatriz didn't share this view. She grew up in a neighborhood with anexos and knew people who had no other option but to send their family members there. Her own father and brother were in and out of them— sobering up in her father's case, staying out of trouble in her brother's. Were they perfect institutions? No. Would she send her own child to one? If she had to.

She confirmed Manuel's claim that anexos were everywhere.

I asked her how many anexos were in Mexico City.

"One thousand, maybe four thousand, maybe more. Who knows? No one can say."

At the time, First Lady Margarita Zavala, wife of President Felipe Calderón, was crusading against drug addiction. Beatriz believed Zavala's campaign, like Nancy Reagan's before her, was a cynical ploy from a government needing to put a positive spin on its disastrous drug war. Zavala's ribbon-cutting ceremonies at a handful of government-funded treatment centers covered up the realities of addiction and health care in Mexico. Accessible professional treatment for the worsening problem of drug addiction simply didn't exist.

"You're the kind of person who can study anexos," Beatriz said.

"Why?"

She took out a cigarette and looked at me. "Because you're an American. You have the luxury of doing whatever you want."

For several days, I thought about Beatriz's provocation. To have the luxury of doing what I wanted didn't just mean that I could study anexos; it also meant I could turn away from them entirely. I wrestled with the decision of what to do. Would I continue my investigation of Health City, whose future everyone seemed to doubt, or dig deeper into the reality of anexos? As much as I dreaded it, I felt myself being pulled toward anexos, and for reasons painfully familiar to me: drugs, troubled kids, frightened and worn-down families.

"It's not a good idea," Manuel said when I asked him to help me enter an anexo. It was June and another attack on an anexo had left six people dead. Manuel insisted I had no idea what I'd be getting myself into. But I pushed back, saying that the attacks on anexos occurred far from Mexico City. Plus, they couldn't all be so dangerous. After all, he put his daughter in one. Manuel finally relented. The next week he picked me up at my apartment and we headed to an anexo named Serenidad, Serenity.

Mexico City is enormous. Its terrain merges with surrounding urban areas, forming a megalopolis of over thirty million people. The farther out a person is located, the more difficult and dangerous life can be. Serenity was in Iztapalapa, one of the densest of Mexico City's sixteen boroughs. Roughly 21 percent of Mexico City's population resides there, two-thirds of whom meet official standards of marginality, which include poverty, malnutrition, and addiction problems, among others. Adding to these issues is the lack of health services, public infrastructure, and schools. In his book *Planet of Slums*, Mike Davis includes Iztapalapa as one of the world's largest slums. It once housed the city's garbage dump. One of Mexico City's largest prison complexes, the Reclusorio Oriente, is also located there.

Given the borough's reputation, I was surprised to find that Serenity was in a working-class neighborhood with paved streets, busy food stands, and small family-run shops. A few men warmly shouted ¡Compañero! as we drove by. It was Manuel's neighborhood, and he seemed to know everybody. The man who ran Serenity was an old friend.

We pulled up to an orange-colored two-story building. I assumed Manuel would accompany me inside, but he didn't move. "I am a chauffeur," he said. "I move people from here to there."

I looked at the building. The anexo advertised itself with a large vinyl banner draped outside: SERENITY. REHABILITATION CENTER FOR ALCOHOLICS, DRUG ADDICTS, AND NEUROTICS.

Manuel tapped the shiny black steering wheel like he was waiting for me to leave. "Just make introductions?" I asked meekly. Manuel stared at me in the rearview mirror for a moment, then opened his door without saying a word.

A young man unlocked a metal gate and escorted us inside. The gate opened onto a neat courtyard framed by two stories of apartments. Kids kicked a ball around, women cooked in a shared outdoor kitchen, an old man read the newspaper. He offered it to us as we passed by, calling it yesterday's news. It was a relaxed atmosphere, and the aromas of food clung to the sticky summer air.

The doors to a few apartments were open and provided glimpses of front rooms stuffed with furniture. The flicker of a television brightened a few of them. Tattered chairs, drying clothes, and buckets of growing flowers and vegetables gathered around each unit. A woman sat in front of her door rolling cigarettes. She offered to sell me one and shrugged her shoulders when I said no.

Serenity was in a corner unit on the second floor. It didn't have just one door, it had three—an iron grille, a metal door, and then a wood one. Unlocking them was a long and noisy process. Our escort talked to Manuel as he fumbled with a ring of keys. I could hear sounds from inside. Somebody was screaming, somebody was crying. Our escort chatted easily. *There's a new chick, young and pretty. One of the counselors was kicked out for stealing food. I'm just helping out till they get someone new.*

I looked at Manuel. He was tall and lanky, dressed in boots and jeans. I suddenly realized I knew almost nothing about him.

———

A sour smell of bleach, cigarettes, and unbathed bodies hit me as soon as I entered Serenity. An oscillating fan pushed the odor from one side of the room to another, over the heads of people—so many people—all sitting cross-legged on the floor. They were *los anexados*, the annexed.

The voice of one anexado shot through a momentary silence. *Who the fuck?*

I glanced around the room. It was about the size of my living room back home in Los Angeles, but it was cramped and dim. In one corner stood a wooden lectern. In the other, a disheveled young man faced a wall. He turned his head to look at me; I could see that he was crying.

The room was about twenty by fifteen feet, with a water-stained ceiling and a cracked tile floor. The cement walls were painted an ugly green and bolts of white caulk filled their many cracks. Curls of yellowing paint hung from the ceiling. A few months earlier, a major earthquake hit Oaxaca and also shook Mexico City. It was impossible to look at the ceiling and not think of it falling.

Nailed to the walls were announcements and handwritten slogans, all ending with an exclamation mark: 5 AM! GET UP! DO NOT TOUCH! LIVE AND LET LIVE! There were large sepia-toned portraits of Bill W. and Dr. Bob S., cofounders of Alcoholics Anonymous, and an unadorned wooden cross. There were no beds or any other furniture that one might expect to find in a place where so many people lived, just tightly rolled blankets and chairs stacked neatly against a wall.

Some of the anexados hung their heads; others looked at me with interest or scorn. They mostly appeared to be teenagers, mostly male. I spotted two young women sitting beside each other. I offered them a faint smile; only one of them returned it.

A man's voice rang out. *¡Órale, cabrón!* The man approached and clasped Manuel's hand in a show of friendship. I looked down, embarrassed. The cracked linoleum tiles had a fleur-de-lis pattern. Out of the corner of my eye I saw a callused toe peeking out of a worn plastic sandal.

The air in the room felt thick and seemed to get caught in my throat. I started coughing. It started off slow and shallow, then developed into desperate gasping. Suddenly, I was holding a cup of water I was afraid to drink. But I drank from the cup, imagining it as a communion chalice. When my cough finally settled, Manuel and I were led to the back of the room, weaving between people's bodies as we made our way. I fixed my eyes on the floor, careful to not step on the anexados' hands or trip on their legs. I felt ashamed of my mobility and wanted to leave. But before I could flee, our guide tapped three times on a closed door before opening it and gesturing for us to enter.

"What's up, *jefe!*" It was Padrino Francisco, the leader of Serenity. Manuel gave him the quickest of hugs, then looked at me. His expression said, *My job is finished.* After a few more words with Padrino Francisco, Manuel left, closing the door behind him.

I glanced around the room uneasily. It was nondescript, like an office for a low-level government worker. There was a microwave and a coffee maker, a banged-up desk with two chairs for visitors. Hanging behind the desk was a dry-erase board dusty with red and blue ink remnants and some framed certificates, the contents of which I couldn't make out. The only thing that stood out was a painting that covered one wall. It showed a naked man. Before I could look any further Padrino Francisco asked me to sit.

He was short and burly, with a receding hairline and clean-shaven face. The skin under his eyes looked bruised from lack of sleep.

"You can ask me anything, *anything*," he said, looking at his watch. I admitted that I knew very little about anexos and didn't know where to begin or what to ask.

"Sometimes it's better not to ask, you know what I mean?"

The painting hovered over me. I saw now that it showed Jesus trying to break thick chains binding his wrists. The palette was dark, except for the bright-red beads of blood running down Jesus's forehead and the startling whites of his eyes. His body was rendered in the classical heroic style, with muscular, elongated limbs, but he wasn't at all serene. He looked wild, with his hands pulling furiously against the chains. It was a bleak image, almost grotesque, and it reminded me of one of Francisco Goya's Black Paintings, *Saturn Devouring His Son*. Goya's painting is based on the Greco-Roman myth of Saturn, or Cronus, the titan who ate his children out of fear of being overthrown by them. It shows a decapitated child in Saturn's hands, whose mouth is opened wide to consume even more of the body. Goya painted it on the wall of his own house.

I asked Padrino Francisco about the painting. He studied it for a moment, then turned to look at me.

"Every person in this place knows that struggle."

"What struggle?" I asked.

"The struggle to survive."

———

I didn't want to return to Serenity, but I felt compelled to. It was like I was pulled down by the force of gravity. The anexo was somehow natural to me, but troubling nonetheless. The multifamily apartment complex was typical of other working-class apartment buildings in Mexico City. It was vibrant, neighborly. Yet it had a room dedicated to locking up young men and women vulnerable to dangers I didn't yet understand.

Rooms to protect people have existed throughout history and are created in response to danger and violence. I understood such rooms in New Mexico. The detox clinic aspired to be a haven of safety, protecting people from the risks of heroin overdose and prison. When I was sixteen years old in Albuquerque, I took refuge with homeless teenagers and runaways in an abandoned railyard building we called the Cathedral. We sought shelter there together, protecting one another from loneliness and hunger. But I had a hard time understanding what was being protected in an anexo. How could life be protected in a place so diminished?

Padrino Francisco accepted my presence at Serenity. I was a friend of Manuel, and therefore a friend of his. My first few visits to the anexo were spent in his office beside the image of Jesus trying to burst out of his chains. Sometimes Padrino Francisco joined me and stared at me with curiosity.

"Just what are you looking for?" he asked.

I thought for a minute, then answered: "The story of this place."

————

The first thing that Padrino Francisco told me was that he inherited his role as *padrino*, godfather, from the man he credited for saving his life—Padrino Alfonso. A construction worker by trade, Padrino Alfonso had helped build many of the pedestrian bridges that span Mexico City's busy streets. It was dangerous work, and crossing them these days is dangerous too. Every year, people are killed crossing neglected bridges, especially in poor parts of the city. Mothers walking their kids home from school, people on their way home from work with bags of groceries: they fall into traffic and are killed.

By his late forties, Padrino Alfonso was too old and broken to compete in a sector saturated with younger workers, at a time when construction projects had slowed dramatically due to Mexico's weakening economy. He comforted himself by drinking, which made his life worse. He spent three years in and out of anexos. After he got sober, he started Serenity to help friends and neighbors like himself.

One of the framed certificates on the wall of Padrino Francisco's office announced the occasion that Serenity opened its doors: May 3, 2001. The Finding of the Holy Cross, a feast day for construction workers. The apartment where Serenity was located belonged to one of the complex's residents, who rented it to Padrino Alfonso for a modest fee. The neighbors in the building welcomed Serenity and the service it provided. There had been a christening party in the courtyard. The initial cohort of anexados was five middle-aged men, two of whom were residents of the apartment complex. They detoxed from alcohol and stayed on for weeks or months, giving their exhausted wives and mothers a break from living with them. Some of the men cycled in and out of Serenity, and a few got sober and went on to establish their own anexos.

Four years after Serenity was established, there were no fewer than ten people in the anexo at any one time. Many were in their twenties and addicted to drugs, not alcohol. The shift in substances corresponded to a particular historical conjuncture. It was a decade after the North American Free Trade Agreement had gone into effect. One of the stated goals of NAFTA was to reduce poverty and inequality in Mexico. In fact, NAFTA dramatically cut segments of the formal work sector that employed laborers and farmers, driving most Mexicans into deeper poverty. Mexico was also still recovering from its 1980s debt crisis at the time NAFTA was implemented, which led to drastic devaluation of the peso in the mid-1990s. Rates of unemployment and poverty skyrocketed, and more Mexicans were forced to migrate up north for work, either in maquilas or in the US, or to rely on the informal economy. A major consequence of the increase of poverty was an increase in the production of drugs as drug-trafficking networks became sources of employment.

The country had faced other crises as well. In March 1994, presidential candidate Luis Donaldo Colosio was assassinated. Colosio was the leading contender to win the presidential election that August. His murder heightened a pervasive sense of insecurity that intensified into the 2000s. It was in this mix that anexos proliferated.

Padrino Alfonso died in 2006, the same year President Felipe Calderón announced the war on narcos. The residents of the apartment building set up an altar for him, the centerpiece of which was a bust of Jesús Malverde, the patron folk saint of construction workers. Malverde famously appears with black hair and eyes, a thick mustache, and a poker-faced expression. According to legend, he lived in Sinaloa in the early 1900s, stealing from the rich and giving to the poor, and he was hanged by the governor for it. Over the past fifty years Malverde has become a patron saint of drug traffickers, too.

Two years after Padrino Alfonso died, Francisco took over as Serenity's padrino. Neighbors in the apartment building affectionately called him *boss* and came to him with their troubles. He was a neighborhood success story, and he earned his good standing through his ties to Serenity, where he was once an anexado himself.

Padrino Francisco described Padrino Alfonso as a good man, always making and fixing things. Once, while talking about the worsening violence in Mexico, he said that Padrino Alfonso timed his death well because, in his own words, there was no way for him to fix the fucked-up situation the country was in.

———

A few weeks after my first visit to Serenity, I began spending time in the little room where the anexados lived. I understood my role as an anthropologist as capturing, as closely as I could, the room's details and rhythms. I approached my time there as an observer, taking notes on the room's physical features. I shied away from looking at or speaking to the people stuck in it because I felt too guilty that I could come and go as I pleased. This asymmetry mirrored the unequal relationship between Mexico and the United States. I was always aware of it, and in many ways it propelled my research forward. I had a nascent understanding that anexos were an effect and expression of a deeper bi-national history. I wanted to understand it, and to render it too.

I drew detailed diagrams of the room in my notebook. I captured the white-washed window that faced the courtyard, the collapsible conference table, and the seventeen folding chairs—not enough to seat everyone in the room, but close. Buckets of dingy water were used for daily cleaning, and bottles of *refrescos*, sodas, lined a shelf above a standalone sink.

The room was sparse, equipped for only the basic functions of habitation. Blankets for sleeping, a sliver of bar soap for washing hands, a worn towel for drying dishes. But Serenity pulsed with voices. I recorded what I heard: talking, weeping, moaning, yelling, singing, whistling, coughing, reprimanding, laughing—sometimes all at once. When a counselor commanded that the anexados be silent, noise from the surrounding apartment complex came through, reminding me that the anexo was not some far-off place, but was situated within a neighborhood, a city. I could hear the outside world from within: children fighting, adults laughing, dialogue from television shows, the high-pitched cries of passing street vendors. Serenity was cradled by this larger community, but the dynamics between them were still a mystery to me.

What is this place? one of my notebook entries reads. *A prison? A shelter? A church?*

I wondered the same thing the first time I went to the Cathedral. The murmur of homeless teenagers laying around the barren freight shop resounds in me still. At any given time, there were between fifteen and thirty of us in that space. The Cathedral was at least five times larger than Serenity, but we huddled together in one corner, our bodies in search of comfort and warmth. We were bored, lonely, and scared, and we were on our own, sleeping near defunct train tracks overgrown with weeds and littered with rusted beer cans.

Memories of the Cathedral returned every time I stepped foot inside Serenity.

———

Inside Serenity, I worried that I took up too much space. I sat in a corner trying to make my body as small as possible. From my position, the room appeared as a diorama dominated by a large wooden lectern. Surrounding the lectern was a blur of anexados. I had to cast my eyes past them, toward the wall opposite me, to help bring them into focus.

They were mostly teenagers and young men in their early twenties: fourteen men and two women. Slowly I began to learn names and people started to talk with me. Luis, a twenty-nine-year-old schizophrenic, had lived at Serenity for seven years and said he'd probably never leave. His mother committed him there before migrating to the United States. One afternoon, he showed me a letter she'd sent him. The paper was wrinkled and torn, as if it had been crumpled and smoothed over many times. The only thing I could make out was the date: September 17, 2008. "My birthday," Luis said.

Eighteen-year-old Bobby insisted he wasn't a *drogadicto*, he just used drugs like everybody else. Bobby had lived at Serenity for just under one year and worried about the day he'd have to leave. There were thugs out to get him. That's why his mom committed him to the anexo—not because he used drugs, he said, but because he was at risk of something more dangerous.

Ángel was twenty. He wanted to leave all the time but couldn't figure out how. Ángel was a bit of a mystery. There were no clear reasons why he was at the anexo. He didn't do drugs, have mental health problems, or worry about his safety. No one ever visited him, and he never spoke of family. It was hard to imagine what kind of life he would return to if he could leave Serenity.

Luis explained, "I learn about the outside from the others. It is a terrifying place. I am not afraid here, only tired."

Bobby: "Yes, I miss my freedom. But there are more people outside who want to kill me than protect me. Hopefully they will forget about me before I get out."

Ángel: "The harder I try, the longer I stay."

Ángel was short and wiry, with a pockmarked face and goofy smile. He was always planning a mass *fuga*, escape. *Come on!* he'd say. *Don't be pussies! Follow me!* Ángelcould hold his hands behind his back and lift them above his head without bending his torso. His natural flexibility made him an ideal escapee, he said. He just needed to figure out how to slither out the door unnoticed. The doors were ajar a few times each day, either to let people pass or to accept donations of food. That's when Ángel would make a go of it. He said if he could escape and make it to the United States, he'd settle in Los Angeles and teach yoga. He'd be like the TV personality Cesar Millan, the Mexican American "dog whisperer" who schooled gringos in how to master their out-of-control dogs. But unlike Millan, whom he called his hero, Ángel would teach rich white ladies what downward dog really meant.

Ángel was Serenity's clown. Every anexo had one. He risked beatings to draw laughter from his peers. Sometimes he sat on the floor with his legs behind his ears. He didn't seem to mind when he was bullied so long as the person insulting him laughed.

Laughter, the philosopher Henri Bergson writes, is "a momentary anesthesia of the heart." It suspends existence so that a world can become different, even if only for a moment. Given the monotony of anexados' days, laughter provided relief from boredom, which was the prevailing mood. Over months, I became aware of Serenity's periods of lightness, of those moments that disrupted the anexo's state of continuous aimlessness. Anexados cracked jokes, usually at someone's expense. The room erupted into laughter when someone tripped or received a blow from a counselor for not being able to hold their bodies in challenging positions during "yoga," the name given to extended periods of lying on the floor with legs in the air. Sometimes Luis laughed for no apparent reason, eliciting more laughter from anexados who called him nuts.

But laughter came to a halt when Padrino Francisco entered the room. He was a serious man who'd had a difficult childhood. He quit school when he was eleven because he needed to help support his mother and two younger brothers. He worked as one of Mexico City's ubiquitous walking street vendors, selling ice pops, fruit, cleaning supplies, and water—whatever was available or in demand. He worked six days a week, ten hours a day, his feet and throat in perpetual states of soreness. He gave his mother the money he earned, but it was never enough.

One afternoon, Padrino Francisco recalled having to wear his father's shoes, which were ragged and too big for him. "What I hated most was they reminded me of that motherfucker," he said. His father deserted the family when he was eight. "I'd rather go barefoot than wear my old man's shoes." But his mother worried that he looked like a "little Indian" without them, making the family appear worse off than they really were, which was already bad enough.

The drug economy expanded. In the countryside, growing marijuana and poppy provided a better living—sometimes the only living—for a rural workforce estranged from their communal lands, called *ejidos*, through privatization by developers in the 1990s. In urban areas, some street vendors were pushed into low-level trafficking of drugs. Padrino Francisco added marijuana, then crack, to his list of goods. Selling drugs did not lift him out of poverty, but he was finally able to save a little money for himself. His first purchase was a pair of new black leather shoes. The day of his purchase, Padrino Francisco walked into a bar and ordered a beer. "*El mundo estaba en mis manos.*" *The world was in my hands.* He was thirteen years old.

Over time, Padrino Francisco moved up the chain of command, eventually overseeing the operation of several *tienditas*, little shops, that sold drugs. The work afforded him some material comfort, but it was dangerous and stressful. He survived several brushes with violence and had scars to prove it: a long gash on a shoulder, a jagged wound on a thigh.

Padrino Francisco's first stint in an anexo wasn't in Mexico City; it was in El Paso, Texas, a key node for drug trafficking. It was the mid-1990s, and he landed at the anexo because the organization he worked for didn't like their people using drugs, and if they did use, they were suspected of stealing the product they were supposed to be selling. "You could drink a bottle of tequila for breakfast," he said. "But a line of coke . . ." The cocaine was for Americans, not Mexicans.

The anexo in El Paso was rough. As soon as Padrino Francisco arrived, his head was shaved, he was stripped naked, and he was dunked into a barrel of cold water. Then he was chained to a wall near a large fan that blew cold air onto his body. For three days he was threatened and starved. Padrino Francisco stayed for a month, got out, and stayed clean, at least for a little while.

He described El Paso as ugly and dirty, but it was where he was making a life. He traveled a bit—to Denver, to Tulsa—delivering and collecting, collecting and delivering. But then his brother, who worked in the same business, was murdered. A few months later, a cousin disappeared. Padrino Francisco drank excessively and started using again, aware of the deadly consequences. What he didn't expect was to be arrested at a bar in Las Cruces, New Mexico. Without papers, he was deported back to Mexico.

Looking at his life back then, Padrino Francisco described himself as *"un perdido muy perdido."* A deeply lost person.

"One thing you need to know, Angela, is that in anexos you are never lost."

———

Mexico long prided itself on not having a drug problem. It was a "transit" country, with drugs flowing northward to the United States. Until relatively recently, the problem of addiction in Mexico was with alcohol. While binge drinking affects all sectors of society (Mexico has one of the highest rates of alcoholism and liver disease in the world), there are resources to address it. Alcoholics Anonymous groups are ubiquitous, as are religious affiliations that emphasize sobriety. There are private clinics for those who can afford them and, for those who can't, respected customs such as making a *juramento*, a vow, to the Virgin to quit drinking. And there are anexos.

The presence of anexos in Mexico City reaches back to the late 1970s. Their development is related to the establishment of Mexico's 24-Hour Alcoholics Anonymous Movement, an unofficial offshoot of Alcoholics Anonymous. As the anthropologist Stanley H. Brandes has documented, AA's extraordinary growth in Mexico, especially among working-class Catholics, defied assumptions about it being culturally tailored to a White, Protestant middle class. Mexico's 24-Hour groups grew out of what its founders called "the necessities of our country," including the "socioeconomic characteristics of marginal alcoholics." These groups offered rooms where poor, homeless, and chronically ill alcoholics could stay while sobering up. While many 24-Hour groups remained aligned with traditional AA, others differentiated themselves further by intensifying their confrontational styles. Endeavoring to provide long-term residential alcohol and drug recovery services for the poor, these offshoots of the 24-Hour movement became widely known as anexos.

In 2011, Mexico introduced substance abuse treatment into its public health insurance program known as Seguro Popular, which debuted in 2004. Although the plan's coverage is extensive on paper, much of the country still lacks the public infrastructure to implement addiction treatment, let alone primary and mental health care services. Fewer than 10 percent of Mexicans in addiction treatment receive government-funded treatment, making twelve-step, religious, and mutual aid groups the principal sources for behavioral and mental health care in Mexico. Public health experts estimate that 90 percent of Mexico's residential treatment for addiction for the poor is provided by anexos.

––––––––

All the anexados I knew at Serenity were committed there by their mothers. The women were like Hortencia; they knew that their children were vulnerable to drugs, and they wanted to protect them from *la violencia*. But there were other reasons women turned to Serenity for help with their kids. I learned one of them while sitting with Padrino Francisco in the building's lively courtyard. Padrino Francisco often took his meals there and, on this occasion, invited me to join him. I was relieved to have a break from Serenity's stifling environment, and I wanted to make small talk with the apartment residents.

A mother and daughter brought us samples of food they were preparing for an upcoming baby shower, which was to be held in the courtyard that weekend. Tamales, camotes, frijoles de la olla. The old man with the newspaper read us the headlines; another politician—the fifth in two months—had been murdered.

One of the counselors came down to announce that Bobby's mother had showed up unexpectedly. She was just beyond the gate, and she was upset. Padrino Francisco ordered the counselor to let her in.

"Padrino!" Bobby's mother cried as she rushed into the courtyard, disrupting its relaxed atmosphere. "I need your help!" She held a boy's hand. It was Bobby's younger brother Gabriel. Both of his eyes were swollen shut and a gash ran down his face. He hung his head while his mother talked.

"The *ratas* stole his backpack and beat him up! They demanded to know where Bobby was. My poor boy. He has autism." The boy shuffled uncomfortably while his mother kept on. "He doesn't speak. And even if he could speak, well, he wouldn't say!"

Padrino Francisco asked the mother what he could do.

"Take him," she answered, pushing her son in front of her.

Padrino Francisco studied Gabriel.

"Are you sure his father didn't do this to him?" he asked, referring to Gabriel's injuries.

"Absolutely not!" she answered, sounding indignant.

Padrino Francisco sighed, then gestured for the counselor to take Gabriel upstairs.

He ordered the mother to come back for her son in two days' time— long enough, he said, for things to cool down at home.

When I returned to the anexo after lunch that day, I found a group of anexados tending to Gabriel's wounds. "It's alright, amigo," Ángel said to Gabriel in an encouraging voice. But Gabriel flinched away from all the attention. It was as if he was being attacked all over again. "Give him some space," Bobby yelled as he looked at his struggling brother. The anexados stepped back, forming a protective perimeter around Gabriel.

When I returned to Serenity a few days later, Gabriel was gone.

———

Most of the days at Serenity were filled with testimony. During this practice, an anexado stands alone behind a wooden lectern facing their peers. At the counselor's command, the anexado is pressed to sink into and dwell upon the misery of their life, recounting scenes from brutal childhoods and relationships, experiences of terrible violence and exploitative labor, and memories of murdered and disappeared relatives. One testimony could last for hours, sometimes all night, and was often accompanied by the anexado yelling, smoking cigarettes, and falling silent or weeping for intermittent stretches. The rest of the anexados were forced to sit silently and listen. They were punished if they slouched or dozed off.

Nineteen-year-old Juan arrived at Serenity badly bruised. During one testimony he talked about the abuse he'd suffered from his father and compared it to the violence of a neighborhood gang that had threatened him since adolescence. "There's always someone who wants to get you," he said. Esme was also nineteen and a sex worker for two years before her mother committed her to Serenity. During one of her testimonies, she talked about having to go into sex work because women were, as she put it, *oprimidas*, oppressed. She went on to say that oppression didn't stop at the anexo's door but continued with the constant harassment from male anexados. The men in the room laughed. "Fuck you!" Esme responded, drawing even more laughter.

Testimonies were not always dark and grim. For some anexados, they provided a space of imagination. Luis was timid and frail looking, and he flinched when men larger than him approached or spoke to him. But during his testimonies he puffed his chest and described victorious fights with bravado. "I knocked him unconscious!" he'd boast. He likened himself to Mexico City's renowned boxer Kid Azteca. "I'm like the Kid," Luis would say while shuffling around the room, taking swings at the air. His audience couldn't help but laugh with him.

Testimonies were also opportunities to chronicle history. Neto was one of Serenity's great *cronistas*. His stories usually revolved around El Hoyo, the Hole, the makeshift neighborhood where he was born and lived for most of his twenty-two years. Located near an abandoned mine, El Hoyo is a settlement built on one of the precarious hillsides that frame Mexico City. Its official name is La Joya, the Jewel. Most of the self-built homes are one or two rooms in size, some with earthen floors and rooftops made of recycled materials. Water is scarce, electricity stolen, and formal employment and public services nonexistent. The renaming of La

Joya to El Hoyo by its inhabitants was more than an ironic gesture. It disrupted the fantasy of inclusion and shared prosperity, realigning the neighborhood's name with its actual conditions.

Neto's testimonies were often animated by *los derrumbes*, landslides. Landslides and flooding are common events for those living in informal neighborhoods along Mexico City's periphery, especially during the rainy season, and Neto survived more than one. However, during his testimonies, he tended to speak of them as one ongoing disaster. "It made a sound. *Whooooosh*. It sounded like that. *Whooooosh*."

After registering the noise of the landslide multiple times, Neto would recall the wreckage that followed the hillside's collapse, beginning with his own body. "There was shit in my eyes, ears, mouth, up to my knees. Thick. I'm walking, nowhere to go, stepping on things I can't see."

At various points, he moved from the first to the second person, as if to enfold his audience.

> You're walking with no pants on.
> You see dogs digging themselves out of the mud.
> There's gonna be lots for them to eat but nothing for you.
> Everything is covered in shit.
> Bags of onions, plastic bottles, broken chairs.

Three generations of Neto's family lived in El Hoyo. Neto recalled the chaos of trying to find each other after the landslide.

> I think I see my mother. You see her?
> Sister was with Grandmother that day.
> Higher up the hill.
> I go up, Mother goes down.
> What do you find?
> People digging, making piles. Taking things.
> *Help me, you motherfucker!*
> *Help me, you worthless piece of shit!*
> I look, faces covered.

I look, see Sister on Grandmother's back.

She is holding a spoon.

———

Since the start of the drug war, there had been a sense that living in Mexico City was like living in a bubble, at least for the middle and upper classes. This feeling of ease and invulnerability to the violence that was spreading through the rest of the country was orchestrated though surveillance cameras, police patrols, and the gentrification of neighborhoods with financial potential. The city government named certain areas *barrios mágicos*, magical neighborhoods, to draw tourists. The upgrading of profitable areas occurred as far larger portions of the city fell into deeper poverty and infrastructural decay. But in the summer of 2011, the feeling of invulnerability was beginning to fade. Masked criminals with assault weapons visited nightclubs in the magical neighborhoods of La Condesa, Colonia Roma, and Zona Rosa. A palpable sense of *inseguridad* spread throughout the capital.

I felt it. Once a day I joined the brigade of hipster moms at Parque España in the Condesa neighborhood. We'd stand around in packs, beneath the canopy of Montezuma cypress trees, while our kids ran wild in the new playground. Tacked to the trees were photocopied signs—photographs of people disappeared, many of them girls and young women. HAVE YOU SEEN HER? the signs cried. The talk among the mothers was easy and light, with updates on vacations and Montessori schools. But no one looked at each other because we were too busy clocking the movements of our kids. And if one were to briefly disappear, hearts pounded and voices rang like sirens. *Rebekah! Luci! Pablito!*

The threat of being kidnapped preoccupied Mexico City's middle and upper classes. Most of these crimes were "express kidnappings," during which an individual is abducted and briefly held in a "safe house" while they and their family members are drained of money. Victims are usually physically unharmed and released within twenty-four hours.

Media and government officials speculated that youth gangs from Iztapalapa were responsible for the crimes in magical neighborhoods.

Even so, studies have consistently shown that kidnappings of all types in Mexico City are far more likely to occur in poor neighborhoods. Like their wealthier counterparts, vulnerable residents of these areas also take measures to protect themselves, like participating in neighborhood patrols and committing kids vulnerable to violence to anexos. But according to formal norms of legality, such methods are indistinguishable from the crimes they seek to deter.

Anexos also engage in abductions, but in a way that cannot accurately be represented as "criminal." Mothers like Hortencia arrange to have their kids abducted and taken to an anexo. They describe their actions as a life-extending gesture—*a prevenir la muerte, a vivir.* To prevent death, to live. It is not a form of fatalism, but a form of realism that mixes practices of care with the violence that has become inescapable.

The fusion of care and violence reflects the burden families and communities shoulder in the contexts of poverty and institutional neglect. Mexico allocates 2 percent of its health care budget to mental health, the vast majority of which goes to its broken psychiatric hospitals. Between 2020 and 2021, the federal government reduced its already meager spending for public health by 44 percent. These cuts occurred at a time when conditions such as depression, anxiety, post-traumatic stress disorder, and substance abuse were skyrocketing, largely because of the cumulative and ongoing effects of criminal and neighborhood violence.

Caring for relatives with mental illnesses or addiction overwhelmingly falls on women, especially mothers. When talking about caregiving, women often express physical and emotional exhaustion, and sometimes hold the government accountable for their troubles. "They should do something," one mother said. "They pay billions for war but nothing to help us live with it." Hortencia often echoed these sentiments. Referring to the government's plan to put surveillance cameras throughout her neighborhood to deter crime, she said, "I wish there were cameras that captured the reality of my life. How hard and lonely it is."

In the absence of professional medical care, poor and marginalized families become what the anthropologist João Biehl calls "the medical agent of the state." Anexos can be considered in similar terms. They provide women relief from the daily labor and emotional drain that comes with caregiving. At the same time, they place additional burdens on women, who must foot the bill for their relative's treatment. Anexos are also sources of women's worries, especially about the well-being of their annexed kids. But the knowledge that they are relatively "safe inside" and might even return home in better shape often outweighs anexos' economic and emotional costs. "I know he is eating and getting help," one woman said of her annexed son. "And me? I don't sleep much because I work all the time, but when I do? Well, I can finally dream."

———————

One morning on my way to Serenity I noticed street vendors and pedestrians wearing thick chains around their necks. I hadn't noticed this in my own neighborhood, the comparatively rich and quiet Colonia Roma, when I set off earlier that morning.

When I arrived at Serenity's apartment building, a counselor named Antonio unlocked the imposing metal gate for me. As usual, the interior courtyard was bustling with activity. Women hung clothes to dry, young children played ball, elderly people sat in the sun. I followed Antonio up a flight of stairs to the second story and watched as he unlocked Serenity's three doors.

Inside, the anexados were in the middle of physical therapy, which meant running in circles and lifting weights made from cement-filled cans. After chatting with Antonio, I took my usual position in a back corner of the room, from which I planned to observe the day's activities. Within an hour, two men carried what I thought was a rug into Serenity. They laid the long, bulky roll on the floor and slowly unfurled it, revealing a thin young woman with flushed skin. One of the anexados exclaimed, "*Órale*, it's Ceci! Ceci's back!" Ceci unleashed a flood of obscenities at her abductors and Antonio. When she was finished screaming, she sat against a wall, held her head in her hands, and cried.

The scene immediately conjured the image of dead bodies, often women's, that are wrapped in blankets—*encobijados*, they're called, literally meaning wrapped up in a blanket. Media depictions show these victims in the trunks of abandoned cars, along desolate rural roads, and in mass graves. But the usual storyline of narco violence didn't seem to apply here, in Serenity. I wasn't sure whether something terrible had just happened, or how to respond to the situation at hand.

I walked around the perimeter of the room and sat on the floor beside Ceci. I introduced myself softly, and she shrugged me off decisively. I remained seated next to her, both of us with our backs against the wall. The anexados finished their exercises, then scrubbed clean and dried the tile floor with tattered rags. The ordinariness of these activities made the earlier event even more disturbing. Eventually, I mustered the will to see Padrino Francisco in his office.

He was organizing stacks of video recordings of anexados' testimonies, which are sometimes sold as a form of treatment literature. "Why do you do this?" I cried. "Why this terrible act of violence?" My heart pounded in my chest and tears filled my eyes. Padrino Francisco looked at me, his demeanor perfectly calm. Finally, he said, "It's just the way we bring you in. And it's very effective because you can't resist."

I waited for him to say more, but he went right back to his recordings. I was angry at him but too afraid to show it.

I returned to Serenity's main room. Ceci hadn't moved and the rest of the anexados were seated in folding metal chairs assembled in neat, forward-facing rows. Their heads were bowed and eyes closed for the daily religious service. Héctor, the oldest anexado at that time, stood before the group and recited a prayer. At first, I thought the prayer was for Ceci, as sometimes prayers are offered for new arrivals. But as I followed Héctor's words, I recognized that he was reciting a prayer for the solemnity of Saints Peter and Paul. *Defend, O Lord, thy servants from all dangers, both of body and soul.* I realized then that it was Saints Peter and Paul's feast day, and that the chains I observed around the necks of pedestrians earlier that morning were a symbol of their suffering.

———

On June 26, 2012, a shoot-out occurred in Mexico City's Benito Juárez International Airport. With its heavy security detail, foreign travelers, and shopping, the airport was promoted as the safest place in Mexico. But the shooting, which involved airport police officers that were also rival drug cartel members, conspicuously raised doubts about the invulnerability of the capital and the alleged goodness of the forces of law and order. Three narco-officers were killed as travelers ran for cover.

Less than twenty-four hours after the shooting, I returned to Mexico City for a round of summer fieldwork. Terminal Two was still very much a crime scene that day, and I tried to steer my young daughters' attention away from the masked federal police and their imposing guns. I was struck by the dissonance between their unsettling presence and the sight of families greeting travelers with bright bouquets of flowers, lovers enjoying long kisses.

A driver held a placard with my name. We piled into his SUV, Benjamin in the front passenger seat and me in back with the kids, their small bodies pressed tight against me.

For a greater part of the year, I had been separated from them. I'd taken a job at Stanford, leaving the girls with Benjamin in Los Angeles to finish out their final year of preschool before joining me in the Bay Area. It was a compromise Benjamin and I struck after countless arguments. He wanted "one more year" with the kids before agreeing to being the commuter parent. Although I didn't admit it, part of me welcomed our separation. I wanted time alone in San Francisco, where I had lived during my late teens and twenties, having fled New Mexico when I was seventeen. I came of age there. San Francisco was where I began healing from being abandoned by my parents, and it would become the setting for the demise of my marriage.

Our apartment in Mexico City was again in Colonia Roma, on a quiet tree-lined street with stately houses. Handing me the keys, the landlady informed us that the owner of our unit was an actress shooting a film in Spain. Assuming paparazzi, I asked if that explained the massive metal gate that separated the apartment building from the street. "Oh no!" she said. The gate was installed in 2008 due to kidnappings. She then bid us goodbye and, while walking away, offered to wash our laundry, babysit the kids, or cook our meals for a small fee. "You don't have to worry about anything while you're here," she said.

A few days later, I took the metro packed with passengers to Iztapalapa. Vendors navigated the crowded aisles hawking pens, batteries, hand sanitizer, and CDs. Padrino Francisco met me at Constitución de 1917, a metro stop commemorating Mexico's progressive constitution. Graffiti was scrawled all around the station announcing *The constitution is dead*.

It was raining that afternoon, as is often the case during Mexico City's summers. In the past, I had experienced the rain as a source of pleasure. I liked having to take cover with throngs of strangers, all of us huddled closely together under the canopies of buildings or the tarpaulins of market stalls. Although a few people would grow anxious and peel off into the street, it seemed to me that most people accepted, perhaps even welcomed, the chance to stand so close and still. But that summer my experience of rain changed.

Mexico City is built on lakes and wetlands drained by the Spanish and modernizing nineteenth-century government administrations, and it has suffered from both severe water shortages and flooding for centuries. At least 5 percent of the city is not connected to the water supply, and one-third of the city lacks regular access to water. During the rainy season, poor areas with inadequate drainage and sewage systems are transformed into "disaster zones," as if the causes and consequences of the season were unexpected. Low-lying neighborhoods contend with flooding, while informal settlements built on the slopes of surrounding mountains, like El Hoyo, experience landslides.

Since my last visit, Serenity had been forced to move to an isolated low-lying neighborhood to evade the municipal Sanitation Department, which kept citing it for violating federal standards for operating a drug recovery center. Previously, Padrino Francisco paid a modest bribe to avoid an infraction. But the citations had become too frequent and the bribes too expensive, making the move to a more remote location necessary.

Our drive to Serenity's new location was long. We passed through parts of Iztapalapa that I had never been to or even knew about, including its industrial zones. There were food processing and beer bottling plants, and plastics, textile, and chemical factories. Standing passengers crammed into microbuses stared wearily out the windows as our taxi passed by them. As we drove, Padrino Francisco explained that sanitation workers in charge of citations had become relentless because they were tied to criminal networks that took a large percentage of the bribe. He couldn't meet their increasing demands.

Meanwhile, the demand for anexos had skyrocketed. Padrino Francisco described a scenario that I saw playing out in the surveillance data: drug addiction, especially to crack cocaine, was increasing in Mexico City, as was the need for drug treatment. Families were increasingly turning to anexos to keep their kids safe from the violence that surrounded drugs. According to Padrino Francisco, the new anexos were less expensive but of poor quality. To keep up, he had to lower Serenity's fees, admit more people, and eventually relocate. This was very hard for him to do; he reminded me that he got clean at Serenity over a decade ago, and that he wanted to uphold the project Padrino Alfonso had started almost twenty years earlier.

We entered a shabby neighborhood of one-story cement houses and pitted asphalt roads. A few of the houses were painted bright primary colors, but most were stained from pollution and flooding. The streets were nearly empty of pedestrians and there were very few businesses. But there were several small chapels dedicated to San Judas Tadeo and Santa Muerte, the saints of lost causes and death, respectively.

Serenity's new neighborhood endured regular cutoffs of water and electricity, a hardship that had been rarely imposed in the former location. The street-level building lacked a gate, and its walls were badly cracked. From the outside it looked abandoned, except for the same vinyl banner, now tattered, advertising the anexo.

That summer, the number of anexados at Serenity was never less than thirty. They were younger than in previous years. Several were new to Mexico City, having fled the violence that tormented their hometowns in the states of Guerrero, Michoacán, and Tamaulipas. One of the recent arrivals was a fifteen-year-old boy named Lalo. He had only been in Mexico City for a few weeks when his mother committed him to Serenity. He recalled:

> Everyone said the capital is safer and there are jobs and things.
> I guess it's true, but I can't tell from here . . . I'm here because
> my mother saw all of the cholos in our new neighborhood and

she was afraid . . . I am her only son. I don't even do drugs or anything like that. I'm just me, and that was enough to land me here.

I asked him how long he expected to be at Serenity. "I don't know. Maybe until the war is over. But that will be a long time, no?"

2

THE LITTLE ROOM

When I was a child, I spent hours in little rooms. In New Mexico it was a shack behind my grandmother's house where thin slices of beef dried on a clothesline, hanging like sleeping bats. In Illinois, I huddled in the dark triangular nook underneath the stairs and listened to the thud of my older brother's footsteps. When we lived in Maine, I spent afternoons in the attic space at the top of the stairway, its ceiling so low I could touch the splintery wood with my hand. And when I was sixteen, back in New Mexico, it was a cubby in the public library, where I spent homeless days worried about homeless nights.

Some psychologists call tight spaces like these secret hideaways where kids assert their independence. For me they were a test of my mother's love. I wanted her to come for me. I'd wait for the door to suddenly open and daylight to rush in. Sometimes I waited all night, only to crawl out in the morning, my hair laced with cobwebs. It was in these tiny rooms that I learned how to see in the dark.

———————

Anexos captivated me immediately. It was like a reflex: small dim rooms filled with troubled kids. Sixteen-year-old César with the mismatched eyes, the gray one wandering outward. Eighteen-year-old Franklin, who tried to distract from his stutter with forearms covered in whirls of black tattoos. Luna la Pensativa, the pensive emo girl, who spent her free time writing out the lyrics of her favorite songs by Depeche Mode. Meche la Machita, the little butch, who was in love with Luna and threatened to kill anyone who hurt her. And Ceci, whose black hair and green eyes reminded me of Kate's.

It was Kate who introduced me to the Cathedral. We were both sixteen at the time. She was homeless and I lived in the Mother Road Hostel, not far in circumstance from her and the kids who made a life for themselves in that grim space with the grand name. The Cathedral was a place of last resort for young people who'd already succumbed to poverty, drugs, and violence. It was also a place of friendship and mutual support, with ratty kids sharing stories and substances to relieve the ache of their abandonment. Truthfully, the place terrified me. I worried that with one misstep I might find myself among its residents, folded into a blanket and sleeping on a concrete floor beside the buck-toothed girl who talked to herself. I wanted to imagine myself far from that crowd, even though I wasn't.

The main difference between anexos and the Cathedral wasn't just one of size. It was that with anexos, there was always somebody on the outside keeping you in. Hard as life was, there was an understanding that someone cared enough to lock you up. The only people looking out for the kids at the Cathedral were the kids who lived there. And they weren't locked up; they were free to roam at their own peril. They had the sense to huddle together, sometimes building a fire in the middle of the colossal building at night, telling stories that ricocheted off the walls while they got high.

In anexos, not everyone was a teenager. Lupe had three kids and annexed her son Miguel at Serenity when he was just twelve years old. Then, when Miguel was in his early twenties, he committed his mother to an anexo to curb her drinking. Efren was in his late forties or early fifties, he couldn't remember. He knew only that he was older than everyone else and deserved their respect. Delia was a thin, wiry woman with a gray braid that ran down her back. People told me not to bother talking to her because she'd lost touch with reality. One afternoon she walked up to me, shaking her finger back and forth in my face, as if clearing the air. "I have not lost touch with reality," she said in a quivering voice. "I cannot escape it."

────────

Delia's reality was Casa San Felipe, a *vecindad* not far from the Zócalo. A vecindad is a housing type common in Mexico City's historic center. It's usually composed of small two-room apartments designed around patios and communal courtyards. A gated passageway separates the building's interior from the street, giving the vecindad a protective, semi-hermetic feel. Some vecindades, like Casa San Felipe, have an anexo.

The anthropologist Oscar Lewis describes what it was like to live in a vecindad, or "slum tenement" as he called it, in the 1950s. His book *The Children of Sánchez* emphasizes the vecindad's strong sense of community. He describes courtyards crowded with people engaged in work and play, chickens and dogs roaming around, women hanging laundry and cooking meals. The inhabitants were poor and proud of their vecindad, a term that also happens to mean *neighborhood*. Many residents are related by blood and godparenthood, and they have lived in the buildings for decades, forging lifelong relationships.

The Children of Sánchez was a bestseller in the United States—but banned in Mexico—when it came out in 1961, and it found its way onto my mother's bookshelf. I must have been thirteen or fourteen years old when I first read it. I was mesmerized by Lewis's description of a family of six restricted to one small room. How did they sleep? Did they have sex? Was it ever quiet? I felt uneasy about how constrained life must have been for the Sánchez family, and yet I craved the sense of belonging the vecindad seemed to enable. The little rooms I locked myself in around the time I read the book were lonely places, places of abandonment. I would never have thought that I would find myself in one of these storied housing complexes, inquiring into the history not of a single family, but of a single room.

Decades later, I taught *The Children of Sánchez* in an anthropology course. This time around, I found myself railing against Lewis's "culture of poverty" theory—the idea that traits like "feelings of marginality" and "helplessness" perpetuated poverty from generation to generation. According to Lewis, Mexico City's vecindades played a role in entrapping its residents in an endless cycle of poverty. His idea persists and is partly responsible for projects that seek to "upgrade" or decimate low-income housing, including vecindades located in the very neighborhoods he writes about.

Delia lived in the vecindad Casa San Felipe her entire life. When we first met, she was fifty-three years old and had been in and out of its anexo for nearly ten years. Delia didn't have problems with addiction; she had schizophrenia. The first signs of her illness emerged in her late thirties, when she began to see and speak to her long-deceased mother. The communal and protective quality of the vecindad made it possible for Delia to live safely there for many years. Neighbors kept an eye on her when she was left home alone. They saw that she ate and invited her to coffee. But her behavior grew more erratic over time, and after much deliberation Delia's daughter committed her to the vecindad's anexo, Grupo Esperanza.

At every anexo I studied, there was at least one anexado identified by padrinos as mentally ill, usually schizophrenic. They tended to be older than other anexados and were often women. One woman was reportedly in Serenity for nearly a decade. I say reportedly because she never spoke on her own behalf. When I tried to make chitchat, she stared at me quietly before turning away. Her thick bangs hung over her face, and she often sat alone with her arms crossed over her chest. "*Sí, señor. No, señor*," she mumbled whenever someone passed her by, whether they addressed her or not. She was excused from most activities but seemed to take some satisfaction in her nightly job drying dishes. Sometimes I wondered if the anexo drove her crazy, or to what extent it exacerbated her illness.

Delia's situation was different. Unlike the other anexados at Grupo Esperanza, Delia was *media luz*, "half-light" or part-time. A few days a week, she was released into the care of her family. She'd eat, bathe, and watch TV. Then she'd return to the anexo, usually without complaint. She called Grupo Esperanza her *cuartito*, her little room, and Casa San Felipe, the vecindad in which it was situated, her house and neighborhood.

Casa San Felipe was named after one of the patron saints of Mexico City. It's located in the working-class neighborhood of Tepito, near the Church of the Immaculate Conception at Tequipeuhcan. A plaque on the exterior of the sixteenth-century church reads THE PLACE WHERE SLAVERY BEGAN, a reference to the subjugation of native people after the Spanish conquest. Today, the church is the site of weddings, baptisms, and feast day celebrations.

The vecindad presented a stark contrast tothe arched façade and domed tower of its neighbor. . From the street it looked like a cement box, squat and sinking. But its interior was very much alive. Gardens and shacks sprouted from rooftops, and doors to new rooms proliferated. Plants dangled from patios and weeds pushed their way through cracks in the cement courtyard. Cats roamed, parakeets talked. The loudest bird lived on the second floor. During the day, when its wire cage was uncovered, the bird repeated the same sequence: *Como quieres. Canta. Cuidado.* As you wish. Sing. Be careful. At night, the courtyard pulsed with the sounds of music, TV shows, and laughter.

In 2013, the building was ninety years old and still incomplete. Many residents had lived there their entire lives. Some remembered when a shared kitchen, laundry area, and bathroom were in the communal courtyard. Over time, private kitchens and bathrooms were installed in the two-room units, many of which were subdivided into even smaller rooms. The rooms had histories, not only in the sense of their changing shapes and occupations, but in their purposes as well.

Casa San Felipe's cuartito was first adjacent to the courtyard. In the 1930s, the room was primarily used for storage. Every day at dawn, aproned women went there to fetch cleaning supplies. Residents of the building woke to the quick brush of the women's sweeping, and the slap and drag of their mopping. Estella lived in the vecindad from childhood. She was in her seventies when she recalled her years of courtyard cleaning. "I remember the girls who cleaned with me. They were my friends. Their names? I can't say. But I see our wet feet."

The cuartito changed over the decades, and its transformations coincided with the crises of the times. During the 1940s, political elites embraced a modern vision for the rapidly growing Mexico City. Vecindades undermined the ideals of economic progress and modernization, and many were eradicated. Displaced people took shelter in Casa San Felipe's little room at night, finding a narrow space to rest among their neighbors' artisanal tools and consumer goods, which were sold on the street.

Prior to the 1950s, most of Mexico's population lived in rural areas. Rapid industrialization led to the growth of cities that attracted migrants from the countryside. At the same time, government policies favored capitalist agriculture entrepreneurs, leading to the displacement of small farmers. During this period, the little room was a temporary shelter for rural migrants with family ties to residents of Casa San Felipe. Meanwhile, efforts to redevelop neighborhoods in Mexico City with financial potential led to the outlawing of street vending, affecting the livelihood of those who still lived in vecindades. To support the vecindad's neediest residents, the little room also served as a pantry.

The mid-1960s through the early 1980s were defined by Mexico's *guerra sucia*, the dirty war. Mexico was the first Latin American country that put into place strategies learned at counterinsurgency schools in the United States, including the School of the Americas. The regime of the Institutional Revolutionary Party met guerillas, political dissidents, and their supporters with brutal violence. They razed villages, pursued mass arrests, and illegally detained and confined thousands of people in clandestine prisons. Anyone committed to a more just social, economic, and political order risked persecution, torture, and being disappeared. According to Carlos Monsiváis, "The guerrillas were lynched with excessive wrath, the bodies were thrown into the sea." Official discourse reduced dissidents to criminals, much as victims of today's narco war are characterized.

Among other repressive policies, the authoritarian government pursued an urban renewal program that sought to bulldoze Tepito's vecindades and replace them with middle-class housing projects. In response, Casa San Felipe's little room became a meeting place for community and political organizing to resist eviction. Arturo, a longtime resident of the vecindad, recalled his father heading over to the cuartito to discuss oppressive policing practices that targeted the neighborhood and residents who made their livings as street vendors. "Our goods were taken away and we were beaten or jailed. The fascists wanted us out."

On October 2, 1968, students and activists gathered at the Plaza de las Tres Culturas, the Plaza of the Three Cultures, in a part of the city called Tlatelolco. Settled in the fourteenth century by the Mexica, or Aztecs, the neighborhood was redeveloped as a massive public housing project designed by the modernist architect Mario Pani in the 1960s. The neighborhood also became the site for the headquarters of the foreign ministry and a national heritage site encompassing pre-Hispanic ruins and a colonial-era monastery. But on that October day in 1968, students gathered in the plaza to protest Mexico's authoritarian political system, widening inequality, and police brutality. Mexico City was preparing to host the summer Olympic Games, which were to open ten days later.

Police, military forces, and paramilitary units descended on the protesters, many of whom sought shelter in the new housing complex. The complex became the stage for the Tlatelolco massacre. While the death toll remains a contested number, most accounts estimate that four hundred people were killed. For decades, the government denied responsibility for the massacre. While there are documents that make a case for government responsibility, no credible investigation has ever taken place and no public officials have been definitively held accountable. It was the last confrontation of the Mexican Movement of 1968, and the movement's legacy continues with an annual Tlatelolco commemoration.

After Tlatelolco, the government doubled down on its efforts to eradicate vecindades, and participation in Casa San Felipe's organizing efforts expanded. Its community meetings quickly outgrew the little room and moved to the communal courtyard. Arturo remembered hanging around in the stairwell with other children, excited by residents' plans to resist displacement. "I learned to stand against injustice, how to respond, with whatever available means . . . The vecindad is more than my home. It is where I developed a social conscience."

On September 19, 1985, an 8.1-magnitude earthquake hit Mexico City and the downtown area was heavily damaged. Buildings collapsed; streets were ruptured. More than ten thousand people died, and thousands more were injured and left homeless. In her chronicle of the immediate after-math of the earthquake, Elena Poniatowska writes that people didn't die because of the earthquake; they died because of "a corrupt government that [didn't] give a damn about people living and working in buildings that can collapse. The government [knew] that many buildings [were] death traps." Several vecindades were destroyed in the earthquake, but Casa San Felipe survived. It was badly damaged, but residents quickly took to fixing its cracked walls and broken stairwells out of fear that the building might be condemned and its residents displaced. Following the earthquake, the little room adjacent to the courtyard became a shelter once more, this time for neighbors who'd lost everything.

It was around the mid-1990s that a spike in drug use occurred. Drug trafficking was never only the domain of large criminal groups but also of small-time dealers who sold drugs within their own neighborhoods to make ends meet. Small-scale dealing contributed to the rise in drug addiction, as well as increased policing of low-income neighborhoods. It was during this time that the little room began to hold round-the-clock twelve-step meetings, called *juntas*, for the vecindad's residents. At Casa San Felipe and elsewhere, these were the precursors of anexos.

Maintaining elements of traditional Alcoholics Anonymous meetings (working the steps, reciting the Serenity Prayer), *juntas* are filled with tes-timonies about issues often shared in recovery settings, like broken hearts and feelings of hopelessness. The testimonies also recount harrowing ex-periences of violence—criminal, familial, or social. Describing his testi-monies at Serenity, Neto said, "I tell my story here. I tell it like it is, all the shit, the pain. Nobody tells me to stop until I get it out of me, you know? It's like a release."

After one of Neto's testimonies of the landslide, he was embraced by his peers. Watching the anexados wrap around him, I was struck by how they held not only Neto, but each other as well. This proximity was ex-periential in its fullest sense, and it was maintained well after Neto had finished his own story of disaster as he became a listener to stories told by Bobby, Angel, Ceci, and others. Their shared suffering gave way to a kind of collective healing—expressive, communicative, resonant. This was not *recovery* in the common sense of the term—the cessation of alcohol and drug use—but something more profound.

———

One afternoon, while sitting in his office at Serenity, Padrino Francisco recalled life in the 1990s: "It was a fucking mess." His mother, Señora Mariana, happened to be at the anexo that day. She visited Serenity from time to time, bringing food and supplies. Sometimes she chatted with the anexados in an encouraging way, reminding them that her son was once worse off than they were and that they too could make it.

Señora Mariana chided her son. "What do you remember about the 1990s? You were too high on drugs. *I* remember." She tugged at the gold crucifix that hung from her neck.

"Everything was *la crisis*," she said. I'd read the macroanalyses: crushing national debt, the privatization of state-owned enterprises, inflation, increases in unemployment. In 1994, the exchange of the US dollar to the Mexican peso was one to four; in 1995, it was one to eight.

For Señora Mariana, the crisis was more than financial. Her siblings, with whom she was close, migrated north in search of work. She stayed in Mexico City, taking care of her arthritic mother. She eked out a living in the same way that many women in working-class and poor neighborhoods did—by buying clothes and household items at cheap rates, then selling these things to family and neighbors. At one point, her two-room household swelled to include an uncle, a cousin, and her cousin's two children. More than money, she worried about her own two sons, both of whom got sucked into a rapidly expanding drug trade. Her fears were well-founded.

"I lost one of my sons. And this one," she said, referring to Padrino Francisco. She shook her head, tears filling her eyes. "When he came back, the first thing I did was commit him to Serenity. I refused to lose another child."

———

In 2004, two years before narco war officially commenced, residents of Casa San Felipe had gathered in the courtyard to celebrate the christening of its anexo, Grupo Esperanza, based in the little room that had already seen so much history. I met the anexo's padrino at a small restaurant a few blocks away. Padrino Francisco was my point of contact for most of the anexos I visited, and he introduced me to many of the people I met and interviewed. He assured me that Grupo Esperanza's padrino was a good man, well-respected by the community, and so trustworthy he'd put his own kids under the padrino's care. In other words, I didn't have to worry about my safety.

Padrino Julio was at the restaurant when I arrived. He called me to his table with a flick of his hand and watched me approach. I steered around the tightly packed tables, apologizing each time I bumped into someone's chair.

"Doctor Garcia," he said, looking me up and down. "From one doctor to another, you don't look like a doctor." I wore jeans and a T-shirt, he a collared shirt and a silver cowboy belt. I told him that I wasn't a doctor.

"But you are a doctor."

"No. Not that kind. You're a doctor?"

"Yes, I'm a doctor. Not that kind." He laughed.

Our first course was a few rice-shaped noodles floating in a bowl of salty broth. Padrino Julio didn't touch his food but got right to the point. "I want to know what you want to know."

As the waitress switched out our plates, I gave him my usual spiel. I was interested in the different ways people treat addiction and wanted to learn how his program worked, how he helped people. While true, I imagined my response wasn't enough to gain his trust. I was a stranger seeking entrance into an underground world. Why should my interests be enough to let me in?

Journalist friends working for American media outlets wondered the same thing. One evening, I joined them for Friday night drinks at a brightly lit place in trendy La Condesa. Getting rowdier with each beer or mezcal, they swapped stories about their latest assignments. Elections, water shortages, kidnappings. One of the heaviest drinkers pestered me for connections. He wanted to get into an anexo and write his own story. I said I'd help but I never did. I didn't want to risk jeopardizing the relationships I'd built over years.

Padrino Julio stared at me from across the table. I started to put away the audio recorder I had presumptuously placed on our table when I first arrived, but Padrino Julio reached forward and stopped me. His hand was confident and heavy. I caught a glimpse of blue tattoos, blurry with age, on the insides of his forearms. He told me to leave the recorder and turn it on. The first recorded words were his. "What makes you think you can understand what we do?" It was more a challenge than a question. "Are your eyes open or closed?" he continued.

"Open," I said, wondering where the conversation was headed.

"You see things with your eyes."

"Yes."

"What do you see?"

"I see what is before me."

"Before you?"

"Yes."

"Do you listen?"

"Yes."

"How do you listen?"

"Yes, I listen."

"What do you listen to?"

"The sounds that are around me. Like—"

"Do you have a weak constitution?"

"Sorry, what do you mean?"

"Do you have a weak constitution?"

"I don't think so. No."

He is not a good man, I thought to myself. *He is humiliating me.* I wanted to flee but I was stuck.

The waitress swept the floor and wiped down the surrounding tables. We were the only people left in the restaurant. She refilled my glass with the juice of the day. It tasted like watered down Kool-Aid, powdery and sweet. A drink for a child.

Padrino Julio whittled me down with more questions. *Do you have asthma? Does the air give you headaches? Do you have difficulty making friends? Are you Catholic? Do you want a cigarette? Where were you born?*

How old are you? I stammered, answering no when I meant yes, yes when I meant no.

"Tell me how it is where you are from," he asked.

"You mean recovery?"

"As you like."

I didn't notice the afternoon downpour until I listened to the audio recording years after the interview took place. A long crack of thunder, rain hitting the street, people running for cover. For seventy-three seconds I searched for an answer to his question. For seventy-three seconds he waited for it.

"The families leave," I finally said. "Not geographically. I mean, they can be right there and still gone. It's not like that here, right?"

Silence. Eighty-seven seconds.

I spoke again. "Where I'm from, families just leave you. They're completely fucked up. But it doesn't really matter, right? Because they leave you."

Silence. Ninety-eight seconds.

Padrino Julio gave an order to the waitress. She responded, closing the restaurant's metal gate, trapping us inside.

I didn't say anything else. I was crying.

———

Padrino Julio reminded me of my father. They were similar in stature, with the same gray-green eyes and wavy black hair. They called themselves doctors, and, although my father was pursuing a PhD in political science, his dissertation was as yet unfinished. And they both communicated through endless questions, a kind of Socratic method that felt like interrogation.

Unlike Padrino Julio, my father didn't want to teach me a lesson. He merely wanted to extract information about my mother, whom he suspected was unfaithful. *Did she leave the house today? For how long? Did she wear lipstick? Receive any phone calls?* The more I answered no, the faster and harder the questions came. My father was convinced that I was withholding things from him, and that I was lying on behalf of my mother. The angrier he became, the more terrified I was. These scenes always ended in the same way—with him walking away, hissing that I was not his child, and me in tears, wondering if what he said was true.

My father is from a Greek military family so proud that his father, my *papou*, named him Ares, after the god of war. One of my memories of my father is of him sitting in a tweed armchair. There were books I needed to read—Greek tragedies by Aeschylus, Sophocles, Euripides. We had a handsome four-volume boxed set, the spine of each book adorned with the image of a Greek god.

I was twelve when the lessons began. I was already a big reader, but too young to fully grasp the heavy books my father placed in my hands. It didn't matter. The Greek tragedies, my father said, were meant to be performed in front of an audience of citizens. He'd sit back in the chair, his eyes a stage light on my face. I spoke the long columns of text, my nail-bitten finger tracing the verses. I had only a dim awareness that all those tragic characters were uttering laments, and that the deceased family members troubled the lives of the living.

I had just started to read part three of Aeschylus's *Oresteia*, *The Eumenides*, when my father moved across the country to take an adjunct job at another university. My mother, siblings, and I remained in our drafty old house in Maine, which papou had bought for us. My father's stint at the university in Maine had been short-lived. He hardly ever produced publications, and his temper drew complaints.

The money my father promised to send from his new teaching position was always late and less than promised. My older brother found a job bagging customers' groceries at the nearest market, the very place that displayed our bounced checks for all to see. It humiliated him. More than anyone, it was my older brother who felt betrayed by my father. He threatened to kill him, but became, in a sense, a version of him—angry, hurt, and vengeful. I took refuge in the attic during my brother's understandable fits of rage. The previous owners of the house had left things there—a pair of old wooden skis, wool blankets, a beveled mirror. It was in the attic, before the mirror, that I finished reciting the *Oresteia* to myself.

The Furies fueled my reading. I was drawn to those daughters of the night whose home was underground, sisters sick with an anger so powerful it dripped like blood from their eyes. I understood that the Furies vengeance wasn't evil or random. It was on behalf of murdered kin. Before the events of the *Oresteia*, Agamemnon sacrifices his daughter Iphigenia to the gods. Ten years later, Agamemnon's wife, Clytemnestra, murders him and his mistress, avenging the death of her daughter. After, their son Orestes murders his mother to avenge the death of his father. The Furies then pursue Orestes for committing the crime of matricide. Once taken, they surround Orestes and avenge the murder of his mother with a binding song to drive him mad.

I imagined our family playing the roles, but in my version of the *Oresteia* my father, Ares, sacrificed me; my mother killed herself; and my brother murdered my father to avenge our deaths. But what of my brother's fate? This I couldn't resolve, not then. The only way I could endure my family's collapse was to turn it into Greek tragedy.

A few months after my father left, my mother found me standing in front of the tweed chair in the middle of the night. I had peed myself and was speaking lines from the Furies' binding song. *Do you hear the Furies' hymn? That which claims the senses dim.* At some point, I fell to the ground. A seizure. It was my brother who drove me to the hospital emergency room that winter night. I stared at him from the backseat of our beat-up Volkswagen Bug. "God damn him," he cried. "God damn him."

———

One of the things that I learned from Padrino Julio is that it's easy to commit a relative to an anexo. All that's needed is someone's signature on a petition. The signature attests that the signee, usually a mother, knows what she's doing. It releases the anexo from responsibility for any unwanted outcome, be it injury, sickness, or death.

Padrino Julio often compared the petition to legal agreements required by hospitals. He told me the story of a seventeen-year-old boy who died in an anexo. His mother claimed the anexo killed him and went to file charges with the police. But the padrino presented the petition she had signed and charges against the anexo were never filed. The mother was sent away.

Some anexos don't bother with petitions, and those that do rarely keep records of anything else. This is neither malpractice nor a a lack of education or expertise in bureaucratic practice. It's an indication of what matters most. In a country that is known for its endless layers of red tape, dysfunctional organizational structures, and constant deferrals, anexos' refusal to keep "risk assessments" and detailed patient records highlights the urgencies to which they must respond. Decisions made by padrinos are highly discretionary. Instead of uniform guidelines, there are allegiances and preferences. A neighbor who appeals to a padrino to take her abusive husband is prioritized over an unfamiliar young woman addicted to methamphetamine. An older alcoholic is refused care while a teenage crack user in trouble with a gang is admitted. These are decisions that padrinos make on the fly. *La cosa más importante*, the most important thing, padrinos often said, was that people had access to protection.

While they may not keep patient records, all anexos keep track of numbers. Amount owed, payment received; payment late, penalty accrued. Payment is usually due the seventh of each month. Most families pay in cash, and those that can't pay with goods: stereos, TVs, tools, a lot of it stolen.

Marta's son was at Grupo Esperanza for five months. She lived in Casa San Felipe and got up before dawn to go to wholesale markets, where she picked up merchandise to be sold at smaller neighborhood markets. When her work was finished, she'd grab a couple of hours of sleep before her next job. On more than one occasion she was held up and the things she was transporting were stolen. I asked her if her son knew how hard she worked in order to pay for his treatment at Grupo Esperanza.

"If he knew he'd tell me to stop killing myself. But if I didn't? Well, it doesn't matter. I've worked like this all my life."

Sometimes mothers barter directly with padrinos. They bring food, or wash clothes and blankets in lieu of cash payments. Having personal ties to a padrino sometimes helps, but only up to a point. Families that don't contribute anything have their kids kicked out, something the kids are often happy about. But there are also those who are just left there and are punished for their parents' apparent abandonment of them. They have to take on more than the usual share of chores—scrubbing floors on hands and knees, days and days of washing dishes, removing waste from clogged toilets. Despite these indignities, they are given room and board and included in daily activities, just like everyone else.

The families who pay on time each month are allowed brief visits with their relatives. At Grupo Esperanza these visits took place Sunday afternoons. I only saw mothers visit their kids. I watched them assess their physical conditions and try to read their eyes. Most of the time they didn't say anything.

One afternoon I asked Marta, who had just visited her son, what kind of treatment he received at Grupo Esperanza. She was quiet for a moment, and then said the anexo provided him with the kind of treatment she could not. *Terapia fuerte*, strong treatment, she called it. Later I learned that strong treatment referred to an unyielding control that often took the form of physical violence. "It's too hard for me to stay strong," she explained, referring to the difficulty of keeping her son in line. It was easier for her to work sixteen-hour days and have someone else handle him.

Many of the women I met were like Marta. They were single, with little to no involvement with the men with whom they'd had children. The fathers were long gone—either because they had left the family, migrated to the United States, or died. This placed a tremendous financial burden on women, who scrambled to meet anexos' weekly or monthly fees.

Hortencia worked long hours at a hotel to keep Daniel in an anexo and out of harm's way. Her labor was the price to pay for his safety and, to a certain extent, her own. On more than one occasion, she described how, when Daniel was in an anexo, she was no longer subject to his erratic and sometimes threatening behavior. "He's not stealing from me. He's not yelling at me. He's not passed out on the couch when I get home from work." He was safe inside the anexo and at a comfortable distance from her.

"Do you visit him?" I asked Hortencia.

"Sometimes," she said.

———————

Not long after our first meeting in the restaurant, Padrino Julio invited me to visit Grupo Esperanza. When I arrived, he called both counselors to the front room and introduced me to them as Dr. Garcia. I said I wasn't a doctor, but they called me one anyway. After our brief introductions, Padrino Julio led me to the second room, where his patients, as he called them, were cleaning.

"This is Doctor Garcia," he said in a threatening voice. "Treat her with respect. No fucking around. Call her Doctor Garcia. Nothing else."

It was midday, sunny outside but dark inside. I scanned the room. The blankets that were used for beds were tightly rolled in a corner, next to spray bottles of cleaning fluids and rags folded as neatly as fine napkins. Metal folding chairs were stacked against the wall.

I always felt embarrassed during my initial visits to an anexo, like a new kid walking into a classroom already in session. But new students usually have a place assigned to them. There was no such place for me at Grupo Esperanza. I stood close to a wall and looked around with a feeling of dread.

The patients at Grupo Esperanza called me Dr. Garcia. They asked me to look at infected cuts, painful bruises, scaly skin. They asked for painkillers for aching backs, antibiotics for urinary tract infections, something to stop diarrhea. I gave up insisting that I wasn't a "real" doctor.

The first thing Rita said to me was that she suffered blinding migraines. Rita was in her early twenties and had been at Grupo Esperanza for three months. She had lived a couple of blocks away from the anexo with her mother, brother, sister-in-law, and niece. With four working adults, the household was financially stable and relatively harmonious, at least until Rita started using drugs. She stopped working and started stealing. Rita's mother and brother worried she'd be killed, or arrested and sent to Mexico City's women's prison, notorious for its abysmal conditions and abuse. They committed her to Grupo Esperanza to protect her from such outcomes.

Rita's migraines made it impossible for her to follow the anexo's schedule and rules. They got her in trouble, she said, especially if she vomited. Rita looked at me with panicky eyes. "I feel one coming."

I needed to talk to the counselor about bringing her medicine. The one on duty that day was Temo. He was cruel and demeaning, especially when he was the only one left in charge. On those days he wore a knockoff Izod shirt and a watch too tight for his hairy wrist. The anexados called him El Reloj, the Watch. I couldn't stand Temo and avoided interacting with him.

But on that day, I needed to. "Rita needs medicine for her migraines," I said, trying to sound unaffected by his noxious presence. "I have the medicine she needs. I can bring it for her, plus enough to store away in case someone needs it later." Temo ignored me and surveilled the room. The patients were cleaning up after lunch, which had consisted of two tortillas and a cup of beans. I said I too had migraines, and all I could do when one hit was lay down and close my eyes. But the medicine helped and would quickly wipe the pain away, I explained. Temo shot me a look of disgust. He told me he didn't care about my fucking headaches and called Rita a lazy fucking whore. I flared with rage. I was afraid of Temo, but I hated him even more.

"Imagine someone standing on your head while you're being electrocuted. That's what it feels like."

Temo looked at me, grinning. I forced myself to not look away from him for as long as I possibly could.

———

The wall between the anexo and the courtyard was porous. Inside, you could hear what was happening in the courtyard. Couples arguing, babies crying, people building things or tearing them down. Different outside sounds conjured different responses among the anexados. Laughter often led to slumped shoulders and forlorn expressions, arguments to clenched fists. Eyes darted around the room every time a cell phone chimed. Music drew relief and, depending on who was left in charge, singing. The sounds from outside were endless and often stirred up anguish and frustration. *Shut up! Shut the fuck up!*

It wasn't just sounds that penetrated the small room. Aromas of cooking and smoke from tobacco and weed floated in the air, whetting appetites and inspiring complaints about moldy tortillas. Smells drew whispers, too. *I'm hungry. It's hard to breathe. My stomach hurts. I can't stop shaking.*

To be separated from the sources of sensory stimulation is not to be cut off from sense. Stuck inside a room, day after day, the senses still change and shift in intensity, just like they do anywhere else. The senses are attentive to life and give it meaning, even when life and meaning seem to have dimmed.

While permeable, the wall was also protective, like skin. Like skin, it felt, and it sensed, the absence of feeling. With movement restricted because of the size of the room, anexados' legs went numb. They'd hop on one foot or bang their calves with fists. "I can't feel it!" they'd shout, their voice full of feeling. In fits of anger walls were punched. Bored or depressed, walls were leaned upon. The walls absorbed and provoked, membranes between worlds.

They were also messengers of another cosmos. In the courtyard, young kids huddled next to the threshold and giggled as they listened to the constant stream of vulgarities coming from the other side. The testimonies they heard were dark and disturbing, the phrase *I'm sorry, I'm sorry* a constant refrain. The kids covered their mouths with small hands and looked at each other, their eyes wide with excitement.

"My brother is in there," one of the boys told me. He looked five or six years old.

"Who's your brother?"

"Pepe. He stole money to get drugs."

"Do you miss him?"

"Not really."

"Do you want him to come out?"

"No. Not yet."

The little boy stared at Grupo Esperanza's metal door. It was secured with a padlock as threatening as his older brother's fist.

————

Delia left the anexo for a few hours during the day. A family member would pick her up and take responsibility for her during her time away. According to Padrino Julio, these outings had happened less and less over the years. Delia's daughter held down two jobs and was a single mother, and her son commuted long hours to work. One afternoon, Delia asked me to sign her out and escort her around the vecindad. She needed fresh air and a bit of sun, she said. Padrino Julio gave me permission to walk with Delia. We strolled around the second story patio several times, passing doors that were mostly closed. A few neighbors stepped out to greet her. We walked down the stairway and stood in the courtyard, where Delia looked up to the low gray sky. "It's so small," she said. "Just a small box."

She was ready to return to the anexo sooner than I expected. I stayed by her side as she slowly approached the little room. We were five units away when she suddenly stopped walking and knocked on a door.

"This was my house," she said, using the past tense.

"It's still your house," I answered.

Delia looked at me. "Is it?" she asked.

"Yes."

She looked at the door in disbelief, then knocked again. No one was home.

————

It was 2013. Things were getting worse. More disappearances, more death, more frightened and exhausted mothers desperate to keep their kids safe. Padrino Julio told me that ten patients were as many as he wanted to take in, but it was getting too hard to turn people away. Plus, there was money to be made.

Grupo Esperanza eventually moved from the little room adjacent to the courtyard to a larger apartment on the second floor. The apartment was the lifelong home of Celia, a serious woman who made her living altering used clothes and selling them good as new. The apartment was an inheritance from her parents, and she had planned to pass it along to her own children. But her son racked up threatening debts, and her daughter was, in Celia's words, a worthless drunk. Celia was in her early fifties when she rented the apartment to Padrino Julio. She gave some of the money to her son and moved to the outskirts of the city to live with her sister, who was paralyzed from the waist down. Celia said her poor sister had an accident before she could have children. "She's lucky that way, at least." She never said what the accident was.

Padrino Julio turned the apartment's front room, Celia's old living room, into an office. An indestructible tanker desk filled most of it, and he spent most of the day sitting behind it, making phone calls. Sometimes he fell asleep in a stained office chair, his shiny black boots propped up on the desk's Formica top.

The walls of the office were crowded with framed certificates that resembled diplomas that might hang in a doctor's office. Most of the certificates were from other anexos. GRUPO LUZ DE VIDA CELEBRATES GRUPO ESPERANZA'S FAITHFUL SERVICE TO THOSE IN NEED. MAY GOD PROTECT YOU. Others were issued from Grupo Esperanza in recognition of itself. These certificates noted the date of establishment, the passing of the torch from one padrino to the next, and messages from grateful families. There were also certifications from government agencies and letters from officials thanking Grupo Esperanza for its service to the community. I assumed those were fake, but never asked.

There was also a small medicine cabinet on the wall, its glass door revealing its contents. Out-of-date packs of amoxicillin, rubbing alcohol, vitamin B_{12}, antidiarrheal medication, bandages, and plastic bottles labeled IBUPROFEN and CLORAZEPATE, which is for alcohol withdrawal. Despite the complaints from anexados about their physical conditions, the medicines remained untouched.

The second room was larger than the office, but the number of people inside it made it feel tiny in comparison. Security bars cut across two rectangular windows, and faded sheets of newspaper covered their glass. The newspaper copy ran right side up, upside down, horizontal, askew.

Windows always do more than intended. They don't just conceal or expose. Uncovered, a window keeps time. Open, it breathes. Obscured by newspapers, it tells stories. A window is always an aperture onto escape, even if barred.

The Mexican artist Martín Ramírez understood this. In the parlance of the art world, Ramírez is an "outside" artist, which is ironic since he was institutionalized in mental hospitals in California for half his life. The outsider-ness of Ramírez's art was not his lack of formal training. It was his immigration status, Spanish language, lack of family ties, and diagnosis of schizophrenia. He was not outside; he was expelled from within. His artist's tools were abandoned objects and trash he collected from the mental hospital: burnt matches, cigarette butts, pencil stubs, wooden tongue depressors, old newspapers. He painted watercolors with his own saliva.

Ramírez drew and painted grids of tiny cells, swerving trains, startled deer. He drew horses with their front legs lifted high in the air, as if about to turn and run. At one point, Ramírez shared one room with more than sixty men. His paintings were his windows, and they looked onto escape.

Ramírez's art gained wider recognition in the 1990ss, and in 2015 the US Postal Service released commemorative Martín Ramírez stamps. I couldn't bear the thought of shrunken replicas of his paintings torn from a plastic sheet, forty-nine cents each. I imagined them crisscrossing the country, Ramírez's entire world affixed to the upper right corner of an envelope stuffed with utility bills. This was not his escape. I bought as many sheets of the commemorative stamps as I could and made a home for Martín Ramírez in a cigar box that still smells of tobacco.

Anexados at Grupo Esperanza and elsewhere often talked about escape. They were either like Ángel, planning a mass *fuga*, or like Rita, looking ruefully into space while listing the things she planned to do when she got out: wash her hair, visit her sister, go to the movies. She would pepper Delia with questions after Delia returned from an afternoon out with her family. *Did you see anyone in the courtyard? What did you do? What did you eat?* Rita was hungry for news, for some sort of experience that wasn't her own. That's why she got high, she said. She liked the escape it offered her.

"Escape from what?" I asked her while we sat on the floor with nothing to do but pass time.

"From worry. There's always something to worry about . . . That's why my mom brought me here. She was looking to escape worry, too."

———

The newly committed anexados were tossed into Grupo Esperanza with only the clothes they were wearing when they were "lifted." Their shoes were replaced with cheap, open-toed black rubber sandals. *Chanclas del oro*, gold sandals, they were called jokingly. The black sandals that were called gold were the subject of constant amusement and frustration. *Try mine. Yours fit better. These fucking things keep falling off. My feet are too fat. Your toes are disgusting.*

One morning a woman in a short, shimmery dress arrived. Her face was painted with bright makeup, and she towered over the counselor while standing in her scuffed high heels. The men immediately started to howl and whistle at the sight of her. "Sheila! Sheila!"

Sheila kicked off her heels and held out her hand as if to be kissed. A counselor pulled a stack of bracelets off her wrists. She'd clearly been through this before. But Sheila's confidence waned when it was time to swap her dress for leftover clothes. She turned her back on her audience and removed her black stockings. Then she reached down and quickly ripped off strips of tape from between her legs. Exposed, she covered her penis with her hands while men shouted vulgarities. She responded with a diatribe and yelled for the counselor to hurry the fuck up and bring her the damn clothes. Her voice was musical but nervous, like notes from a flautist with trembling lips.

Sheila was from a small city in the state of Puebla and had moved to Mexico City at sixteen to escape the stigma of being feminine and gay.

A hairdresser and entertainer in shows in the Zona Rosa, she wanted to be a *mujer completa*, a complete woman, but didn't have the money for surgery.

One afternoon, Sheila told me about the abuse she and other trans women endured at the hands of police. "We're easy prey," she said. "Even women discriminate against us, usually because we're more beautiful than they are."

Beauty was important to Sheila, and she often requested products from me. Pantene shampoo, "American" soap, mascara. She urged me to take my hair out of its ponytail and let it fall past my shoulders. "Why hide it?" she said as she styled my hair with her hands.

———

Every day, two collapsible conference tables were assembled three times: at seven in the morning for breakfast, noon for study, and six for dinner. At mealtimes the tables were pushed together. The anexados sat in regular spots, day after day, elbow to elbow. Newbies and troublemakers sat on the floor.

Two anexados were assigned cooking duties each night, one of whom was often Delia. Sometimes this meant doling out a dish prepared by a neighbor, usually a woman with a kid or husband locked inside. Other times it involved chopping whatever vegetables were on hand, like carrots and squash, and tossing them in water for soup. Meat was a rarity and sorely missed. Everyone lost weight.

Sometimes Padrino Julio would join and sit at the head of the table. On those rare occasions, everyone was well-mannered, and his patients spoke only when spoken to. But it was usually two counselors left in charge. Talk at dinner was loose and lively. People gossiped about goings-on in the vecindad—so-and-so hooked up, a neighbor went missing, another one was going to get his ass kicked. Counselor Lorenzo was a news junkie and reported some of the latest headlines. A major topic of conversation that summer was the arrest of Miguel Treviño Morales, the leader of Los Zetas cartel. The Zetas were known for making "stew" out of their victims' bodies, and some of the more obnoxious anexados joked about the Zetas' methods while slurping down their soup. President Enrique Peña Nieto claimed the arrest of the kingpin was a victory, a sign that law and order was finally being restored. The anexados called the president a pussy and a crook.

One evening, the conversation focused on which objects people missed most. Weed, alcohol, food, a real bed. "My high heels," Sheila said.

It was Pepe's turn. Pepe had facial piercings and two sleeves of tattoos. For some reason the counselors had let him keep his jewelry, which no one dared call jewelry. Nor did anyone try to rip it off during the frequent brawls he always won. I often thought about Pepe's little brother in the courtyard and the way he said he didn't miss him, wasn't ready for him to get out.

"I miss Sheila's ass," Pepe sneered, drawing an outburst of laughter from the men around the table.

Mari was next. She was seventeen and flirted with everyone, possibly in an effort to protect herself. She sighed and said she missed her hairbrush. "I'm sick of brushing my hair with my fingers." Sheila nodded in agreement, then looked down at the newbie sitting on the floor. "What about you, sweetie?"

Minutes after his arrival at Grupo Esperanza, Nicolas was renamed *Catorce*—fourteen, his age. It was his first time in an anexo, and after two weeks he still looked shocked to find himself there. He was delicate and soft-spoken and the target of constant insults, especially from Temo and Pepe. Catorce's dark eyes darted around the room, confirming his permission to speak.

"I don't know," he said.

"How about dick?" Pepe smirked.

Sheila immediately shot back. "Shut the fuck up."

Catorce sat cross-legged on the floor and stared at his bowl of soup. He closed his eyes for a minute, like he was making a birthday wish. When he opened them, he said, "I miss my phone. So I can check Facebook."

Catorce's mother committed him to Grupo Esperanza when she'd had to leave town unexpectedly. There were family matters she needed to attend to, and she didn't want to leave her son alone. He'd already started drinking and smoking pot, and she worried he'd get into trouble. She reasoned that the anexo would keep him safe and teach him a lesson.

She said she would return for him in a few weeks, but weeks turned into months. The start of the school year was quickly approaching and there was no indication that Catorce would enter ninth grade on time. He appeared increasingly anxious and, in a small voice, asked Padrino Julio if he'd received any news from his mother. "Not yet" was always the answer.

———

Most houses have rooms with names: bedroom, living room, dining room, kitchen, bathroom, laundry. If the owners are wealthy enough, the house might also have a room for recreation, another for study. The names of rooms distinguish one from another. They divide a day's activities and indicate whether the room is occupied by one person or more. The names of rooms structure the lives they sustain.

The anexo is a room attached to a house. Like a house, it is also a space for living. But the anexo provides no prescribed map or schedule for the day. In this sense the anexo is *unschooled*, to use Roland Barthes's architectural term. It makes its own way.

I was fourteen when my father left Maine. Soon after, my mother fell into a deep depression and rarely left her room. I felt as if I lived alone that summer, reading during the day, frightened at night. The place I felt safest was the attic. It was musty and dim, lit by a single light bulb with a pull string. I lay on the floor atop of the leftover blankets and stared at the rafters, listening for signs of life.

Summer ended and my family tried to reunite one more time. We joined my father in Idaho. The last house we shared was a lime-green Victorian. It belonged to another professor on sabbatical, and it was stuffed with objects from his travels: African textiles hanging on cream-colored walls; Zulu baskets and masks assembled in glass display cases; and wooden fertility sculptures as tall as my little brother. My father followed us from room to room screaming, "Be careful! Don't break anything!"

It was our family that was breaking. My father began an affair with one of his students and my mother returned to New Mexico, leaving me and my siblings in Idaho. With my mother gone, my father and his new girlfriend rented a big house in one of Boise's gated communities. They took my younger sister and brother to the new house, but not me. I learned about their plans on moving day, which was also April Fool's. The girlfriend was the one who broke the news, informing me, dryly, that there wasn't enough room for me in the new house. We were alone in the living room, under the watchful gaze of the African masks. She was wearing her tight, neon-colored workout clothes, and I was dressed head to toe in black, sleeves pulled over my razor-blade scarred arms.

"But where will I go?" I asked her, choking back tears.

She handed me an envelope with four hundred-dollar bills, one for each week of April. She told me that I was lucky to have the whole house to myself for one month. "Every fifteen-year-old in the world would die to be in your shoes," she said, suddenly trying to sound upbeat.

"But what will happen in May?" I asked, my voice desperate. She didn't say, and neither did my father. He was outside, waiting for his girlfriend in his new sports car, my younger siblings sitting clueless in the back seat.

One April afternoon, shortly before my alone time in the Victorian was up, two women paid me a visit. They wore vintage kimonos, had buzz cuts like Buddhist monks, and had bland smiles on their faces. "You must be Angela," one of them said as she extended her hand. "We're Helen and Anne."

They explained that they had heard about my situation and, for reasons unknown to me, wanted to see if there was anything they could do to help. I startled them, and myself, by admitting that I would soon be homeless and needed a place to live.

I lived with Helen and Anne, rent free, until I completed my sophomore year at Boise High. What I remember most about that time was the parties Helen and Anne threw almost every evening. Their guests smelled like patchouli and played drums on the floor, tripping on mushrooms or LSD. Some called me *sweetie* or *angel* and showered me with unwanted affection, while others appeared discomfited by my dark presence, or by the attention given to me. Lacking a bedroom of my own, I would slip away into Helen's room and lie on her mattress on the floor. I'd cry silently, listening to the strangers in the other room. After the end of the school year I returned to New Mexico, leaving my younger siblings behind with my father.

There, I found my mother pregnant and living in a one-bedroom apartment with a family friend. I slept on the living room sofa for a few weeks and watched my mother prepare the place for a new child. I felt invisible and pushed out.

I stopped going to school when I was sixteen, just weeks after I had started my junior year of high school. Ceci, one of the anexados at Serenity, was also sixteen when she stopped going to school. The *preparatoria* she attended didn't prepare her for anything, she said. Plus, she couldn't imagine a life after school, so why stay?

Her parents were unhappy with her decision to drop out but appreciated her help in their small stationery shop. She worked under the watch of her mother, tidying inventory and managing the place while her mother took on extra work selling plastic food containers to neighbors. But the help didn't last long. Within a few months Ceci started partying and staying out several nights a week, worrying her parents.

My mother supported my decision to drop out, reasoning that I was smart and independent, better off taking my GED and going directly to college. I got the GED but didn't go to college. Like Ceci, it was difficult for me to imagine a future. I spent my days drifting between other people's houses while waiting for a room to open at the Mother Road Hostel. While I waited, I passed my unschooled days walking up and down Albuquerque's Central Avenue, passing a row of divey motels and junkies shooting up under Interstate 25's overpass. I'd rest in Old Town's grassy square and watch tourists awkwardly browse the spread of turquoise jewelry Native women laid out every day. The Native women had their usual spots on the ground and so did I.

Crossroads Motel and the Hiway House were two of the motels I passed on my daily journeys. They were owned by the same family and, after I'd made several inquiries about work, eventually hired me as a maid. Five days a week I slowly pushed a cart stacked with thin towels, toilet paper, diluted cleaning solution, and deodorizing spray. My shift was from eight in the morning until three in the afternoon—the same hours as a school day. Moving from motel room to motel room I'd think about which class I'd be in if I still lived at home with my mother. Calculus, AP English, social studies.

Motel travelers checked out early in the morning to hit the road. Those with no place to go stayed past check-out time and left only when forced to. The difference in the travelers' departure times gave me an hour or so during my shift with nothing to clean. I'd grab a library book I had hidden between towels, close myself off in one of the rooms I just cleaned, and read. I schooled myself in those dingy motel rooms while the sounds of fighting and sex crossed their thin walls.

Finally, a room opened for me at the Mother Road, which was an early twentieth-century house with arched doorways and wood-framed windows. Mine was a corner room on the second floor. It fit a twin bed, a small dresser, and a chair. Hanging above the bed was a paint-by-numbers seascape. The painting upset me, because it recalled Maine. One morning I took it down. When I returned from work that day the painting was back on the wall and a note had been left on my bed. DO NOT REARRANGE THE ROOM.

"My bed is a small boat lost at sea," Gaston Bachelard writes. I felt lost in that bed, in that room. My dreams were of all the spaces I once lived, beginning with the first house, a one-bedroom apartment in Albuquerque that faced Iron Avenue. Somewhere there exists a photograph of my mother standing in its tiny front yard of gray rocks. She wore a dress, brushed by the wind to one side, revealing legs slender and young. She looks into the camera, her unsmiling stare a mystery to me. But in the dream image, I am in her arms, swaddled, cradled, safe.

———

The first floor of the Mother Road Hostel gave the impression of a single-family home. There was a grand entryway, a living room, a dining area, and a kitchen large enough to fit several people cooking for themselves at the same time. The woman who ran the place patroled the common areas, making sure everyone cleaned up after themselves and nobody stole anything. I was the youngest boarder at the hostel and felt ashamed to be there. I lied about my age and my circumstances, taking on the persona of an adventurous young woman, which I was not. When I wasn't at work, I stayed in my room, venturing out only when the wood floor outside my door stopped creaking. I had very few possessions with me—some clothes, a picture of me and my siblings in our old backyard in Maine, one of the wool blankets from that house's attic, and the boxed set of Greek tragedies.

Curtains heavy and thick hung at the edges of the window. I usually kept them open during the day. But sometimes I closed the curtains, turning daytime into night, blocking out the sight and sound of cars driving up and down Central Avenue. In the darkness, I saw tiny blinking lights, like hundreds of fireflies dancing in my room. A ray of warmth spread through my body. And then I was gone.

———

Grupo Esperanza had a daily schedule it followed, and intervals of cleaning filled most of it. Wake up at five in the morning, clean the room, then oneself. Eat a roll or tortilla, sometimes with beans, and clean the room. Exercise and clean the room. Eat a midday meal, if there was one, and clean the room. Study, give testimony, and clean the room. Make and eat dinner, clean the room. Offer more testimony, then clean the room once more. People went to bed around ten at night and slept on the floor for a few hours before the day began again.

Lo mismo, the same, is how anexados referred to their days and the events that took place within them. If I asked, what are you doing today? they inevitably responded, *Lo mismo*.

What did you do yesterday? *Lo mismo*.

How did you sleep last night? *Lo mismo*.

What are you cooking today? *Lo mismo*.

For some anexados, *lo mismo* led to profound boredom or hopelessness. Néstor was in his early thirties. Day after day, he shuffled around Grupo Esperanza in his sandals and spoke in a low, monotonous voice, earning him the nickname El Zombi. He hadn't always been like that. When he first arrived, he cracked jokes one minute, then complained loudly the next. During daily exercise he lifted weights like he was training for a fight. But as time wore on his muscles atrophied and his personality dampened. *Dispirited* was how I described him in one of my notebooks.

In *The Gay Science*, Nietzsche asks, "What if some day or night a demon were to sneak after you in your loneliness and say to you: 'This life as you now live it and have lived it, you will have to live once more and innumerable times more; and there will be nothing new in it, but every pain and every joy and every thought and sigh and everything immeasurably small or great in your life must return to you, all in the same succession and sequence.'" Nietzsche recognizes that the prospect of eternal recurrence, as he called it, is a devastating one. But it is also a way to recognize life exactly as it is, and this recognition brings with it a potential for change. "If this thought gained possession of you," Nietzsche writes, "it would change you as you are or perhaps crush you."

For some anexados, the sameness of days offered a space for thought.

"It's strange, isn't it," Rita said to me one afternoon. "The world is strange."

"What do you mean?"

"I mean, I never thought about it before, but now, here. I mean, how did it get this way? How did we end up in here? Look at Catorce. It isn't right. I mean, he's fourteen years old, for fuck's sake. Where does he go from here?" Rita paused and looked around the room. "Where do I go?"

———

"Study" meant reading. Metal folding chairs were set in neat rows that faced a table and battered copies of the Big Book—the textbook of Alcoholics Anonymous—or the Bible were doled out. When there were more people than books, people read in pairs. Some anexados enjoyed reading and were good at it, but most struggled. There were people who learned how to read in an anexo and others, like Delia, who forgot.

Omar usually sat at the head table. He was in his late twenties and had spent half his life in anexos. Anexos are hierarchical in structure, and Omar had graduated from being a regular anexado to being the *encargado*, the anexado in charge. Many encargados move on to become counselors, then padrinos. Omar was on this path.

Omar performed his duties according to the counselor in charge of training him. If it was Lorenzo, Omar was calm and encouraging. If it was Temo, Omar paced around the room, drawing his skinny right arm into a punch position. Omar humiliated his peers and turned their obedience to him into a sign of weakness. *¡Eso! ¡Eso!* Temo cheered. If Omar wasn't cruel enough, Temo humiliated and punished him.

Temo usually left the room during study hourto sit in the front office. If he stayed, he forced Omar to call on the weakest reader to read out loud. The class held its breath and the anexados shrank in their seats. *Not me. Please, not me.* Temo laughed and insulted people who slowly sounded out words. But Omar was gentle when he was left in charge alone. "Go on. Don't feel embarrassed," he'd say.

One afternoon, Omar called on Sheila to read a page from First Corinthians. "I'm not feeling good, Omarcito," she said. "Will you ask someone else?"

Sheila stopped going to school in fourth grade. Reading was hard for her, but Omar insisted. He told Sheila to read just one passage. She could decide which one.

Sheila stood up reluctantly. Her hair, once an ebony halo around her face, was thin and gray. Her skin was darker than when she arrived, her face scarred by acne. Her breasts were gone, her fingernails bitten and bumpy. Sheila hated the way she looked and called herself names before anyone else did. *Ugly horse, perverted skank, sad hag.* She used to say she was beautiful.

Omar patiently watched as Sheila flipped through the pages. She took a deep breath. "And I will show you," she said quietly, "a still more excellent way."

————

There was a television. A heavy wood-grained box with bent antennas and a channel dial that clicked. At some point someone called it E.T.— probably after the alien in the Steven Spielberg movie. The name stuck.

The TV sat on a cart next to the door to the office, the only door in the room. Every once in a while, it was wheeled out for sports or a dubbed American crime show. One afternoon it was Catorce's turn to fetch it. He moved cautiously, looking from side to side to make sure the teetering bowls and plates stacked on the cart's bottom shelf didn't crash to the floor.

Five weeks had passed since Catorce arrived. He kept to himself and spoke when he had to. The only time he chose to be close to anyone was at night, when he slept between Sheila and Rita. He felt safest between their bodies, with the women curled in on him, forming a cradle for him to rest.

Catroce flipped the channels, pausing briefly to display each program until counselor Lorenzo settled on something he wanted to watch. *No, No, No. Keep going.* News programs, cooking shows, soap operas, and commercials flashed by. Everyone waited in expectation, hoping Lorenzo would finally land on something. But nothing appealed to him. He told Catorce to wheel the TV back to its place by the door.

There were long stretches when there was nothing to do. "Empty hours," they were called. Some filled it with talking, flirting, or arguing, sometimes with themselves. Others sat against a wall to think or space out. Catorce stood by the windows and read the sheets of newspaper taped onto the glass, his small dark head following the directions of the words.

During one of the empty hours, I walked over to him. It was the closest I'd ever been to him, and I was alarmed by how he looked. His cheeks were shrunken and his eyes, so open and alert when he arrived, were small and red. I never saw him cry, but he looked like he'd been crying for months.

"Is it hard to read like that?" I asked.

My proximity startled him.

"No." He turned back to the writing on the window.

I asked if he was getting enough to eat. He said yes.

I asked if he liked to read. He nodded slowly.

I looked at the window. Coupons, cartoons, crooked politicians on newspaper sheets, yellow and brittle like blistered skin. One sheet torn from *La Crónica de Hoy* showed a picture of María Félix, back when she was the leading actress of Mexico's Golden Age. She is wearing a black lace dress, and her glossy hair falls in waves. Her head is slightly tilted, and her lips are about to smile. Mexicans still say María Félix has the most beautiful face in cinema. The article said she'd died a day earlier from heart failure.

3

HEAVEN

The very first time I visited Mexico City was in October 2006, two months before newly elected President Felipe Calderón declared war on drug traffickers. Benjamin was participating in the city's international book festival. At the time, I was five months pregnant with twins. Mexico City would be our last trip together before our daughters were born.

Our hotel room looked onto the Zócalo and faced the National Palace. White tents filled with books blanketed the plaza, where an immense Mexican flag rose from its center. All night it flapped, sounding hoarse and tired. We slept with the tall-shuttered windows open so that I could listen to the city's sounds. Piercing whistles, the melancholy tune of an organ grinder, people shouting advertisements, church bells. I laid in the hotel bed, anxious about motherhood, finishing my dissertation, finding a job. I wanted to stay in that hotel room forever.

For the first couple of days, I joined the masses at the festival and roamed the aisles of books. Table after table showcased titles on the rise and fall and rise of the Institutional Revolutionary Party, which maintained control of Mexico's government for seventy years, from 1930 to 2000. There were books on the consequences of NAFTA, the origins of drug cartels, and biographies of narco celebrities. Panels of writers discussed topics like US-Mexico immigration politics and gender inequality. The mood was serious and political, but I was light-headed and emotional, the altitude and my hormones making me weepy. I browsed the colorful selection of children's books, my hands cupping my heavy belly. For a long time, I watched an author read a book to a group of children. She was young and attractive, and a child sat on her lap as she read aloud to her rapt audience. *What kind of mother would I be?* I wondered. At the time, I was terrified that my love for my daughters would diminish as they grew older. Isn't that what happened to me, with my own parents turning away from me when I reached adolescence? When the author was finished, the children begged her to read it once more. For some reason I hoped she wouldn't, but she smiled and read it again, her voice just as enthusiastic, her audience just as attentive.

The festival and old friends took up a lot of Benjamin's time and I often found myself alone, mostly by choice. I blamed my lack of sociability on my "condition." What was my condition? Something more than enormously, uncomfortably pregnant. I stayed back in the hotel and sat in front of the window, watching contingents of campesinos protest around the perimeter of the Zócalo. *Land! Education! Health care!* I felt disconnected from the place I was in, from my own body, even. Sometimes I went up to the rooftop bar to read or gaze at the Metropolitan Cathedral and government palaces. The Mexica capital Tenochtitlan was entombed beneath the great square. Something was entombed within me—a deep sadness and fear that I would fail my daughters as my mother had me.

Toward the end of our trip, I forced myself out of my room and wandered around the neighborhoods surrounding the Zócalo on swollen feet and with no particular destination. On my last excursion, I headed east, down streets lined with old colonial buildings, cracked and crumbling, their balustrades draped with drying laundry. Shops on the ground floors sold cheap household items, school and party supplies, and jewelry. The merchandise spilled onto the sidewalks, where street vendors took over with even more for sale.

I maneuvered around the crowds, faces blurry with activity, merchandise a wash of colors and shapes. A cacophony of sounds pulsed around me. My belly grew heavier block by block, and the babies kicked my stomach so hard my shirt fluttered. I was disoriented and tired. But instead of returning to the hotel, I walked deeper into the unknown neighborhood, toward streets dense with people and away from the life that awaited me.

The thought that I was putting my pregnancy at risk crossed my mind. I was hot, diabetic, and far from the hotel. Thirsty, too, as sweat gathered in the deep crevice between my breasts and belly. But the thought that I'd never walk those chaotic streets again compelled me forward. I needed more time to be anonymous, to be a woman unafraid of getting lost, a woman who could see and listen to the world.

———

Porfirio Díaz was obsessed with Paris. During his dictatorship between 1876 and 1911, he modeled Mexico City's architecture after the European capital's neoclassical and beaux arts designs. The Zócalo was the center of the city, and the streets closest to it formed its wealthiest residential areas. The aristocracy boasted mansions, paved streets, gardens and squares, and elegant shops, representing a civilized, European Mexico. Modernization of the capital was vital to Mexico's inclusion among industrialized nations, and to project an image to foreign companies that it was a safe investment. Meanwhile, the countryside was the main source of wealth for the city, and Mexico's small ruling class owned much of the land upon which over half of all Mexicans lived and toiled.

By the turn of the nineteenth century, Mexico City's population had exploded and neighborhoods close to the plaza divided. The areas to the west remained a "City of Palaces," while the areas to the east became crowded with poor artisans and laborers. Tens of thousands of rural peasants landed there, having been forced off their lands by railroads and mining companies financed by US capitalists. Mexican elites lamented the "loss" of the Zócalo to these groups, who were characterized as loiterers and thieves. They abandoned their aristocratic mansions for newer suburbs to the west, and some of their deserted homes became vecindades for artisans, laborers, and their families. A topic of endless scorn, reporters described vecindades as "gloomy and festering . . . dank caves" crammed with a dozen or more people per room, all of them filthy, diseased, and immoral. Many vecindades were in the neighborhood Tepito.

The *barrio bravo*, Mexico City's fierce neighborhood, is infamous. It's the home of street markets and Santa Muerte, prizefighters and smuggled imports. The historian Pablo Piccato describes it as having an "unholy bond" with the Mexican state. Its reputation is that of crime and violence, bravery and resilience. In Netflix's wildly popular Spanish-language series *Ingobernable*, Tepito is the home of ex-prisoners, political victims, drug smugglers, and corrupt politicians. Tough and good-hearted women protect their families and their neighborhood, even taking up arms to do so. Tepito is a reality and a myth, one that tourists pay to see on walking tours.

The anexo Grupo Centro was in one of Tepito's vecindades. Over the last century, the building's rooms were subdivided into smaller and smaller dwellings, many without kitchens or bathrooms. The ornate figural elements on the building's facade were chipped beyond recognition, and ivy climbed its deep cracks.

When I first visited in 2014, the building was home to dozens of families and street-level shops that specialized in *miscelánea*--plastic containers, hair accessories, cleaning supplies, and the like. At the back of one of these shops was a shower curtain that covered a bolted metal door. Beyond the door was a narrow flight of stairs that led to Grupo Centro's own heavily bolted entrance. At all hours of the day a man stood guard in the grim stairwell, monitoring traffic between Grupo Centro and the world outside.

The anexo was composed of two high-ceilinged rooms. Both rooms had tall, arched windows that faced the street below, with missing glass panes plugged up with cardboard. The loud hum of activity from the street penetrated the anexo, creating a passage between inside and outside. Sometimes a single voice from the street would break through, eliciting an anexado's response. *That sounds like so-and-so. Is he calling me? What did she say?*

I was introduced to Grupo Centro by Claudio, one of my research assistants. He was from Tepito and had friends and relatives who had been committed at the anexo. At that time, I was reluctant to start researching another anexo. I had made plans to split my time between Serenity and Grupo Esperanza. Serenity's condition had deteriorated since my last visit, partly because of the rainy season, one of the worst in years. Its walls were crumbling, its ceiling buckled. The anexados were constantly repairing it. Ángel said he was learning skills to become a construction worker in the US, if only he could figure out how to escape. Meanwhile, the number of anexados at Grupo Esperanza had increased. Rita and Catorce were still there. Rita had resigned herself to being forever stuck in that room. Catorce was fifteen now and more despondent than ever. I was inclined to focus my attention on them, to better understand how confinement in these rooms shaped their outlook on the world. But Claudio insisted I'd learn a lot from Grupo Centro, especially about the war.

I thought I was educated on the subject, having read many books on the drug war's history and consequences, even teaching courses about it at Stanford. My courses took a long view, reaching back to 1620, when the Spanish colonists banned the use of peyote and pulque. But the course content really began in 1912, with Mexico signing onto the new Hague International Opium Convention, which inspired the 1914 Harrison Act in the United States, the foundation of US drug law in the twentieth century. After signing the convention, Mexico deepened its involvement with international drug control regimes. At the same time, drug trafficking increased, and new trafficking corridors and methods proliferated. Profits skyrocketed.

In the late 1930s, the psychiatrist Leopoldo Salazar Viniegra challenged Mexico's prohibitionist approaches to drug use. Salazar worked with drug users at hospitals in Mexico City and witnessed how prohibition not only failed to prevent drug addiction, but also enriched drug traffickers. He also insisted that Mexico lacked sufficient resources to treat addiction, pointing out that Mexico's wealthier counterpart, the United States, was also unsuccessful. An early advocate of legalization, he proposed state control of morphine, reasoning that such an approach would curb the illicit traffic of drugs while giving users an incentive to seek ongoing care from physicians.

Salazar's plan of legalization and medical treatment was as radical then as it is now. It was adopted and went into effect in 1940. But US pressure forced Mexico to quickly rescind the policy and return to its prohibitionist stance. Leadership of drug control moved from the public health authorities to the attorney general's office.

The governing party, PRI, fostered an arrangement between authorities and cartels, even establishing a "pax mafiosa" that allowed cartels to engage in drug trafficking at the US-Mexico border. In exchange for bribes, corrupt officials granted protection from one or another rival cartel. They had two conditions for such protection: the cartels were to abstain from public displays of violence against Mexican citizens and refrain from selling drugs within Mexico. As the scholar Viri Ríos puts it, "International drug trafficking was considered a business, and domestic drug selling was viewed as a crime."

Traffickers' identification with and devotion to Jesús Malverde spread in the 1980s. On both sides of the border, they turned to the bandit-saint for protection. Los Cuates de Sinaloa's *narcocorrido* "Mi Santito Preferido" ("My Favorite Little Saint") captures the significance of Malverde for those working in the drug world:

> Don't leave me, Malverde
>
> . . . .
>
> And you've always protected me
> My cargo comes over
> Safely to the United States
> That's why you, Malverde
> Are my favorite little saint.

During the PRI's regime, criminal violence and domestic illegal drug markets remained relatively contained. This changed in 2000 with the election of President Vicente Fox from the right-wing National Action Party (PAN). Most scholars agree that the oppositional parties led to the breakdown of criminal protection and increased violence. In the last several years, Fox has called the war on drugs a "total failure" and argued that legalizing drugs is the best way to control criminal groups.

The scale of violence and catastrophe of the drug war are unseen in the history of modern prohibition. The United States is the largest con-

sumer of drugs imported through Mexico, with the largest prison population in the world. The United States is a decisive protagonist in *la guerra*,
contributing firepower, customers, and for-profit prisons. Mexico, Juan
Villoro writes, contributes the dead.

But there was still so much I didn't know, especially the extent to
which *las violencias*, the multiple forms and spheres of violence, had
become integral to the lives of people from poor and working-class communities. Not just murders and disappearances, but kidnappings, extortions, robberies. Exploitative labor, repression, impunity, scarcity, and
displacements caused by fear. These violences did not just affect life; they
constituted it.

It was Hortencia who first taught me this. It took me years to understand the significance of her claim that all she could do was witness the
brutal attack on her son Daniel in case she "needed to make a report."
There were no organizations or institutions that could help her, no one
to actually submit a report to. Hortencia's only option for ensuring Daniel's safety was to participate in and witness his kidnapping. When she recounted that harrowing event to me, she wasn't just describing the scene
of a crime, nor was she providing an example of what has been called the
normalization of violence in Mexico. She was clueing me into something
more profound. Violence did not just strip away her ability to care for
Daniel—it had become the way to care for him.

The idea that violence can be a way to provide care is not entirely new.
In the United States, parents send their troubled teens to military-style
boot camps, mothers of addicts are encouraged to practice tough love,
and women and children are beaten under the guise of "learning a lesson." It would be easy to liken Hortencia's scene of kidnapping to such
examples. But Hortencia's story is not reducible to punishment, "education," or abuse. Embedded in the practice of care that she described is a
specter of narco violence that shapes day-to-day life in Mexico, especially
for the poor. Caring for Daniel meant engaging with criminal imaginar-
ies and practices—the very kind Hortencia sought to protect Daniel from.
The violence of war and motherhood had become intertwined, opening
a profound ethical ambiguity. What should one do when the only avail-

able forms of care inflict abuse and do not promise healing? What about Hortencia's own vulnerability to violence? Who cares for the mother?

———————

Rafa was Grupo Centro's padrino. He was tall and muscular, with close-cropped hair and black eyes. Two fingers were missing on his left hand, giving his arm a claw-like appearance. There was an intensity about him that made me uneasy. It wasn't just his mangled hand; it was also his voice. He never raised it. Nor did he shout obscenities, not even *chingado* or *puta*—words that peppered nearly every sentence spoken by every other padrino or counselor I knew. It was impossible to listen to Padrino Rafa's measured voice and not think that there was a volcano within him, about to explode.

My research assistant Claudio conducted the first few interviews with Padrino Rafa and I pieced them together to develop a picture of his life. It wasn't easy. Most of the recordings were of Claudio's own nervous chatter, of him filling uncomfortable stretches of silence with dirty jokes and talk about sports and women. At one point, he talked about me—how naive I was, how privileged, a total pushover. He said the money I paid him was decent and that he was sure he'd fuck me by the end of summer. I appreciated that Padrino Rafa didn't egg him on. I never mentioned that part of the tape to Claudio, partly because I figured he wasn't the only man I worked with who talked about me in those terms.

Despite that, I learned a lot about Padrino Rafa from the interviews, not just from what he said, but also from what he didn't. He was from a city near Pachuca, Hidalgo, about an hour north of Mexico City, where he grew up in a working-class neighborhood with both parents and five siblings. He had problems in school—learning was difficult and fights were frequent. His parents wanted him to go to college, but he quit school after finishing ninth grade.

His girlfriend Maribel was pregnant by then. They married in the church, then moved in with Rafa's grandmother, who ran a nursery out of her home. The sounds of toddlers drove Rafa crazy, and he soon got a job as a pizza delivery man. When the owner of the pizza franchise realized Rafa was reliable, he gave him added responsibilities—small quantities of drugs were taped to the bottom of Rafa's pizza boxes.

Throughout Padrino Rafa's teen years, his parents worried he was falling into a gang. They encouraged him to return to school, even offering to enroll him in a private high school so that he could make it to college and provide for his family. But he said no, partly because he knew his parents couldn't afford it. A military base was located near his grandmother's neighborhood. Tired of the sounds of crying toddlers and with no future in sight, he enlisted in the Mexican army at seventeen, becoming an infantryman. He was following in the footsteps of his beloved older brother, Mateo.

Rafa served before the army "left the barracks" to lead the narco war. The armed forces, like local police forces, have long been infiltrated by crime groups. Cartel leaders often serve in military divisions, and many receive training in the United States. As in the United States, the Mexican military draws heavily from the poor and working classes. Soldiers are poorly paid—and therefore easy targets for crime groups embedded in the military who offer more money. Rafa left the army after two years. When Claudio asked him what he did for work after the military, Rafa answered, "Whatever needed doing."

The Mexican military doesn't just fight violent cartels, it comprises and protects them. Narcotrafficking in Mexico is integrated into many segments of society—including policing, political organizations, and commercial operations. To do "whatever needed doing" could have meant countless things. Padrino Rafa didn't disclose the exact nature of his work to Claudio. He was more forthcoming when asked about his experiences in anexos.

He wasn't the first padrino to report having first gone to an anexo in the United States—in his case, in Laredo.

"Laredo or Nuevo Laredo?" Claudio asked, differentiating between the cities on either side of the US-Mexico border.

"Laredo."

"What were you doing in Laredo?"

"Whatever needed doing."

"Who committed you?"

"My brother."

A ten-month age difference separated Rafa and Mateo. From what I could gather from the interviews, Rafa followed his brother Mateo to Nuevo Laredo, Tamaulipas, which lies on the banks of the Rio Grande, across from Laredo, Texas. Between 2002 and 2006, Rafa worked and lived on both sides of the US-Mexico border, with some stints in other parts of Mexico.

The anexo in Laredo was one room in a neighborhood with dirt roads and cement block houses. Most of the anexados were Mexican, but there were also a few Latinos from the United States. One memory stood out for Rafa. It was of a teenage junkie who'd shit his pants and could barely speak a word of Spanish. Most of the other anexados were older alcoholics. Rafa watched this teenager in the throes of detox and felt sorry for him. "I told him, 'The worst will be over soon.'"

Mateo checked in on Rafa by phone a couple of times a week. The calls were brief, but grounding. "He'd say, 'You ready, bro? One more week and I'll get you out, bro.'" But then the calls suddenly stopped. Rafa never heard from or saw his brother again.

———

I visited Grupo Centro after piecing together Claudio's interviews with Padrino Rafa. At the time, around fifteen anexados lived there—a small number given the anexo's relatively spacious size. The anexados were mostly young people from Tepito, and like the anexados of Grupo Esperanza they were sometimes from the same block or apartment building where the anexo was located. They often already knew each other.

Padrino Rafa and I met in his office, which was where one-on-one counseling sessions, Padrino Rafa's business meetings, and anexados' visits with relatives took place. Every night female anexados were moved in there to provide them with privacy and safety.

It was orderly, with a sofa and a TV—more like a studio apartment

than an anexo. Anexados were in charge of maintaining the place under the watchful eyes of counselors. They swept and washed the floor
and cleaned the tiny kitchen area that was in one corner of the room. Its
two-burner stove and utility sink were visually hidden by two walls that
reached only halfway up to the tall ceiling. On the day I visited, I could
hear two anexados washing the morning dishes. Padrino Rafa ordered
them away.

He was in a contemplative mood, having just returned from a reunion
with Padrino Gonzalo, the man he credited with saving his life. An 8×10
photo of the two men hung from the wall. It was a kind of graduation
photo, with Padrino Gonzalo and Rafa standing side by side. Padrino
Gonzalo's face is smiling, while Rafa's is deferential and serious. The occasion was Rafa's promotion from anexado to counselor at Nueva Vida,
New Life, Padrino Gonzalo's anexo.

The promotion of an aneaxdo to counselor depends on a variety of
factors: the length of an anexado's stay in an anexo, their good standing and commitment to "clean living," and their interest in making a life
within the world of anexos. Most anexados just want to leave and reenter
the larger world. They wait for their releases, which usually come about
when relatives stop paying for their stays.

Padrino Rafa wanted to talk about his time at New Life. The anexo, he
said, was nothing like Grupo Centro. New Life was in a desolate neighborhood on the outskirts of Mexico City, near defunct factories and with few
neighbors or services around. Padrino Rafa called it a "strong group," not
a *grupo fuera de serie*, the designation for anexos that were "outside the
norm" and that engaged in useless violence. The anexos I visited always
differentiated themselves from *grupos fuera de serie*, emphasizing that
their forms of discipline and punishment were selective and purposeful,
not indiscriminate and senseless. This distinction signaled a belief in the
restorative potential of violence. As one padrino explained, the therapeutic
practices of "strong groups," which ranged from hitting to humiliation,
transformed relations between anexados for the better. These choices
played a crucial role in collective healing and were meaningful attempts to
come to terms with anexados' individual and shared vulnerabilities.

By the time Rafa landed at New Life, he'd been in prison and in and out of anexos for over a decade. He was using drugs, stealing, and causing and getting into trouble. His now ex-wife heard an advertisement for New Life on a radio program. The advertisement emphasized New Life's spiritual dimension. She believed that was what Rafa was missing and arranged to have him committed there for three months. At first, New Life reminded Padrino Rafa of prison. There were around one hundred and twenty male anexados sharing one large concrete room. He was beaten, humiliated, stripped naked, and deprived of food and blankets. What he described to me sounded like torture. Such spaces and practices have in fact been singled out as torture by human rights groups that seek to close anexos. They cast all anexos as "prisons" or "labor farms," obscuring their diversity and the struggles of poor families who must make decisions about how to care for their relatives. From the point of view of many Mexican women who turn to anexos, the indiscriminate condemnation of anexos does not protect the people within them; on the contrary, it makes them more vulnerable to the consequences of untreated addiction, violence, and criminalization. While discussing human rights groups' criticisms of anexos, one mother I talked to put it like this: "Would they rather I abandon my child?"

Padrino Rafa was aware of criticisms leveled against anexos' use of "strong treatment." He insisted his experience at New Life was something different from torture and abuse. Yes, there were forms of severe punishment, but not only for breaking the rules of the anexo. There were also incitements to restore the capacity for pain. "Back then, I couldn't feel pain. I couldn't feel guilt. I couldn't *feel*," Padrino Rafa said.

His assertion that he couldn't feel was not unique. Padrinos and anexados often described a sense of numbness that resulted from years, sometimes lifetimes, of violence. The injuries accumulate. The pain deepens. Then it seems to disappear.

Many social scientists and psychologists argue that the continual and worsening violence in Mexico has led to its normalization. Children fight more in school. Everyday language includes words from the narco lexicon. Women experience increased incidents of violence at home and in the streets. These are just some oft-cited examples of the normalization perspective. The problem with this view is its assumption that the violence that pervades Mexico breeds tolerance for it. It ignores the populace's courageous efforts to put an end to the war. And instead of focusing on state insufficiencies that allow for bad actors' impunity, it suggests marginalized citizens are complicit with violence.

Padrino Rafa's assertion that he "couldn't *feel*" points not to normalization but to victimization. This does not mean that he did not commit or witness terrible acts. Instead, it means that his experience with violence had left him apathetic and isolated, because there was no community in which he could acknowledge his pain and share it with others. There was no space or shared language with which to suffer and grieve.

The author Cristina Rivera Garza writes about "the deep sorrow that binds us" as a way to describe contemporary Mexico. She says that there is an urgency to find a new language from which to speak about the violence, and she calls on her fellow Mexicans to say, "I suffer with you, I grieve myself with you. We mourn us." For Rivera Garza, language is the "humblest and most powerful force available," and she envisions a practice of writing that is entwined with grieving. Rivera Garza lost her sister Liliana to femicide. Reflecting on her writing practice since her loss, she says, "I do not want to avoid suffering. Quite the opposite. I want to think through and with pain, and to painfully embrace it, to give it back its beating heart."

Rivera Garza's powerful vision of expressing and sharing pain resonates in unexpected ways with the practices of anexos. One of the things anexados often reflected upon was their proximity to others—not only in the sense of space, but also within life experience. During and after testimonies, they identified with each other in deep and profound ways— through physical gestures such as nodding, holding, and touching; quiet conversation; and simply by looking at each other. The pain suffered in anexos was experienced in the presence of people who knew the same horrors and losses. It was shared.

Some of the practices Padrino Rafa described enduring at New Life reminded me of Los Penitentes, a Catholic brotherhood that has been active in New Mexico since the nineteenth century. To atone for their sins, the penitents practice penances that bring pain to the body and humiliations. The parallels with New Life were striking. Padrino Rafa described the entire group of shirtless men kneeling on bottle caps while holding their arms out in the form of the cross. Counselors lashed their bare backs if their arms began to fall. Anexados were forced to kneel and wash the feet of all present. They also had to recite long prayers, repeatedly. The purpose of these practices wasn't just the discipline and punishment of anexados; it was also to accessthe "truth of being-in-common," to use Jean-Luc Nancy's phrase. For Nancy, being-in-common is both an articulation of community and a force for it. It is an ethical mode of coexistence that emerges through ongoing communication and sharing, which for Nancy is the basis of politics.

Every Holy Week, thousands of Mexicans pour into Iztapalapa, the borough where Serenity is located, to enact and identify with the Passion of Christ for millions of viewers, including the anexados at Grupo Centro, who watch the televised event. The ever-increasing realism of this collective rite of agony—which includes painfully young penitential Nazarenes carrying massive wooden crosses, the bloody scourging of Jesus, the Crucifixion itself, and the emotional wailing of Mary,—is both theatrical and real. It evokes the suffering in Mexico in palpable and dramatic ways, and it challenges a sensibility that shudders away from willing and elaborate engagements with pain.

In recent years, the passion play of Itzapalapa has garnered media attention and criticism for becoming too commercial and too violent. Vendors sell T-shirts and religious paraphernalia while thousands of police and additional security forces surveil the scene. But the passion play's transformations, performed each spring since the mid-nineteenth century, extend far beyond questions of consumerism or security. Today, the passion play serves as a staging of the agony that stems from *la violencia*. Many participants carry large placards of murdered or missing relatives and crowds gather to hear speeches denouncing violence. The self-inflicted pain that is willingly endured cannot be experienced without reference to the ongoing pain of war.

Far from normalizing violence, people seek a common language with which to suffer and grieve the wounds violence inflicts. They do this, as Nancy writes, "*in* common, *with* one another." Whether through writing, strong therapy, or religious reenactments, they actively engage with and reimagine the vulnerability and pain wrought by violence. Testimony in anexos is a language that allows those who suffer to express pain with and for others. Reflecting on testimony during his time at New Life, Padrino Rafa said:

> You listen to the same story over and over. Different men tell-
> ing the same story. You begin to remember, to recognize. I felt
> pain that went deeper than my own skin. I wasn't speaking, I
> was listening. And I cried for myself, for my family, for all of
> us. And nobody laughed or beat me or robbed me or called me
> a faggot, because if they did, they got punished. I cried and
> they listened.

———

The first testimony I observed was at Serenity. A boy of eighteen stood be-hind a lectern before his seated peers. My first impression was that he ap-peared isolated and alone. This impression was amplified by his story—an abusive father, a battered mother, an older brother gone. Over time, my attention shifted from his testimony to the audience's quiet unity. They were immersed not only in the anexado's story, but in its sonority—his anguished cries, his bitter anger, his gentle weeping. Their imposed si-lence was not a privation, but a resonance. This reverberation seemed to bind the anexados together in an act of listening that I had not encoun-tered before.

In his book *Listening*, Nancy makes a distinction between hearing and listening. "Isn't the philosopher someone who always hears . . . but who cannot listen . . . who neutralizes listening within himself, so that he can philosophize?" Nancy suggests that the philosopher's mode of hearing is closed upon itself because it is primarily aimed at transmitting thought and meaning. He proposes a different kind of listening, one that is attuned to sound and its reverberations. "To listen," he writes, "is to enter that spatiality by which, at the same time, I am penetrated, for it opens up in me as well as around me." Like permeable walls, the listening self who is opened by sound can't be understood through traditional dichotomies of self-other, interior-exterior. Instead, the listening self is one whose sounds resonate with and toward other subjects of resonance. In actively listening, we open ourselves up to the resonances of the one who speaks, and the one who remains silent. We become witnesses to each other and forge what Nancy calls "a community consciously undergoing the experience of its sharing."

As at Serenity, the delivery of testimonies filled most of each day at Grupo Centro. During one testimony, a young man who went by the name Cabrito, little goat, recalled an afternoon when gunmen rolled into his grandmother's small town in the state of Michoacán. He had traveled there with his mother, who wanted to see her own ailing mother and convince her to leave her war-torn town and move to the capital, where it was safer. In a rhetorical form common among anexados, Cabrito spoke in the present tense and took on the identities and perspectives of his mother and grandmother. Intersubjective and relational, his testimony expressed an understanding of, and an identification with, multiple lives.

> Come home with us, *Mamá*.
> No, no. I stay here.
> There's nothing here for you, *Mamá*, nothing.
> Don't be stupid. Everything is here for me.

Cabrito's grandmother refused to leave. She was born in that small town, raised eight children there. Her husband and two of her children were buried there, and she would be, too. Cabrito saw that his mother's pleading was pointless, so he went outside for a walk. His grandfather had been a barber and ran the local shop where men used to gather to talk and primp. He wanted to see if the shop was still there and buy some snacks for the long bus ride home.

It was the middle of the day and very hot. Cabrito recalled the sight of kids, not much older than him, dressed in school uniforms. There wasn't much else to see. His grandfather's barbershop was now the town's *tiendita* with poorly stocked shelves—a few vegetables, soft drinks, potato chips, and random toys. His mother was right, he thought, there was nothing here. Cabrito said he couldn't wait to get home and see his girlfriend, smoke some weed, and have sex, drawing laughter from a few of the anexados and a couple of lewd comments. "Shut up and pay attention!" a counselor yelled.

"*Había un mal.*" Something was wrong. Cabrito said he noticed the SUV right away because it looked out of place, but before he could respond with his feet, the shooting started.

"*Ppppppppppp.* It sounded like that. *Ppppppppppp.* You hear? *Ppppppppppp.*"

Cabrito kept registering the sound of bullets spraying into the air, like he was caught inside of it and couldn't get out. Eventually, he collapsed onto the lectern and started to cry. "*I'm hit, I'm hit, fuck, I'm hit!*"

He wasn't the only one. When it was over, three people had been killed.

The audience of anexados were moved by Cabrito's pain, which echoed long after his testimony was over. Day after day, the delivery of testimony enabled the anexados to contemplate a sensorial vision of the human condition, creating bonds of coexistence through the outpouring of grief.

————

Ceci's entrance into Serenity, rolled up in a rug, had left an indelible impression on me. When I learned that her parents had committed her to the anexo a second time, I was drawn back in. I barely recognized Ceci when I returned to Serenity. Her long black hair was was cut short and two hoops pierced her lower lip. Her skin was lined with thin vertical scars from elbows to wrists. Ceci was injuring herself. She was also using meth.

Around 2010, public health officials in Mexico noted the rise in methamphetamine use among youth, coinciding with the increase in the production of the drug in Mexico. Ceci fell into a group that used the drug. She stopped working at her parent's stationery shop completely and rarely came home. When she did, it was usually for money. But her drug use wasn't the only reason her parents had recommitted her to Serenity.

Ceci's previous stint at Serenity had been when it was in an established working-class neighborhood. When I saw her again, Serenity was in a worn-down area on the edges of Mexico City. She called the place a fucking shithole and insulted everyone around her, even if it got her in trouble. She looked hard and aggressive during these bouts, but most of the time she just sat against the wall and cried, her tiny frame closed in on itself. Whenever I tried to engage her in conversation, she'd wipe away her tears with the palm of her hand and walk away.

Ceci was covered in bruises. There had been an uptick in violence in her neighborhood. The circumstances of her assault were uncertain, but her parents were afraid it was related to their inability to pay a monthly extortion fee that allowed them to operate their business in an area that was under the control of a criminal group.

The assault took place the very month Ceci's parents were late paying the *piso*. Worried the attack was a message, her parents committed her to Serenity while they scrambled to make payment. This meant they were racking up debts with the anexo, too, but Padrino Francisco was willing to give them time to pay the five hundred pesos he normally charged for one month. According to Padrino Francisco, more and more young people were being committed to Serenity under circumstances like Ceci's.

The extortionists hounded Padrino Francisco, too. He had to factor these fees into his own monthly costs. In 2011, he said he only charged families to cover costs of necessities like rent, food, and occasional bribes to Sanitation Department workers. In 2014, he had to factor in extortionists and neighborhood security, parties that were often one and the same. Faced with the threat of violence, individuals and families would fall prey to increasing demands for money—not only from criminal groups, but also from the police and armed forces who patrolled neighborhoods, ostensibly to protect them.

One afternoon, I visited Ceci's parents' stationery shop. It was a tiny space, no larger than a single-car garage, with a pull-down metal door. When I arrived, Ceci's mother was seated behind a glass cabinet filled with school supplies. She was alone and watching a show on a television affixed to the wall.

"Can I help you?" she asked.

I told her how I knew her daughter.

Ceci's mother paused for a moment, then asked if I had children. I told her I had two daughters.

"Then you know. No mother wants to make the decision I had to make," she said.

Ceci's mother told me that she called Padrino Francisco every day to speak with her daughter, but Ceci always refused her calls. The silence filled her with grief, but she hoped that Ceci was safe and that their relationship would eventually heal.

"There is hope when your child is alive. No matter how difficult things are, there is hope."

At Grupo Esperanza, I found solace in the friendship Rita and Sheila had forged. One afternoon, I arrived there to see Rita lying with her head in Sheila's lap, her eyes closed. Sheila looked down toward her friend's calm face and murmured a lullaby as she rubbed her temples. *Sana, sana, colita de rana. Si no sanas hoy, sanarás mañana. Heal, heal, little frog's tail. If you don't heal today, you'll heal tomorrow.*

Sheila had become something of a mother to Rita and Catorce. She swatted Pepe's hand away when he reached out to grab Rita's butt, and she told Temo to go fuck himself when he insulted Catorce. She also reminded Catorce that he was committed to the anexo because he was loved. When the time was right, his mother would come for him. She was careful to not say when that might be.

Sheila's own story remained a mystery to me. I never learned who committed her to Grupo Esperanza or who paid for her stay there. She didn't talk about her parents or childhood. But during one of her testimo-

nies, she wept while remembering all the girls lost to AIDS and violence.
A few days later she was gone. This wasn't unusual. Some people stayed
in anexos for long periods of time, years even, while others disappeared
after a few weeks or months. Sheila had been at Grupo Esperanza for five
months. I asked what happened to her and if there was a way for me to
reach her. No one could say.

After Sheila left, Rita's eyes got red from crying and Catorce was more
despondent than usual. By then, Catorce had a seat at the dinner table,
next to Rita. The spot where Sheila once sat was empty. She seemed a
Marian apparition—Our Lady of the Vulnerable. I hoped that she had
someone to protect her.

———

On my daughters' sixth birthday, I received a 176-page report, *Mexico's
Disappeared: The Enduring Cost of a Crisis Ignored*. The report by Human
Rights Watch documented 249 disappearances that occurred over a
six-year period—from the start of the drug war in December 2006 to the
start of Enrique Peña Nieto's presidency in December 2012. Of the documented cases, 149 were classified as enforced disappearances involving
state actors, including the army, navy, and federal and local police. The
report referenced was a provisional list, compiled by the Federal Prosecutor's Office and the Interior Ministry, of more than 25,000 "disappeared"
or "missing" individuals during that same six-year period.

I read the report while my daughters waited for me in their colorful
kindergarten classroom in Oakland, California. I was supposed to bring
the class cupcakes to celebrate the big day. My reading the report made
me late to the party, and I felt pangs of sadness as I watched their expression of worry fade into relief when my daughters saw me. They each wore
cardboard crowns in the shape of six candles. The children sang happy
birthday to them and then my daughters helped me pass treats to their
classmates. On the walk home from school I held on tightly to their small
hands.

I knew disappearance was a reality in Mexico, but my references were largely statistics from the media. It wasn't until 2012, when Mexico's Movimiento por la Paz con Justicia y Dignidad (Movement for Peace with Justice and Dignity) started its trek across the United States, drawing attention to the human suffering caused by the US-backed drug war, that I began to understand the epidemic proportions of disappearance in Mexico. According to the latest figures, more than a hundred thousand people have disappeared.

I closely followed the movement, which was founded by the acclaimed poet and novelist Javier Sicilia in 2011, after the murder of his son Juan Francisco, a university student, and six of his friends. Sicilia wrote a final poem to his son.

> The world is not worthy of words
> . . . .
> And the pain does not leave me
> Only one world remains
> For the silence of the righteous
> Only for your silence and for my silence, Juanelo

Sicilia vowed never to write another poem again. He took his pain and rage public, demanding justice for his son and all victims of the war. In an open letter, he called for an end to the bloodshed and impunity by invoking the Mexican saying *"estamos hasta la madre"*—literally "we've had it up to our mother." His grief mobilized a victims' movement across Mexico. A march from Cuernavaca traveled to Mexico City, culminating in a massive demonstration in the Zócalo in front of the National Palace. Other caravans soon followed, including one that crossed the border at Tijuana and stopped in more than thirty American cities before arriving in Washington, DC. I watched tearful mothers emerge from the crowds in Los Angeles and approach Sicilia with photos of their young sons and daughters.

Sicilia, along with victims across Mexico, spoke the name of their dead and disappeared, forging what John Gibler called a "rebellion of names in a war of anonymous death." These mobilizations placed suffering at the center of public discourse. On May 10, 2012—Mothers' Day—mothers marched in Mexico City, wearing T-shirts and holding placards bearing photos of their children. They demanded the government meet with them, demanded recognition and justice. The Mothers' Day march has since become an annual event. These nomadic mothers walk not only to draw attention to their disappeared children, but also because they keep searching for them. Each year, the number of mothers grows.

———

In her documentary poem *Antígona González*, Sara Uribe draws on the Sophoclean tragedy *Antigone* to reenact the devastation of those victimized by criminal violence in Mexico. Commissioned after the discovery of a mass grave that held 196 people in San Fernando, Tamaulipas, the book includes testimonies from family members of the victims and fragments of news stories that also tell the story of all the bodies that are missing. The story follows Antígona as she searches for her disappeared brother Tadeo, retracing his route, promising to keep going until he is found, whether dead or alive. She is Sophocles's Antigone, full of grief for her brother Polynices's death, who is refused a burial rite by the leader of the city, Creon. "I will bury him," Antigone declares, and she does, thereby acknowledging his life and her own irreplaceable loss.

But there is no justice for Antígona, who, like so many women in Mexico, roams a landscape of violence, erasure, and loss, with no end in sight. "I didn't want to be an Antigone // but it happened to me," she says. At the end of the book, Antígona is reunited not with her brother, but with all the other grieving women who keep searching. The last line, a challenge to its readers, is a translation of Sophocles's tragedy: "Will you join me in taking up the body?"

———

On a Sunday morning in May 2013, a mass kidnapping or "lifting" occurred in an off-hours bar called Heaven. The bar was in the touristy Zona

Rosa district, a government-designated "safe neighborhood" in Mexico City where such things were not supposed to happen. The missing were thirteen young people, mostly between the ages of sixteen and twenty-six. Twelve were from Tepito.

Within hours of the mass kidnapping, the families of the missing reported the crime to the Ministry of Public Security, which was located only two blocks away from Heaven. They had an eyewitness, another boy from Tepito, who saw the abductions take place in broad daylight. Yet despite multiple reports and the eyewitness, the crime didn't garner an investigation for a week. During that period, the families staged public protests against the authorities' indifference. Each day they marched from Tepito carrying images of the missing and placards announcing that the authorities and the state did not care about them. ¡Ya es mucho tiempo y nada ayuda! ¡Ayúdanos a encontrarlos! So much time has passed and you haven't helped! Help us find them!

Meanwhile, in Tepito, large banners that read ¿LES HAS VISTO? (Have you seen them?) were draped across market stalls and apartment buildings. The banners described the identifying physical characteristics of each disappeared: round face, mole, cracked tooth, thin lips, pierced ears, black hair, light skin, tattoos of names in Hebrew, tattoos of Santa Muerte and the Virgin of Guadalupe, tattoos of hearts and diamonds, tattoos of tears.

Mexico City's prosecutor and mayor referred to the youth as "absent," not disappeared. They said the crime was an act of retaliation between rival gangs based in Tepito and was not related to drug cartels, concluding that what happened at Heaven was not a cause for concern among citizens or visitors to Mexico City. Their response drew fury from the residents of Tepito, who staged even larger protests in turn. I watched marches and vigils, which were composed of generations of relatives, almost entirely women. Some carried framed photos of their relatives, others large signs that had the names of the disappeared. They moved through the streets slowly, shouting a phrase that has become a somber refrain throughout Mexico. ¡Hasta encontrarlos!

Within weeks of the kidnapping at Heaven, the number of anexados at Grupo Centro in Tepito had doubled. I was there the afternoon Magi arrived. The men that delivered her to Grupo Centro immediately took her into the second room, where Padrino Rafa and the counselors were waiting. Everyone else was in the other room, with a more senior anexado named Mario left in charge. Mario had been in and out of anexos for more than a decade and had spent seven months at Grupo Centro. He couldn't imagine life beyond anexos, but he was determined to change his position within them by becoming a counselor and eventually a padrino. Part of his training involved repeating the commands of Grupo Centro's counselors. Mario carefully raised his voice an octave above theirs to signal his lesser status. On this particular occasion, he was leading the group in its daily reading of recovery literature.

I heard Magi before I saw her. She screamed obscenities and demanded to go home. Some of the anexados chuckled and wondered who the new girl was and whether she'd be attractive. Eventually, her screams broke into sobs. When I left the anexo that evening she was still crying in the second room.

I finally met Magi when I returned to Grupo Centro the following week. She was small and thin, with long black hair that she tied on top of her head, only to let it loose and tie it up again. She was dressed like a typical teenager: tight jeans, sneakers, and a T-shirt that read THE RAMONES. To my surprise, the counselors didn't call her offensive names, as they did with other newcomers, and she was permitted to sit in a chair, not on the floor. I figured that she must have been Padrino Rafa's relative, or the child of someone important. In fact, she was the cousin of one of the persons abducted from Heaven and a friend of others.

It was now July, and hope that the disappeared would be found alive was fading. Cut off from the news, Magi asked for updates. I hesitated to say anything because I worried it might upset her. The truth was there wasn't much to report, which was also upsetting. Sometimes, after seeing Magi at Group Centro, I walked by Heaven. The walls were still plastered with images of the disappeared and handwritten messages to them. Scrawled in block print, the messages assured the disappeared that they weren't forgotten, and that their families would keep looking for them and fight for justice.

———

One afternoon, Magi described the day she was "lifted" and taken to Grupo Centro. She had been working at her family's market stall in Tepito. Typically, her mother or aunt worked with her, but on that day she was mostly alone. In the evening, her aunt returned to relieve Magi, telling her to pack up and head home. Little did she know that her mother had arranged for Magi's kidnapping.

> It happened so fast. I was hot. I could barely breathe . . .
> No . . . I couldn't move.
> I heard laughing . . . doors opening and closing . . . My heart pounded so hard it hurt me . . .
> I thought, *My god, this is it. I am going to die. This is it . . .*
> I kept thinking, *Is this is what happened to him? Will anyone find me? Are they taking me to the same place?*
> But I landed here. I landed here. I'm here.

Landing in the anexo meant not being disappeared and killed. It meant being seen by, and included in, a community of people similarly situated. Of course, this community was not freely chosen; it was shaped by coercion, violence, and tragedy. But Grupo Centro provided a protective space for Magi, Cabrito, and others to live together.

Three months after they were abducted from Heaven, twelve of the thirteen bodies were found in a concealed grave in Tlalmanalco, on the outskirts of Mexico City. Nine were decapitated. As news of the discovery spread, so did the narrative that the victims must have been involved in crime, as if that justified their brutal deaths. Their families angrily rejected this idea. In the days that followed, they spoke to television reporters, describing their murdered relatives as young, dedicated parents or students—good, hard-working people, people loved and missed.

Magi learned of the fate of her cousin and friends while she was at Grupo Centro. Many anexados tried to console her and often repeated the phrase "it could have been any one of us." Others were frustrated by all of the attention she received, pointing out that they had suffered similar tragedies but had received none of the fuss. A shrine was created, and a memorial service was held, during which anexados offered prayers, expressed feelings, and threatened revenge.

Estamos hasta la madre.

In the fall of 2014, shortly after my return from fieldwork in Mexico, I taught my signature undergraduate class called Drugs. On the first day, the students filed into the sunny classroom dressed in athletic shorts and flip-flops, carrying their Nalgene water bottles with the Stanford logo.

The first class proceeded as it normally did. I started off with "Two Questions on Drugs," an essay by Gilles Deleuze. In it, Deleuze asks about the moment when drug use shifts from something vital to something deadly. "Does it necessarily happen very quickly?" Deleuze asks about the turning point from life to death that so often accompanies drugs. The students looked at me thoughtfully as I read aloud from the text. I told them to be prepared to discuss the essay the following week.

Two days after my first class, more than one hundred students from Raúl Isidro Burgos Rural Teachers' College who had been traveling by buses from Ayotzinapa, Guerrero, to Mexico City were stopped in Iguala. The students were mostly from rural peasant families and were on their way to the capital to join an annual march commemorating the Tlatelolco massacre in 1968. Midway through their journey they were attacked by the police, who allegedly took them to be members of a gang. The assault lasted for several hours. Six people were murdered, and forty-three students were disappeared, their whereabouts still unknown.

I walked into the classroom the following week and watched my students, the same ages as those killed and disappeared in Mexico, drop their backpacks to the floor and sit at their desks. They were in good cheer and chatted casually. The dissonance between what occurred in Mexico and the atmosphere in my classroom left me numb. I set my lecture down and stepped away from the lectern.

"Does anyone want to talk about happened in Mexico a few days ago?" I asked.

The room was silent.

"Does anyone *know* what happened?"

More silence.

I looked around the classroom, waiting. Finally, one student raised his hand.

"There was another massacre in Mexico," he said.

I couldn't proceed with the class as I had planned, but I didn't know what to do. I felt helpless and enraged.

Stanford is nicknamed "The Farm" but apart from its horse stables, there's really nothing farm-like about it. Year-round, the lawns are vibrant green and soft as velvet. The palm trees are perfectly groomed, and the grounds of the eucalyptus groves are swept clean. The original campus buildings and courtyards, a blend of Romanesque and mission revival designs, cast a golden glow in the evening. My office was in the oldest part of the campus, not far from Auguste Rodin's six *Burghers of Calais*, bronze figures with despairing gestures and expressions of doom.

I often stayed on campus late into the evening, waiting for Bay Area traffic to die down before my commute home. My office faced the courtyard in the main quad. From my window I watched the cleaning crew push their carts from building to building, just like I did when I was a motel maid as a teenager. I always left my office door ajar so Juan, one of the janitors responsible for the anthropology building, could reach in to fetch my wastebasket without having to knock. One evening he asked if we could talk.

Juan said that his coworker, a groundskeeper at Stanford, was the uncle of one of the forty-three disappeared students. He called Stanford a "powerful place" and asked if we could help the affected families, who resided in both Mexico and the United States. Many of the service workers at Stanford are from Guerrero and Michoacán, states in Mexico where criminal violence is most intense. It hadn't occurred to me until then that they were suffering the tragedies I spent my afternoons lecturing about. But what could we do to respond to their suffering? Could we do anything at all?

I arrived before any of the students for the next class meeting and rearranged the desks into a circle. Class couldn't go on as planned, I told the students. What occurred in Iguala demanded a response, and we would spend the quarter trying to provide one. Some of the students sighed in disappointment. I invited them to leave, and a few did.

All around the world, students were making videos in solidarity with the disappeared students and their families and uploading them to YouTube. They were holding teach-ins and vigils at their campuses. For many young people, the disappearance of forty-three students in Iguala was the event that revealed the horror of the war in Mexico. For the first time, they were motivated to do something.

The response from Stanford was slow. It wasn't just that the pristine campus was far removed from the world's messy realities; it was also the institutional barriers to organizing and dissent. "Free speech" was limited to one hour a day in White Plaza, an empty space akin to a pedestrian parking lot in the center of the university. All events, including protests, needed advance approval from the Office of Student Engagement.

I had no experience organizing *manifestaciones*, as they are called in Mexico. I learned with my students, turning our class into a ten-week teach-in and protest. We spent Monday learning about the drug war and Wednesday demonstrating against it. Students carried hand-painted signs (#ITWASTHESTATE, FIND THEM, STOP THE DRUG WAR), chanted into bullhorns, and formed sit-down blockades. We partnered with centers and affinity groups across campus and held teach-ins and vigils, some of which were covered by local Spanish-speaking media. The uncle of the disappeared student was at the center of these events, carrying with him an iPad that showed photographs of his nephew. "He wanted to be a teacher," he'd say, unable to hold back tears. "Help us find him."

But raised consciousness and resistance seemed to die down almost as quickly as they emerged. By the end of the quarter, the sounds of protest were replaced with the celebratory boom of Stanford's marching band. The big game was on the horizon. Massive signs draped over hallowed buildings in the main quad read BEAT CAL, a reference to the Stanford football team's rivalry with UC Berkeley. The Farm had moved on.

But Mexico hadn't. On a gray morning in November 2014, thousands of people gathered around Mexico City's golden-winged Angel of Independence. Simultaneous gatherings took place at the Monument to the Revolution and the Plaza of the Three Cultures, sites where the intensities of state repression and opposition are still felt.

The point of convergence for the three contingents was the desire to turn disappearance into presence, presence into a process of transformation. The basic method: reconnecting people in space and time. In the afternoon the crowds released themselves and flowed through Mexico City's broad avenues and cobblestone streets. As they moved, they chanted. *¡Vivos se los llevaron, vivos los queremos! You took them alive, we want them returned alive!* They were specifically referring to the disappearance of the students, but also more generally to Mexico's *guerra sucia* and the narco war. It rained lightly, and there was an aroma of marijuana mixed with copal.

The three protests came together in the Zócalo. Black-and-white images of the dead and disappeared accompanied the living. At night an effigy of the Mexican president was set afire, casting a sphere of light into the vast darkness. The fire evoked the memory of the disappeared and inspired a sense of collectivity among those who were present. The people gained courage through their connection, knowing it might not hold. The burn of the fire nurtured their hope, and in its turbulent flames they caught a glimpse of change.

Across the Zócalo, a group of demonstrators confronted police standing guard in front of the National Palace. They threw Molotov cocktails, stones, even rockets, and set fire to the palace's ancient front doors. Riot police moved forward—shields in one hand, weapons in the other. They sprayed tear gas and water; they struck demonstrators indiscriminately with steel batons. People screamed, *No violence, no violence,* but the police wouldn't stop until they cleared the Zócalo. The demonstrators resisted, and as they were pushed back and beaten up, they counted the numbers one through forty-three.

The repetition of those numbers sent a tremor through the chaotic night. It was a reminder and a challenge to the demonstrators that the movement *must* survive, even as it was being shattered.

In his memoir of the October 1968 Tlatelolco massacre of student demonstrators in Mexico City and the tumultuous decade that preceded it, Paco Ignacio Taibo II addresses the difficulties presented by the very notion of "the movement." "We didn't know what the movement was," he writes, "but it was growing . . . a tidal wave that just kept growing and growing." Taibo recalls the relationships, ideas, affects, and actions that gave expression to the desire for liberation, one met with increasing levels of state repression:

> All we knew was that there was a Movement and that it had to be defended against those who sought to destroy it with clubs and bazooka fire, and protected from those who wanted to suffocate it with words, slow it down, halt it. We knew that we had to make it grow, nourish it, and take it beyond itself.

The book's title, '68, delineates these efforts in relation to the darkness of a particular historic juncture. At the same time, Taibo carries '68 forward, like a pre-illumination of things still in the making. In the context of the mass protests in 1968, Taibo says that such a quest "meant violence, repression, fear, prison, assassination." However, it also meant "the reengagement of a generation of students with their own society, their investment in neighborhoods hitherto unknown to them, discussions on the bus, a breaking down of barriers, a discovery of solidarity among the people." When Taibo writes of "the *tremendous force* of our four hundred dead . . . images of the wounded being dragged off by their hair . . . memory of blood on the wet ground," he speaks of the generative force of darkness.

I arrived back at my hotel that night to find two men guarding its doors. Throngs of demonstrators continued to run down the street, away from the besieged Zócalo. Some held their heads as if they were being struck from above, while others looked nervously over their shoulders. "Show us your key," the guards demanded before opening the doors.

The hotel was the same one that I had stayed at in 2006, when I was pregnant with my daughters. Once again, the tall-shuttered windows in my room opened onto the Zócalo. There were still hundreds of demonstrators below. Some confronted the police, their bodies surging and retreating in furious waves. But most had already been rounded up, and they sat with their hands tied behind their backs. The rhythmic counting from one to forty-three continued, echoing off the ancient buildings that framed the plaza, ricocheting across the city. For several hours I took comfort in the chants, until they were replaced by the morning calls of church bells and street vendors. But a sonic memory continues to resonate, and it cannot be erased.

4

MOTHER OF SORROWS

I visited Hortencia again a few months after she had committed Daniel to an anexo named Grupo Amistad. It was a few blocks away from her home—close enough for Hortencia to easily visit her son, and far enough for her to feel some distance from him. Several mothers I talked to described wanting to be both near their kids and away from them. Anexos provided a space where this tension could be resolved, at least for a little while.

I was leaving Mexico City the following week and brought small gifts to say goodbye—a tortilla española from the fancy shopping center near my apartment, a bag of candy tied up with a bow, and a pair of my earrings she had admired. A fiftieth wedding anniversary party was in full swing in the courtyard when I arrived. Balloons hung from patios and mariachis performed. People danced around Armando and Josefina, the elderly couple at the center of the celebration. They were dressed as they may have been decades ago, with Armando's blue guayabera pulled tight against his belly and Josefina's white dress hanging loosely from her small frame. El Gordo y La Flaca, Fatso and Skinny, they were affectionately called. They danced close, their well-practiced movements trailing the music by several beats.

Hortencia's neighbor Lupe rushed over when she saw me and immediately led me to a banquet of food. Rice, beans with pork rinds, and mole de olla filled large ceramic bowls. A towering white-frosted cake stood at the end of the table, surrounded by kids with excited eyes. "Eat," Lupe commanded as she fixed me a plastic plate of food. She slapped on a few corn tortillas for cutlery and watched me eat until the plate was clean. Her six-year-old daughter held on to Lupe's leg, sucking her thumb.

A few women came over to talk. They'd seen me before and wanted to know who I was. I told them I was a researcher from California studying anexos. "Anexos!" they exclaimed, surprised by my topic of study. They were accustomed to researchers and reporters in their neighborhood, but they usually investigated Tepito's culture of street vending and crime.

Tepito's residents and vecindades have long been stigmatized as impoverished and dangerous, and valorized as scruffy and dignified. The jubilant atmosphere of the courtyard didn't fit the stereotypes. One of the women who'd come over to talk with Lupe and me playfully warned, "Everything and nothing you hear about Tepito is true."

Her name was Carmen. She was a hefty woman, with short-cropped hair and a bosom so large she couldn't help bumping into people with it. She named the countless anexos she'd committed her five kids and husband to—*Grupo Amistad, Grupo Luz de Vida, Grupo Juventud, Grupo Bravo.* The list went on and on. "When they're in an anexo, I have my little vacation." The women laughed. By then I knew that women sometimes commit family members to protect themselves from domestic violence, or to give themselves a break from the daily burden of caring for an addict or alcoholic. In addition to keeping others safe, anexos provided women a brief respite from the daily onslaught of work and abuse. They provided women safety—not from criminal or neighborhood violence, but from violence within their own homes.

Another woman in the group interjected and said her husband was in the anexo in the vecindad.

"Here?" I asked. I hadn't known that there was one.

"Of course!" Carmen interjected. She went on to explain that the owner of the apartment had saved enough money to move out of Tepito and into a middle-class neighborhood. For years, he rented his unit out to residents who needed storage space. Then, in 2010, the building association assembled and decided it was time to turn the unit into an anexo. Their decision was prompted by a shooting in the neighborhood that left six teenagers and young men dead. According to residents, they were returning home from a shrine devoted to San Judas Tadeo, Saint Jude, patron saint of hopeless cases, a pilgrimage site for those who are poor or addicted to drugs. The police dismissed the killing as gang related and didn't investigate further. Carmen said that the residents of Tepito were deeply shaken by the massacre. The establishment of an anexo in the vecindad was one way to provide its residents the safety the police would not. About half of Grupo San Judas's anexados were from the vecindad. "Outsiders" were charged higher fees, a portion of which was funneled back into the association's coffers and used to pay for things like building repairs, security, even parties.

The owner of the unit and the anexo's padrino were at the anniversary party, and Lupe wanted to make introductions. She scanned the crowded courtyard in search of them. Carmen joked that they'd be easy for me to identify. All I needed to do was look for the two men dressed in the most expensive clothes.

———

Everyone who lived in the complex was invited to the party, but Hortencia wasn't in the mood to attend. She worked two jobs, six days a week, her long days divided between cleaning rooms and waiting tables at two different hotels near the Zócalo. It was supposed to be her day off, but she had cleaned that morning too, covering for a friend who couldn't make her shift.

Hortencia's gray work frock hung from the balcony and her door was open when I arrived. "Come in," she said as she tidied the front room. When I stepped into her apartment, I thought of the two servers who had pushed their way in just a few months earlier. Daniel was still in the anexo Hortencia had committed him to.

We sat on the sofa with our bodies angled toward a sputtering fan. It was early September and hot. Hortencia wore a white tank top, her pink bra peeking through its fabric. A tattoo of a crown capped her left shoulder, and her swollen ankles were strung with flower tattoos, their green and red ink bleeding into her skin. Strands of gray streaked her long black hair. She caught me looking at her and smiled.

"How old do you think I am?"

"Thirty-five," I guessed.

"¡Ay! I didn't have Daniel when I was a child! I'm a respectable thirty-eight!"

The three-year difference mattered. Hortencia was fourteen when she met Daniel's father, Rey. At fifteen, she was pregnant, and a mother at sixteen. A few months before Daniel was born, Hortencia moved in with Rey and his family. Their home was the same apartment where Hortencia would go on living with Daniel, long after Rey and his family were gone.

The apartment used to be crowded. In addition to Rey and Hortencia, there were Rey's parents, his brother, and a constant stream of relatives from Morelos. Rey's family was close, warm, and they welcomed Hortencia without complaint. His mother Anselma doted on her during her pregnancy and after, and neighbors brought baby clothes and toys, filling the already stuffed apartment with light blue. Living in the vecindad with Rey and his family was the first time in Hortencia's life that she felt cared for and safe.

"Do you know what my name means?" she asked me. "It means *hydrangea*. The flower." She took a framed picture off the wall and placed it on my lap. It showed different types of hydrangea—French, Pinky Winky, Tea of Heaven, Little Lamb. The picture was a birthday gift from Anselma. "She gave me many gifts," Hortencia said. The greatest gift was home.

The upbeat music from the courtyard filled the dim room. It was only the fourth time I'd visited Hortencia there and each time I'd found her to be the same way—reserved, a bit melancholy.

"I never had a *quince*," she said, referring to a quinceañera, the celebration of a girl's fifteenth birthday. A *quince* is a major affair, marking a girl's passage into womanhood. Families pour their resources into it, often more than they do for a wedding. Hortencia's fifteenth birthday passed by unannounced. It was nothing to celebrate, she said. At the time, she was four months pregnant and living with her older sister Cecilia elsewhere in Tepito.

"And you? A quince? A sweet sixteen?" Hortencia smiled, but her brown eyes were suddenly narrow, defensive.

We were close in age.

"No." I didn't tell her that there had been nothing for me to celebrate at fifteen or sixteen, either.

———

That afternoon I visited Hortencia was some thirty years after Mexico City's massive earthquake. The two anniversaries—the earthquake and the celebration in the courtyard—were intertwined for Hortencia. Hortencia was ten when the earthquake hit. She lived with her parents in Colonia Doctores, a working-class neighborhood close to the Centro. Her family was relatively well-off—they owned their apartment, which had a private bathroom and kitchen, and her father had a steady administrative job at the Secretariat of Government. Despite these advantages, Hortencia's childhood was hellish. She was unwanted, born a decade after her four sisters, all of whom left the house as soon as they could.

"My parents were alcoholics," she said plainly. "My mother drank until she blacked out. That's when my father abused me." Hortencia recalled the abuse without reservation or tears, but she wasn't numb. At times, her voice and shoulders trembled. The joyous music from below seemed to make these memories all the more upsetting.

She called her father pathetic, but also frightening. When he touched her, he compared her to her own mother. Hortencia was good, her mother was bad. Hortencia was pretty, her mother no longer was. Hortencia made him proud, her mother was an embarrassment. Sometimes he cried pitifully and apologized—for what, he didn't say. When sober, he was cruel. He said Hortencia was just like her mother, whom he openly despised. Meanwhile, Hortencia's mother barely looked at her. She knew what was happening and drank herself to unconsciousness so she wouldn't have to deal with it.

"My mother didn't protect me."

Hortencia's memories of her parents' abuse were tied up with the earthquake. She was preparing herself for school, pulling on the pants her mother made her wear underneath her school uniform. Brown pants under a gray and blue plaid dress—the ensemble of a girl whose mother was ashamed of the abuse at home. Her father hadn't yet left for work. He sat at their kitchen table drinking coffee and smoking a cigarette, as if nothing had happened the night before. She remembered that the radio was tuned to a show about local politics. "That's what he listened to. Politics," she said. In 1985, Mexico was in a grave economic crisis, saddled with international debt and high unemployment. Austerity measures caused living standards to plunge. Then the earthquake happened. The unfathomable damage it caused made the very idea of "living standards" pointless.

Earthquakes are a lethal reality in Mexico City, and children are well acquainted with them. They feel the tremors and practice emergency drills at school. Hortencia's teachers called them natural events. But for her, the earthquake that devastated the city that September morning was a punishment from God for her father's sins.

"We lived on the second floor. Our building had five. How I wished my father had been crushed under floors and floors of concrete." Their building was badly damaged but deemed habitable. A block away, a four-story apartment building completely collapsed.

After the shaking stopped, everyone who could ran out of their building and into the street. Hortencia and her parents ran, too. Dogs were the first thing she noticed. They seemed to be everywhere, skulking around, their skinny bodies covered in white plaster. They looked like ghosts, she said. Then she noticed her mother's foot. At some point during the rush to the street she had injured herself, and her ankle bone jutted out of her skin.

Find help! Find food! Find something to drink! Hortencia's mother yelled. Hortencia obeyed and went searching while her parents stayed behind. I asked why her father hadn't gone in search for help.

"Why did she make you go?"

"Because my mother wanted me to get lost."

Hortencia remembered being overwhelmed by the commotion and thinking she still needed to go to school. She found herself next to a *panadería*. The windows were busted out and the contents of the shelves were scattered on the ground, covered in dust. She licked a roll, hoping it was sugar, but it tasted metallic. She brushed the rolls off and headed back toward her parents.

"At first I couldn't find them. I didn't cry. You'd think a child my age would cry." She looked at the people running around her in a frenzy, at the able-bodied men and women working to rescue those trapped beneath collapsed buildings. She remembered that the city was filled with the sounds of shouting, wailing, helicopters churning. The phrases *Help me!* and *Over here!* were repeated for days.

She finally spotted her parents. "They were on the ground, close, like sweethearts. I'd never seen them like that. I thought, maybe things will be better now. Or maybe I should tell someone my parents were dead. Or I am an orphan." Instead she stood there, twenty, thirty feet away, thinking *What should I do, where should I go, will anybody help me?*

A woman appeared. "She asked me if I was okay. I told her, yes, I'm okay. Her hair. It was white and her face was bleeding, just below her eye, like she was crying. She asked me if I was lost. I pointed and said, look, my parents are just over there."

After the earthquake, Hortencia never lived with her parents again.

Officials claimed the earthquake killed five thousand people, but residents of hard-hit neighborhoods called that a lie. One of the padrinos I knew, Padrino Mike, claimed that there were "fifty, sixty, seventy thousand people dead, homeless." Padrino Mike ran Grupo San Hipólito, an anexo downtown. During one of our conversations, he recalled how, at the time of the earthquake, he was working construction in Dallas. The earthquake left his mother permanently disabled, and relatives and friends were buried under the rubble.

It took Padrino Mike over a week to make contact with his family. He and his coworkers, also undocumented immigrants from Mexico, listened to Spanish-language radio whenever they could. They filled each other in with occasional updates—such-and-such building was destroyed, so-and-so was killed or missing. They felt helpless and wanted to return to Mexico, but it was too risky—they might never make it back to the United States and they needed to make money to support their families back home. So they remained in Texas, building luxury condominiums during the day and drinking and worrying in their shared apartment at night.

Padrino Mike remembered sitting in a bar in Dallas, watching the first ladies of Mexico and the United States standing side-by-side on TV. Their backs were turned away from the pitiable scene of men and women scrambling up a collapsed building, searching for survivors.

The earthquake was like the narco war. The real problem wasn't just the collision of tectonic plates or, in the case of the war, rival cartels. It was, as Elena Poniatowska writes, the corruption and neglect of governments who couldn't care less about poor people. "We've always had to take care of our own," Padrino Mike said.

————

The oscillating fan blew Hortencia's hair off her face. I watched her stare at the chair where Daniel had sat, passed out in a drug-induced stupor. Committing Daniel to an anexo was her way of caring for him, but such care came with risks. Hortencia remembered the night the servers came into her house to take Daniel away, how they beat him and threatened her. She worried about the kind of treatment he might be suffering in the anexo. Would he come home physically and emotionally scarred? Would he resent her so much he'd never return? "There was nothing else I could do," she said. The anexo was her only option.

"Do you think Daniel knows you sent him to the anexo because you wanted to keep him safe?" I asked.

Hortencia closed her eyes and slowly shook her head. "I think he will hate me. At least for a little while."

Someone stepped inside Hortencia's apartment unannounced. It was a young woman with a baby slung on her hip. *Come down, floja! There's so much food! Don't be lonely like that, tensita! Bring your friend!* Hortencia's voice perked up. "The party will go on all night! There's no rush. I'll be down soon. I promise!" When her neighbor left, Hortencia told me she had no intention of going to the anniversary party. Instead, she talked about her marriage to Rey. She took out a small white photo album from a the top shelf of a dresser drawer.

"We were married in Jiutepec, in Morelos," she said, opening the album to the first page. Below the plastic protector was a photo of Hortencia and Rey dressed in ordinary clothes a few days before the wedding. "Have you ever been to Jiutepec?" I admitted I hadn't. Rey's father was from the small industrial city and the "destination wedding," as Hortencia sarcastically called it, made it possible for his extended family to attend. She expected that Jiutepec would be out in the sticks and that her future father-in-law's family were peasants. She imagined cauldrons of soup, thin tamales, and mosquitos. She was wrong.

Rey's uncle Enrique was the one who threw the reception, and he was by no means a peasant. His house was a four-bedroom ranch. His coiffed wife presented Hortencia with a party dress. It was mauve, with large sequins glimmering around the neckline. The reception was also lavish. There were three wedding cakes and meats of every kind and cut. The family hired a professional photographer and a live band played covers of beloved *boleros* and *rancheras*. Hortencia had never experienced anything like it.

At that time, she knew very little about the extended family and was surprised by their wealth. She was also surprised by how easily Rey fit in to it. It was as if he'd lived in such a comfortable setting his entire life, not in a cramped two-room apartment in Tepito. It turned out that the relationship between the two places was closer than it appeared. Rey's family moved pharmaceuticals and car parts from Jiutepec to Tepito, where they were sold on the black market. Hortencia never questioned why Rey and his father would go away for a couple of days and then return with enough cash to shower the family with gifts. Nor did she inquire about the contents of the apartment unit the family rented as a storage space.

What she did know was that Anselma was a beautician. She cut and dyed hair out of her home and gave women elaborate updos and makeovers for special occasions. She tried to teach Hortencia her trade, but it was hopeless. Hortencia couldn't braid hair or apply the right balance of eyeshadow, so she worked with her sister-in-law in one of Tepito's *tianguis*, the market stalls that crammed Tepito's streets. They sold bottles of perfume named after famous Americans.

"If Anselma was here, she'd have fixed up Josefina," Hortencia said, referring to the woman celebrating her fiftieth wedding anniversary in the courtyard below.

Men at her own wedding reception asked Hortencia to dance and Rey, who never showed jealousy, encouraged her to say yes. They were family after all, and everyone was kind to her. But Hortencia didn't want to dance with men she didn't know. I suspected her reluctance had to do with her father, but she said it was because she worried about Daniel.

"Everyone was passing him around like a ball, like a game. All these strangers holding him up into the air, calling him *little man*. I didn't like it. I didn't like it at all." She worried about losing sight of Daniel, or that he might fall and get hurt. But it was Rey that she lost. Five years after the wedding, he was murdered. I never asked Hortencia about the circumstances that led to Rey's death.

A year after he died, Rey's parents moved to Morelos, leaving Hortencia the apartment. Anselma visited her and Daniel regularly, always arriving with gifts from the extended family. Hortencia told me that she was thankful for their love and support, but she stayed away from Morelos. She never explained why.

Another neighbor came to the door. This time it was Lupe, the same child still wrapped around her leg, thumb in mouth. Lupe marched in and said she'd had enough of Hortencia's antisocial behavior and that my research could wait.

"I'm not going to leave until you leave with me," she announced, her arms crossed over her chest.

Hortencia relented. She put on the earrings I'd brought her and brushed her hair. In the stairwell, two teenagers nodded off from some kind of high. Lupe gave them a little kick and called them lowlifes as we passed them by.

The courtyard was even more crowded than it was when I arrived. People talked and laughed and sang the lyrics to the mariachis' songs. Within seconds, Lupe was suddenly gone from our side. I spotted her a few minutes later chatting easily with neighbors.

Hortencia, on the other hand, was tense. A few people approached her and planted a kiss on her cheek or made small talk before quickly drifting off. Carmen half-jokingly greeted her as "the snob." When Lupe reappeared with two plates of food, one for Hortencia and the other for me, I ate both. It was obvious to me that Hortencia wasn't comfortable with parties, something I understood. I was relieved when she suggested we go to the Zócalo. I followed her as she pushed her way through the courtyard with determination, making sure to give the celebrating couple a smile and congratulations as she passed them by.

We took Jesús Carranza, one of the streets clogged with stalls where people sold everything from barrettes to engine parts. People said hello to Hortencia as we passed by. Sometimes she returned their greetings, more often she ignored them. I wasn't put off by her lack of sociability. It felt natural to me. It seemed that one-on-one conversations were easier for the both of us.

I stopped at a stall that sold *milagritos*, tiny religious votives made from cheap metals. They were in the shapes of body parts for every form of injury and sickness, people lost or in need of help, and sacred hearts. Each figure represented a history of vulnerability, hope, and faith. I told Hortencia that I grew up with *milagritos* in New Mexico and watched my great-grandmother use them for petitions. When my mother was pregnant with me, my great-grandmother sewed them into her clothes—breasts, hearts, lungs, bellies, as well as tiny persons kneeling in prayer.

"You were wanted," Hortencia said.

I wondered if what Hortencia said was true.

The little miracles shimmered on the vendor's table like a treasure trove. I ran my fingers through them instinctively.

"You touch, you buy," the seller said. She scooped up a cup of *milagritos*, tied them in a small plastic bag, and handed it to me for fifty pesos.

————

As we approached the Zócalo the stalls gave way to walking vendors and street performers. We passed a young violist playing Beethoven's "Für

Elise," his instrument's tattered case filled with tourists' gold coins. A few yards away an elderly organ grinder played a melancholy tune. Occasionally someone tossed a small silver coin, the one of lowest value, into his limp hat.

We headed toward the Metropolitan Cathedral. Hortencia said she went there for its quiet and cool air. I sat near her, in front of the golden Altar of Forgiveness, famous for its sculpture of Christ, his skin darkened by the sin and suffering of his devotees. Hortencia didn't close her eyes or kneel like the others around us, nor did her lips move to words of prayer. Instead, she sat silent and still, with her open eyes fixed straight ahead. About fifteen minutes passed before we left the cathedral.

"Did you pray?" I asked her.

"Of course I did," she snapped, like the answer to my question was so obvious it shouldn't have been asked.

———

Each time I visited the cathedral, I'd slip into one of the pews that leads to the Altar of Kings, pull down the prayer bench, and kneel. Sometimes I tried to pray, but usually I pretended to do so while stealing glances at the cathedral's baroque details. The angles of the cross, the curves of the nave. Radiant gold, dark shadow. It was a place of refuge and violence, built on the Templo Mayor, the main temple of Tenochtitlan, which was destroyed by Spanish colonists.

I took my mother to the cathedral one summer when she stayed with me in Mexico City, ostensibly to take care of my daughters while I worked. I promised her an exciting vacation in exchange for her help and did my best to deliver. I rented the nicest apartment I could find in Colonia Roma, took her to tourist spots, the "best" restaurants, Oaxaca. When we visited the cathedral, it was midway through her stay and things were not going well. She complained relentlessly about Mexico City's noisy crowds and suffered from headaches that required multiple naps a day. She was terrified of leaving the apartment alone, yet she felt like a prisoner in it. She was driving me nuts. But whenever she talked about wanting to leave early and return to her isolated trailer in New Mexico, I felt nervous and afraid. No matter how difficult she was, I wanted her to stay.

The air was thick with grime that day and it stuck to our skin. My mother was tired and cranky and wanted to return to the apartment. She didn't need to see the inside of the cathedral, she said, the exterior was impressive enough. But I suggested we take a quick rest inside, promising her it would be quiet and cool.

My mother is Catholic. When she was a child, Sunday mornings were spent in a church made of thick, minimally adorned adobe walls. It was her grandmother, Margarita, who took her to Mass, because her own mother was usually too hungover to go herself. Among my mother's few cherished memories of her childhood is that of her and her grandmother walking to church. They'd proceed along the *acequia*, the irrigation system that fed the neighborhood crops. Along the way they gathered wild greens for the night's dinner. Years later, my mother would try to relive the memory, walking me down the same path.

As soon as we entered the cathedral my mother was thrown into a state of awe. She looked up toward the ceiling, her mouth slightly open, bronze face glowing. I loved seeing her this way, in this rare moment of grace.

Almost immediately an elderly man approached us in the church. My mother looked at him kindly, thinking he needed help. Instead, he scolded her for not removing her sun hat. It was a thrift-store find she'd bought for her trip to Mexico City, white and wide, like something Jackie O would wear. That's how she described it to me on the phone a few nights before she arrived. My mother ripped the elegant hat off her head and apologized to the old man. Humiliated, she turned to leave, but I grabbed her arm and held her back, insisting that she take a quick look around, insisting she just had to see. She looked at me with wet eyes, yanked her arm away from me, and rushed toward the cathedral's massive wood doors, the white sunhat crumpled in her hand.

I ran after her, desperate to catch her, as she pushed through the crowds, fleeing the shameful scene. We made it out of the square and stood near the entrance of the Best Western hotel. "When I was a child,

I wore a mantilla to church," my mother cried. "If I forgot it my grand-mother pinned a wrinkled Kleenex on top of my head. Oh, I didn't do anything wrong! It's just different here! I didn't do anything wrong! I didn't do anything wrong!"

All I could do was try to appease her. I suggested we get a cocktail at the hotel's rooftop bar. "It has a beautiful view, far from the crowds," I promised. My mother wiped the tears off her face, fixed her hat back on her head, and stared at herself in a compact mirror.

We took a table that looked onto the Zócalo. A summer downpour was about to burst from the low gray sky. My mother placed her hat on the portable coat rack, shook out her thick, dark hair, and lit a cigarette. She loved that she could smoke in bars in Mexico City and joked that it was her favorite thing about the place.

I noticed a group of businessmen checking her out, which annoyed me but delighted her. My mother is a beautiful woman, compared her whole adult life to Raquel Welch. At forty-four, she married a man half her age. A decade later, she was anxious about her fading good looks and was relieved when men noticed her. But she hoped these men wouldn't come over and try to strike up a conversation. She wouldn't know how to respond.

My mother grew up listening to her parents speak Spanish but was convinced she could never speak it herself. "It was beaten out of me," she'd say, which was true. In the 1950s and 1960s, speaking Spanish was a cause for shame. Schools didn't teach it and punished students for sharing a joke or secret in the mother tongue. In parts of New Mexico, White and "Spanish" establishments were separated by ethnicity. My mother's parents wanted her to speak English like the neighbors in their white neighborhood, which they moved to when she was a child, leaving the barrio behind.

In Mexico City, people addressed my mother in Spanish, and it pained me when she'd look at me to translate. She was flustered whenever dialogue was necessary, especially in bars, where we spent considerable time together, even with my kids. Back home, she worked as a bartender and was brilliant at her job. She memorized customers favorite drinks and birthdays, put women at ease when their husbands or boyfriends flirted with her, and poured cocktails like a dancer. She could hold three different conversations at the same time.

During her trip to Mexico City, my mother needed bars, cigarettes, and at least three cocktails a day. Drink in hand, her shoulders would relax, and her face would soften. She'd scan the room, the scenery, and notice things besides her own misery.

"Look at how grand the Metropolitan Cathedral is! What a spectacular view! Do you feel a chill in the air? I think the rain is about to come. What a relief it is that we're safe here, isn't it?"

———

Growing up, my mother wasn't safe. There was an uncle. Whenever he visited her parents' house, he'd call for my mother and her two sisters. He wanted to know how they'd grown. Since he was blind, he touched them. One by one, the girls were forced to stand before him and remain still as he explored their developing bodies. He started with the crown of their heads, then touched their faces with his large, chafed hands. Slowly, he'd move down the neck, the shoulders, then brush against their breasts.

My mother told me stories about the abuse she suffered. I was her trusted confidant, even when I was a child. One afternoon, Uncle Johnny visited my mother's house while I was there. She welcomed him in a voice I'd never heard before, so high-pitched and nervous. The three of us sat together at the kitchen table. I wondered if this man with the dark glasses was the one who'd hurt her. "Let me see how you've grown, Angelita," he said to me. My mother shot me a worried look but said nothing. I refused my great-uncle's advances while my mother's eyes filled with tears.

I knew things about her childhood. Like how by the time she'd come home from school, her parents had been home drinking beer for hours. There was no family meal, just bits of food my mother and her sisters stole from the kitchen and ate in their shared bedroom, careful not to take too much or make a mess. Their bedroom was adjacent to the living room, where their parents drank, watched game shows on TV, and argued.

When the three girls were in their room, they tried to keep their voices and the record player low to avoid upsetting their parents, who constantly complained that they were too loud.

By the time my mother was a senior in high school she was engaged to be married. It was her ticket out, she told me. Every weekend, her sisters crawled out of their bedroom window and into the blue New Mexico night. My mother stayed home and listened to music. She needed to protect her reputation, she said, to be seen as a wholesome bride.

When she was alone, she listened to records she loved but her sisters hated, like Simon & Garfunkel and Joan Baez. Though she didn't often say it aloud, she was opposed to the Vietnam War. Such a view was not only unpopular in her parents' house, but a cause for beatings.

I knew all about the beatings—my mother told me about each episode, sometimes the same story multiple times. One memory haunted her. She was alone in her bedroom, listening to the Supremes, trying to drown out the sounds of her parents fighting in the next room. She turned up the volume on one of her favorite songs—"Shake Me, Wake Me (When It's Over)"—and danced in the narrow space between her and her sisters' beds.

"I didn't hear my mother scream for me to turn the music down. I didn't hear the door swing open."

Her mother stormed into the room, slapped her multiple times, scratched the record silent, and slammed the door shut on her way out. When my mother repeated this story to me, I imagined her holding the sides of her battered face, refusing to cry.

"What happened next?" I asked her, even though I already knew the answer.

"I put on my bright-orange miniskirt with matching tights."

Sometimes, my mother demonstrated how she concealed her bruises with foundation and powder, adding a touch of blush to one side of her face to balance out the signs of her latest injuries. She taught me how she ironed her hair, curling the ends upward like a smile. I remember staring at our reflections in the bathroom mirror—me dolled up like Mary Tyler Moore, my mother in her worn bathrobe, her face bare and drawn. She'd grown her hair out so long it covered her chest like a thick black blanket. "You look so pretty," my mother would say to my reflection. All I wanted to do was protect her.

To this day, my mother locks herself in her bedroom and smokes cigarettes like a teenager. When I was a child, she locked herself away for days, sometimes weeks at a time. I'd tap on her closed door and tell her I'd made dinner, to please come out and eat. She'd either ignore me or say she'd join later, but rarely did. Eventually, she'd burst through the door and head to the grocery store or public library, show sudden interest in my schoolwork, and sing while watering the houseplants. I did everything I could to keep her from locking herself back up in her bedroom. I wanted her to stay outside of the room, to remain in the open, with me.

Over time, I also began to hide—in closets, attics, outbuildings filled with my grandfather's rusty tools. The difference between my mother and me, I think, was that I hoped to be found.

———

Between 2001 and 2006, seventeen young women disappeared in Albuquerque. Some were from my mother's South Valley neighborhood. I was used to seeing MISSING flyers, brittle with age, posted on electrical poles and in small businesses. They included photos of the disappeared women and descriptions of their physical characteristics. Hair colors, skin tones, moles, tattoos. Some of the flyers listed the cell phone numbers of worried relatives. *I am her mother*, one read. *Please help me.*

The little media attention that was paid to the disappeared women in Albuquerque focused on their involvements with drugs, sex work, or gangs. The victims' families were outraged by such coverage and argued that it made it seem like the victims were responsible for crimes committed against them, justifying the lack of an adequate police response. The families told reporters of having to search for their disappeared relatives alone.

In February 2009, a woman walking her dog discovered a human femur bone in a desolate area on the edge of the city. She reported her discovery to authorities, and within weeks the bodies of eleven women and girls were found in shallow graves in the same area. They were between the ages of fifteen and thirty-two. One of them had been pregnant.

The grave was just a couple of miles from my mother's house. Stricken, my mother called me in Los Angeles, where I lived at the time. As we spoke on the phone, I could hear low-flying aircraft circling the area. They were looking for disturbances in the dirt, my mother said. I listened to her weep while I looked at my own daughters napping soundly in a shared crib.

It took nearly a year to identify all the remains. As news trickled in, makeshift memorials began appearing where the disappeared had lived or worked. One was on Central Avenue and Atrisco, an intersection not far from my mother's house. The memorial's handmade white cross read MÓNICA: IN LOVING MEMORY and was surrounded by plastic flowers.

At the time, an antifemicide movement in Ciudad Juárez was gaining international visibility. Activisits and mothers of femicide victims from Mexico traveled to Albuquerque to console the devastated families. An event organized by Albuquerque's Center for Peace and Justice brought attention to a shared plight. The mothers in attendance—some from Albuquerque, others from Ciudad Juárez—shared stories of searching for their daughters and pleading with law enforcement to help. Posters that read JUSTICIA showed photographs of female victims from both sides of the border.

I visited the location of the West Mesa murders in February 2022, thirteen years after the initial discovery of the bodies. Resting against a wall near the crime scene were twenty handmade wood crosses representing twenty women. Some of them note the date a victim disappeared and declare FOUND HERE. Other crosses exclaim STILL MISSING.

To this day, no one has been arrested for these crimes.

———

Women and girls disappear in Mexico, and if they are found alive it's a *milagro*, a miracle. If they are found dead, their bodies show signs of torture. More often than not, they don't come back, and their fates remain unknown.

Crimes like these are all too familiar in the state of Mexico, a sprawling metropolis of industrial cities and informal settlements that wrap around Mexico City. Between 2011 and 2012, 1,258 women and girls were reported disappeared there, over half of whom were between ten and seventeen years old. During the same period, 448 women were reported murdered. The majority of these crimes took place in Ecatepec, a municipality of two million people that borders the northeastern part of Mexico City.

Ecatepec wasn't always dangerous. The city dates to the precolonial era and its name is derived from the Nahuatl words *Ehécatl*, the name of the Aztec wind god, and *tepētl*, for "windy hill," a reference to the gently sloping hill that watches over the city. For centuries, Ecatepec was an agricultural community. Paintings from the nineteenth century depict clear skies, fields of crops, colonial haciendas, and a glistening, distant lake.

Things changed dramatically in the mid-1940s, when modern industrialization took hold of Mexico. After the Mexican government passed tax credits for international industries to establish themselves outside of Mexico City, many US companies set up shop in Ecatepec. The communal lands and fields of Ecatepec were transformed into factories, and people from impoverished rural communities flooded the city in search of work. By the 1970s, there were more than two hundred thousand residents, the majority of whom worked in factories for companies like Procter & Gamble, General Electric, and Jumex, a Mexican juice company. Today, there are two million residents, making Ecatepec the most populated suburb of Mexico City.

Many of the US-owned factories that drove Ecatepec's growth are now dormant, having moved to the northern border after NAFTA went into effect. But Ecatepec's population continues to grow, fueled by the arrival of people from rural provinces searching for work in Mexico City and desperate citizens displaced by the violence of the narco war. Ecatepec is now a dense and chaotic landscape filled with new and defunct factories, modern corporate offices, working-class neighborhoods, and precarious settlements that climb higher and higher up the windy hill.

Public protests against the murder and disappearance of women in Ecatepec were taking place at the same time that the "maquiladora murders" in Ciudad Juárez were commanding international press attention in the early 2000s. Yet, until recently, the crimes against women and girls in Ecatepec have garnered little attention. This is partly because the Mexican government has minimized the problem of femicide, issuing vague "gender alerts" and calling for the "respect" of women. Officials, including President Andrés Manuel López Obrador, consistently discredit national and international agencies investigating the extent of gender-based crimes.

Soon after I began my study of anexos, I began collecting articles and reports on Ecatepec's femicides. I had a sense that what was happening in Ecatepec was related to the anexos I was studying in Mexico City. Year after year, my femicide file grew.

In 2014, the bodies of at least twenty-one people were discovered during the drainage of the Grand Canal, part of a channel system on the outskirts of Ecatepec that diverts water and sewage away from flooding the capital. Sixteen of the bodies were women and girls and showed signs of torture. Civil agencies disputed these numbers, stating that there were forty-six bodies, the majority female. The discovery and the discrepancy between the two figures unsettled me. I called Beatriz, the social epidemiologist who encouraged my research on anexos, about the *femicidio* taking place a mere fourteen miles away. She told me to never trust the government's numbers. "The real figures will never be known," she said. "How could they be in a world where the lives of women don't count?"

———

I met Karina at Grupo Centro. She was from Ecatepec and had sought refuge in Mexico City with an aunt who lived there. Karina was eighteen and her aunt committed her to the anexo after she started hanging around Plaza de la Solidaridad, a popular hangout for street kids in Mexico City. According to Karina, she needed to "clean up her act." This meant getting a job and contributing to the household, which Karina thought was impossible. "Look at me," she said in a soft voice. One of her eyes showed evidence of stitches and a scar ran down her cheek. Both were wounds from an assault she survived in Ecatepec a year earlier.

Grupo Centro wasn't the first anexo she'd been in. She'd also been in one in Ecatepec, a anexo for women and girls. Karina talked about it during one of her testimonies. She dreaded giving testimonies because it forced her to face her peers, exposing her face. She'd try to conceal her scars by letting her long hair fall over her eyes. Face covered, she'd describe how her mother committed her to an anexo shortly after the attack.

"My mother made me disappear," she said, looking down at the floor. "She hid me in the anexo."

The anexo she described sounded like a women's shelter, and in many ways it was. It helped women meet their immediate and long-term needs, whether those were a period of protection from dangerous households and neighborhoods or an escape plan from those places. There was an awareness of the significance of gender, too. Girls and women were endangered *because* of their gender.

Karina's description of the anexo in Ecatepec reminded me of the other anexos I knew. Instead of a padrino, a *madrina* called the shots. All the women and girls were crowded together in one room. There was a daily schedule, although this one started later, providing the women more time to sleep. Most of the day was taken up with testimonies, and everyone was expected to deliver them, even children. The main difference about the place Karina described was the absence of physical discipline.

Karina's mother, Lydia, showed up at the women's anexo a few weeks after she'd committed her daughter to it. Karina described the events leading up to her mother's arrival.

Karina's father worked for a company that bought and sold metal. Once, on his way home from work, he was abducted and held for ransom. Lydia gave the criminals everything she could to secure his return, but she worried it wasn't enough. To protect herself from harm, she committed herself to the same anexo she had placed her daughter in. The anexo, Karina said, was a "shithole," but they felt safe there, at least for a little while.

Two of Lydia's sisters lived in Mexico City. They pooled their money to pay for Lydia and Karina's stay at the anexo for one month. When the month was up, one of the sisters took Karina in, but both sisters were unwilling to take Lydia. It was too risky. What if the gang who kidnapped her husband followed her to Mexico City and hurt the sisters' families, too? Lydia returned to Ecatepec. At the time of Karina's testimony at Grupo Centro, her mother was okay, but her father had yet to come home.

———

Much of Ecatepec is an unruly mix of poor and working-class neighborhoods. When seen from above, it appears to be a great sea of one-room cinder-block houses, some of them painted in bright pastel colors and roofed with sheets of corrugated metal. Many of the houses appear unfinished and abandoned.

Every morning, microbuses carry tens of thousands of women from Ecatepec to Mexico City, where they care for babies, clean houses and hotels, and staff restaurants. Thousands more travel by the metro line that connects Ecatepec to Mexico City, or on the public cable car. The Mexicable was inaugurated with much fanfare in 2016—the same year that Mexico had the second-highest murder rate in the world, second only to war-torn Syria. The elevated cable car glides over giant photographic portraits of disappeared and murdered girls and women, whose haunting images are plastered on the sides of concrete homes and apartment buildings. There is one portrait of an adolescent girl with sad eyes and furrowed brows; another of a woman looking down and to the side, gently smiling.

El Río de los Remedios, the River of Remedies, cuts through Ecatepec and reaches into Mexico City. Much of the shallow canal is cased in concrete and dotted with putrid islands of garbage and sewage. In the past decade, the river has become a liquid grave for disappeared women. One of these femicides led to the establishment of Casa Dolorosa, an anexo where women sometimes disappear themselves, and their daughters, to live. Named after the Mother of Sorrows, it's located in one of Ecatepec's poorest neighborhoods, a place where water is delivered once a week in steel-drum barrels, garbage is collected by a horse-drawn cart, and tangles of electrical wiring crisscross rough dirt roads.

Míriam founded the anexo in 2015, nearly two years after her daughter Yeni's body was discovered on the bank of the River of Remedies. Yeni had been missing for three weeks and, during that time, Míriam had convinced herself she was still alive. After Yeni was found, Míriam went silent. Her son worried she'd had a brain aneurysm, but it was grief that took her voice away.

———

In many ways, Casa Dolorosa doesn't exist. It sits on a street without a street sign, in an unnumbered building, and doesn't announce its presence in any way. It's just a room on the second story of Míriam's concrete house, an addition her husband Ulises constructed for what they'd hoped would be a growing family. When Yeni was alive, she and her son Ever lived with her parents on the first floor, while her brother, his wife, and their two children lived on the second.

I went to Casa Dolorosa in the summer of 2016. Manuel drove me to and from the anexo and Araceli, a research assistant from a local university, accompanied me. As we drew closer to the anexo, I suddenly felt afraid and grabbed Araceli's hand. "It's okay," she whispered.

Míriam welcomed us into her home with a tight embrace, cups of instant coffee, and plates of scrambled eggs. Her husband was still asleep on their pull-out sofa, snoring loudly beside five-year-old Ever. One of the first things Míriam said was to call her by her first name. "Here, we are all madrinas."

We sat at a folding table pushed tightly against a concrete wall. Míriam angled a lamp to look through the provisions she had asked me to bring. "Go to Walmart," she said a few days before I visited. I did as I was told and bought towels, blankets, rolls of toilet paper, plastic cutlery, bars of soap, menstrual pads, shampoo, naproxen, ointment for bug bites, boxes of instant ramen, and a piñata-sized bag of candy. Míriam touched each item, counting quietly. When she was finished, she placed the lamp on the table and sat down. The light of the lamp was no stronger than a candle, giving the room a shadowy atmosphere.

We talked for an hour or so, our conversation guided by Míriam's thoughts. She spoke in a low voice so as not to wake anyone. She woke up early every morning, she said, before anyone else, to think and pray, not just over the loss of her daughter, but for every daughter.

Míriam said that Ecatepec used to be a good place to live and have a family. Her husband Ulises worked at the factory for La Costeña, a Mexican canned food company. She did, too, until Yeni was disappeared. Now she took care of her grandson. I looked at him sleeping soundly next to his grandfather, dressed in nothing but a pair of Spider-Man underpants.

Daylight began to filter in through the barred window, illuminating a small shelf on the wall. It held stacks of mismatched dishes, a display of old greeting cards, and small plastic figurines of Jesus and Pope Francis. Earlier that year, Pope Francis had delivered a mass in Ecatepec. It was during the Lenten season, a time of reflection and repentance. Míriam wasn't among the hundreds of thousands of people who went to see the Pope's outdoor mass, but she listened to it on the radio. In his homily, Pope Francis spoke of the corruption of the elite and called for an end to inequality. More important to Míriam was his message about the invisible suffering of Mexico's poor: "How often we experience in our own lives, or in our own families, among our friends or neighbors, the pain which arises when the dignity we carry within is not recognized."

I didn't ask Míriam to talk about the circumstances surrounding Yeni's death, but she did. I sensed from how she narrated the story that she had done so many times before.

"She was late. We waited two, three hours. We waited and she didn't come home."

Yeni had just started working at a chemical plant in the northwestern part of Mexico City. She was excited about the job, which paid more than her last one, which had been caring for three toddlers for a middle-class family who lived in Mexico City. The family had regularly accused her of stealing food; the chemical company provided a generous midday meal for free. During orientation, a manager described the opportunities for workers to move up the ladder into higher-paying positions. Yeni dreamed of moving to a condominium in Las Américas, one of the well-lit gated communities in Ecatepec with two-story condos and running water. Life would be safer there.

"Yeni always left for work by six in the morning to make sure she arrived by eight," Míriam said. Like all women in Ecatepec, she avoided walking alone. She went to the bus stop with a group of women from the neighborhood. They carried everyday objects to defend themselves—pipes, knives, screwdrivers. They felt safer when they were together.

Yeni made it to work that day but fell into danger on the way home. One of the women in their group reported that she'd peeled off from the group. There were rumors that she had boyfriends. Míriam didn't believe any of it. She said her daughter would never choose to walk alone, not for any man. "And even if she did," she added, "she should not have suffered for it."

"*Mi hija*," Míriam said in a low voice, "she was very likable. She had many friends. But it isn't true that she had many boyfriends. The police, the president, they always blame the women, even little girls. *Mi hija*, Yeni. She always had self-respect. We taught her she was worth more than gold."

During her lunch break, Yeni sent her mother a text Míriam would never forget.

> *Estoy bien mamá*
> *Me tratan bien.*

I looked at Ulises, Yeni's father, sleeping on the sofa while Míriam described the night Yeni didn't come home. Ulises walked up and down the street, she said, knocking on his neighbors' doors. He begged for their help and gave them his cell phone number. "He told them to hold on to her and to call him immediately, that he would come for her." All of the neighbors promised. Nobody contacted him.

They posted signs in the neighborhood. ¿LA HAS VISTO? Have you seen her?

The signs showed a photo of Yeni and included a description: the clothes she was wearing the day she disappeared (blue jeans, white shirt, black shoes), her slim build and *café*-colored eyes, a small mole near her nose, the friendship bracelet she never took off, which was a gift from a childhood friend. The sign for Yeni looked like all the signs for Sofía, Gaby, Diana, Julia—all over Ecatepec, all disappeared.

For weeks, Ulises and Míriam retraced Yeni's route from their house to the bus stop, looking for clues. They contacted authorities every day—police in different parts of the municipality and organizations dedicated to finding missing people.

"We reported and reported and reported. But nothing happened," Míriam said.

They pushed for an investigation but never knew if one was opened. They took to social media, starting a Facebook page dedicated to finding Yeni, and emailed inquiries to nonprofits. Friends, family, and activists told them to never give up.

The weeks passed.

In the present, Míriam stopped talking about Yeni as Ever started to wake up. "Good morning, little prince," she said, her voice tinged with grief. She pointed a remote control at a TV. A cartoon show lit the room.

There were rustling noises from above. Wooden stairs connected the two floors. Beneath the stairs were neat columns of provisions—many of the same items she had asked me to bring. "From the *feministas*," Míriam said.

For decades, women have been confronting violence against women and girls in Mexico, taking on the misogyny, impunity, government corruption, and inaction that perpetuate abuse and femicide. These efforts span from visualizing the faces and names of victims through public art and social media to *marchas* and demonstrations across the country. Every year, mobilizations grow in frequency and levels of participation, and some have garnered worldwide attention, like the enormous photographic portraits in Ecatepec, or the thousands of red shoes that filled the Zócalo, commemorating women disappeared and murdered. On International Women's Day in March 2021, there were back-to-back mobilizations in Mexico City, including the projection of the word FEMICIDIO across the Presidential Palace and participation in a strike called "A Day Without Us." These highly publicized actions have undoubtedly helped to open the world's eyes to the brutality of gendered violence. But hidden from view are the everyday efforts of women to keep each other safe, to survive.

———————

It was time to go upstairs. Míriam knocked on a trapdoor and we climbed into the room. It opened onto a scene of women and girls folding blankets. There were nine women, seven teenagers, and four children under the age of nine, including two boys.

The room had cinder-block walls, one of them with a small window cut into it. A tarp was nailed over it, casting a bluish glow throughout the room. On the opposite wall stood a large, pink-colored wooden cross. Painted down its post was the word JUSTICIA. Justice.

I wasn't sure what to call the people I saw. *Anexadas? Madrinas? Víctimas?* A quick glance around the room showed them in various states of pain. There were swollen black eyes and bruised arms, scarred and nervous faces, expressions of exhaustion and grief, as well as distrust. However, not everyone appeared so hurt or wary. A few women and girls smiled and offered a hello. The littlest children sat cross-legged on the floor or stood behind legs, hiding.

Míriam introduced us to the group, calling us friends. She encouraged people to talk freely with us, promising them that they didn't have to worry. When the introductions were over, the women returned to folding bedding, talking quietly to each other, their voices nearly a whisper. I brought a few children's books out and set them on a small round table, where there were stubs of crayons and colorful hair scrunchies. One of the little girls asked to brush my hair. Another asked Araceli if she was a boy or a girl. Most of the women watched our interactions with the children with set, unsmiling faces. I fought back tears, feeling guilty for wanting to cry.

———————

There's a story by Ursula K. Le Guin about a city named Omelas. In this city, the personal happiness of its residents depends on a child being hidden away in a small broom closet. The closet is dark and fetid, and the child's naked body is covered in festering sores. The residents of Omelas are fully aware of the child's condition and they understand their relation to her. What to do? Some of the residents of Omelas reason that the child is too destroyed to ever experience anything like happiness, that her misery and their good fortune is part of the natural order of things. Others cry at the injustice of the child's suffering but do nothing. And still others walk away from the city of "happiness" to somewhere new, but the narrator does not say where this place is because "it is possible that it does not exist."

About an hour into our visit, Míriam told the women to gather for an announcement. I sat on the floor, next to a woman who appeared to be in her early twenties. "I'm Rosalía," she said. "I'm Yeni's friend." I was struck by her use of the present tense and nodded in acknowledgment. Rosalía had been at the *casa* for nearly a week. "It's not where I want to be," she said. "But I'm safe here."

I looked around the room, at the community of women. One laid her head on the shoulder of another woman; another took a restless toddler off her mother's lap, giving the mother a break. A few of the women held hands, while others folded their arms tightly across their chests. One wore a pastel-colored household apron over her clothes. She stared at me with a weary expression. I wondered what scene she had fled before arriving at Casa Dolorosa.

Míriam stood in the middle of the room and let out a heavy sigh. There was a perceptible shift in the atmosphere. It seemed to have darkened and grown still.

"Yesterday I had to turn away three women," Míriam said. "Today there will be more. Madrinas, this is a safe space for you, but it's temporary. You have to make plans."

Silence.

Míriam continued. "This is a safe place for you to rest, to gather strength. But you cannot stay here." She looked around the room and waited for a response. Slowly, a few of the women began sharing ideas of which relatives they might call upon, or whether they could risk going to the police. The name of a shelter came up, but one of the women shook her head no, as if she'd had a negative experience there, or perhaps it no longer existed.

———

Araceli was comfortable making small talk with the women. She was from Gustavo A. Madero, a Mexico City borough that borders Ecatepec and that shares many of its conditions. She had family and friends in neighborhoods whose names some of the women recognized. She was an out *lesbiana* and at home in her body—tall, wide, and healthy.

I wasn't. I was sick again and weighed twenty pounds less than I had the year before. In twelve months, I'd suffered two rounds of pneumonia, several bouts of the flu, and clusters of seizures. One specialist led to another, and the diagnoses piled up, as did the medications. Meanwhile, my marriage was falling apart. The distance between Benjamin and I was both physical and emotional. I returned to Mexico City that summer partly to escape the pressures that were building in my life, including a growing sense of my own physical vulnerability.

Casa Dolorosa seemed full of heightened vulnerability. The room was born out of women's exposure to violence. They took refuge there, sometimes with their children, with the full recognition of the fragility of life—their own and each other's.

"Embracing the other's vulnerability means that the subject cannot avoid recognizing his own fragility. This acceptance is a force," writes Anne Dufourmantelle. Within the anexo's enclosure, this force was not an expression of weakness but of resistance against femicide. The space of safety that was opened by women and girls' vulnerability constituted a common project where mutual support and care were possible.

Míriam said it was time for a *junta*. Immediately, I could sense that this meeting wouldn't be like ones in the other anexos I knew. There was no lectern that faced neat rows of chairs, no counselors surveilling the room. The women didn't appear impassive or broken down. They seemed gentle and afraid. Míriam called upon a young woman named Edith to give testimony. I tried to concentrate on her story, but only certain words seemed to jump out at me. *Hitting, searching, crying, home.*

I felt feverish and needed to lie down. Míriam poured me a small cup of Pedialyte and suggested I rest downstairs, where it was cooler. But I couldn't possibly leave. I sat on the floor, next to a woman with eyes the color of night. That's what I wrote in my field journal, anyway. She asked me if I wanted to know about her daughter. I said yes. The only thing I remember her saying is *Mi hija está viva. Mi hija está viva. Mi hija está viva.*

Around three in the afternoon, Míriam appeared with a small white cake. One of the girls at Casa Dolorosa was celebrating her thirteenth birthday. She wore jeans with pink flowers sewn on the back pockets. We gathered around her and sang "Las Mañanitas" in quiet unison. There were two candles. The birthday girl blew them out with one quick breath.

5

THE LOWER DEPTHS

Albuquerque is 5,300 feet above the distant sea and during the summer the city feels too close to the sun. The fortunate stay indoors, their air conditioners and swamp coolers churning. The Mother Road Hostel didn't have either. During the day, the heavy damask drapes were pulled shut against the windows in a losing effort to keep the heat outside. At night they were flung open to let in the still-hot air. Day and night, the rooms in the hostel stayed dim. Residents complained they lived in an oven.

I looked forward to my job cleaning rooms at the motels on Central Avenue because lodgers always left the air conditioners on full blast when they departed. Room to room, I'd lean my face close to the air conditioner's metal grille and listen to the compressor sputter. To this day I cannot sleep without the hum and breeze of a fan.

Back then I walked to and from work, which meant crossing under the I-25 overpass, a shady refuge for the down-and-out. Raggedy men sat high on the slanted concrete and hollered at me as I passed them by. I hoped they wouldn't stumble down toward me or notice my quickening pace. One day, the voice of a girl rang out. "Hey!" she yelled. I stopped and watched as she crawled down the concrete slope like a crab, her scraped knees peeking out from beneath her oily jeans.

"Hey," she repeated, her voice smaller this time. Traffic passed over our heads. "Do you have some food?"

She looked about my age, with short black hair and a yellow bandanna tied around her neck. Kate.

Milton's diner was just a short walk away. Sometimes I met my mother there for lunch. She'd bring my new baby brother and try to convince me to come home, living, as she finally did, in a house with enough room for me. I'd tell her I'd think about it, knowing it was too late. I was getting by and making plans to take my GED exam and attend community college. I didn't need her anymore.

Kate and I slid into a red vinyl booth. She was like a dark-haired Jean Seberg but more interesting, with her chipped blue fingernail polish and a backpack carrying her only belongings. From behind the tall menu, she admitted that she didn't have any money. I told her not to worry, I had just enough.

We split a patty melt and french fries. Kate talked while she ate, telling me stories about nights spent in cemeteries and old cars down on Fourth Street, west of downtown. "But then I found the Cathedral," she said. She wanted to take me there. I assumed the Cathedral was a church of some kind, maybe a Mormon temple. Instead, Kate took me to the abandoned rail yard.

Immediately, I understood why she called the old freight shop the Cathedral. The deserted building was grand, with high metal ceiling beams and walls made up of small rectangular windows, some amber, others green, a lot of them busted out. Light filtered through them, brightening the blackened concrete floor. I looked up, toward pigeons and rooftop holes. Chandeliers made of rusted beer cans hung still in the air.

There must have been thirty teenagers there. Most of them were lying around on blankets and gave me glazed looks. A few kicked around a deflated soccer ball. Kate called them her "tribe." I accepted the offer of a joint and I wanted to be among them. But the Cathedral frightened me. It was too large and empty of a space, and I was too close in circumstance to the people who lived there. A trapped bird fluttered helplessly across the length of the building, seeking a way out.

After our first encounter, I began looking for Kate on my way to and from work, always carrying with me money for lunch at Milton's and books to share. Weeks went by without seeing her again. I thought about going to the Cathedral but was too intimidated by my memory of the scene. I finally gave up on the idea that I'd ever see her again.

One afternoon I found her standing on Central Avenue, grinning. She smelled strongly of marijuana and looked like she hadn't slept for days. This time, I took her home with me, sneaking her into my room at the Mother Road. I listened nervously as she washed herself in the bathroom down the hall. I gave her a fresh set of clothes and turned away from her as she dressed. Right away, she noticed the boxed set of Greek tragedies on my dresser. "Read to me," she said.

Embarrassed, I stood reading from *Oresteia* while she laid on my narrow bed, her long arms crossed behind her head, watching me. When she fell asleep, I went downstairs, returning with crackers and apples, the only food left in my designated cupboard. For a long time, I stared at her face. Her thick eyebrows ran straight above her dark lashes and her lips were naturally red. When she woke up, we ate our little dinner, both of us sitting cross-legged on the bed, smiling shyly. Night came and neither of us suggested she leave. We lay down together, facing each other, our bodies touching.

We began to spend every night together, clandestinely in my room at the hostel. When night fell, I'd sit outside, looking for Kate walking down Central Avenue toward Mother Road, her dark silhouette lit by the headlights of passing cars.

One night, Kate showed me the tracheostomy scar she hid behind the yellow bandanna. She thought it was ugly, but I found it beautiful, like a crescent moon. She also wore a silver pendant of Saint Jude. PRAY FOR US was inscribed along the lower edge. The pendant had been her father's, a heroin addict and Kate's only parent. She began wearing it after he died. She also attended school less and less, and eventually moved from Santa Fe to Albuquerque, where it was easier to get by on nothing.

Within a few weeks, Kate got a job cleaning rooms at one of the motels I worked at. We smiled when we passed each other on the landing, both of us pushing our cleaning carts. A few times she tried to coax me into one of the empty rooms for a kiss, but I always hurried away, too afraid of losing my job. Eventually, we pooled together enough money to get a studio apartment. The elderly woman who owned the place affectionately called us *girls*.

Kate and I readied our new home with things we stole from the motels we cleaned. Sheets and towels, a clock radio, and an endless supply of cheap toiletries. Eventually, I got a job as a baker at the Artichoke Café, one of the coolest restaurants in Albuquerque at the time. I'd crawl out of bed at five in the morning and let myself in to the empty kitchen to make the day's baguettes. Kate and I practically lived on day-old bread slathered with butter and jam. After discovering French New Wave cinema at the artsy movie theater, we talked about moving to Paris together. *Je t'aime*, we'd say to each other whenever we parted.

Within a few months Kate started spending time at the Cathedral again. I joined her on a few occasions and watched, bored, as she and her friends tripped on acid. I always left before dark, terrified of the bats that darted above our heads, a source of wonder for her tribe.

Kate's time at the Cathedral quickly became a source of tension between us. I complained that the place smelled of piss and was infested with rodents, and I even accused her of bringing home germs. She called me a judgmental recluse with a stick up my ass. Kate started staying out all night, and I grew jealous and resentful, imagining her hooking up with unwashed guys while I worked at the bakery. Distracted, I'd burn my forearms while pulling loaves of bread out of the oven. Before long, I learned that Kate was following in the footsteps of her father, shooting heroin into her veins.

––––––

Drug addicts in Mexico and the United States have been devoted to Saint Jude, the patron saint of lost causes, for decades. They call on him during periods of desolation. The believers aren't necessarily Catholic, but they approach the saint with shared stories of pain and powerlessness. Some of the male heroin addicts I cared for at the detox clinic in New Mexico decorated their bodies with tattoos of Saint Jude. A small altar dedicated to him sat beneath the large canopy of a cottonwood tree close to the clinic, near the banks of the Rio Grande. Votive candles surrounded his ceramic statue, and a tangle of rosaries hung from its neck. Affixed to the tree's trunk were weather-worn photographs of locals who had overdosed and died on heroin. Some afternoons I accompanied detoxing patients from the clinic down to the altar. Used syringes pierced the hard ground. The shrine to Jude was a shooting gallery, too.

According to the New Testament, Saint Jude Thaddeus was one of the twelve apostles of Jesus. One of his attributes is an axe, symbolizing the way he was killed. After his martyrdom, pilgrims came to his grave to pray, seeking intercession in matters of despair and suffering. A shrine to him in Chicago is a pilgrimage site. During my visit there, recovering addicts expressed their devotion to Saint Jude to me. "He helped me quit drinking," one woman said. "I pray to him every day to help me in my sobriety. And for my daughter. Don't let her go down my path."

In Mexico, the veneration of San Judas Tadeo, as Saint Jude is called there, is centuries old. In Mexico City, a church now partly dedicated to him dates back to 1599 and was one of the first churches in New Spain. The Church of San Hipólito sits on the site of the *Noche Triste*, the Sad Night, a reference to a battle that resulted in the military retreat of Hernán Cortés and his troops. After the conquest of the Mexica empire, Cortés ordered a temple be built on the battle site as a memorial to the Spanish killed in battle. The building of the church was finally completed in 1740. What stands today is a massive baroque structure officially named after Saint Hippolytus, or San Hipólito.

Mexico City experienced what some scholars describe as a sudden mass devotion to Saint Jude in the early 1980s in the wake of Mexico's debt crisis. Widespread despair worsened after the earthquake of 1985. It was around this time that San Hipólito Church was flooded with new congregants and became a site of pilgrimage for people seeking relief from economic and personal hardships.

On the twenty-eighth of each month, thousands of poor and working-class Mexicans crowd around the Church of San Hipólito to worship Saint Jude. Many of the pilgrims wear green and white clothes, the colors of the saint's robe, and some carry life-sized statues of him strapped to their backs or baby-sized statues cradled in arms. The devotees stand in long lines to attend one of the round-the-clock masses, their bodies pressing toward the church's massive wood doors, which are badly tilted because the church is sinking into the ancient lake bed upon which Mexico City is built. Vendors hawk plastic flowers and figurines of Saint Jude. While Saint Jude appeals to people of all ages, the majority of *sanjuderos* who gather on the twenty-eighth are teens or in their early twenties. Many avoid the crush of churchgoers and stand around smoking pot or drinking beer. *Chemos* sit in ratty clothes, inhaling chemical solvents and glues for a buzz that disappears almost as quickly as it hits.

On one of these occasions, I found myself standing next to a cluster of teenagers, one of whom reminded me of Kate. "Buy us some cigarettes?" the girl asked, her red lips grinning. Next to her was a young man so thin his tattered jeans hung like drapes. His gaunt face was painted stark white, and delicate wisps of green glitter ran across his cheeks. He teetered. I worried he might collapse.

The girl noticed my concern. "He just got out," she explained. Just out of an anexo, she meant. She pointed a chewed-up finger down Callejón Zarco, a street that runs adjacent to the church, and said, "Over there. Grupo San Hipólito." I was struck that an anexo was in such close proximity to the church and named after it, too.

After a long silence, the boy with the glittery skin started to talk, his words emerging in dreamy couplets. "From inside, Hipólito. I can hear, you hear. Sounds. You know the date. Because the sounds." We fell silent and listened. Microphones announced prayers, the reedy cries of street vendors clashed against *banda* and electronic music, whistles pierced, and church bells clanged.

"How long were you in there?" I asked him.

"Twenty-eight times," he said,

Walking in Colonia Roma, I passed little flickering lights on a tree. It was one of the street altars that dot the city, appearing on sides of roads, next to taxi stands, in markets, by street food vendors, and on top of phone boxes. This one was dedicated to San Judas Tadeo. Set inside a glass case, the altar was beautifully maintained, with a figurine of the saint, shiny tinsel, and fresh white gardenias. Curtains made from green netting hung in front of it, giving it the appearance of a miniature theater.

The altar reminded me to follow up on the anexo named after Saint Hippolytus. I called Padrino Rafa, whose anexo was not far from the Church of San Hipólito, and asked if he knew about Grupo San Hipólito and whether he could get me into it. Many anexos were linked to one another through padrinos' informal networks. Padrino Rafa made the connection and arranged for a server to escort me to the anexo the following week.

I met the server in front of Papas, a grimy take-out place that specializes in french fries. He was young and looked like he could be one of my students. His name was Ramiro.

Callejón Zarco is a one-way street crowded with cars. Most of the buildings are dingy concrete structures, their walls smeared with the residue of smog and graffiti. Every block or so, a nineteenth-century building remains: grand houses turned into tenement apartments with ornate second-story balconies draped with drying clothes.

Ramiro stopped in front of a building taller than the others on the block. Chunks of its facade had crumbled away, revealing layers of pink, green, and gray cement. He unlocked a small steel door and ducked through it. I followed him down a short, dark alley, through an empty room, out its back door, and into a small courtyard, where two women sat chatting on plastic chairs. One of them teased Ramiro as we passed by. "When are you going to marry me, handsome?" The women laughed.

At the end of the courtyard was a steel spiral staircase that we climbed single file. The steps were so badly corroded that some of the slats resembled torn brown lace. The staircase reached up to the building's flat rooftop, but we stopped on the third floor. Ramiro led me down a long hallway of burned-out lights and metal doors, each with a peep hole that clocked our movements like spying eyes. A few of the doors were cracked open, letting out a sliver of light. Every once in a while, a child stepped into the hall. *What are you doing, Ramiro? Who's she, Ramiro?* We finally stopped at a closed door that looked no different from all the others. Ramiro took out his cell phone and made a call. "Here" is all he said. Then he left, his job of transporting me finished.

The door opened onto a woman standing in the threshold. She stared at me as she took a bite of a cereal bar. After a long pause she invited me in.

"I'm Madrina," she said, gesturing to a puffy sofa. "You live in California?"

I told her I lived in Oakland, adding that it was near San Francisco.

"I know where Oakland is," she snapped.

The sofa faced a TV tuned to a talk show. It suddenly occurred to me that Ramiro may have taken me to a safe house and not an anexo. In Mexico, a safe house is not safe. It's where people who've been kidnapped are held until they, their families, and their friends have been drained of money.

Madrina took a small cell phone from her jeans' pocket. "She's here."

———

My first weeks at Grupo San Hipólito were spent in that room. It looked like a typical working-class living room, with lots of furniture and a big TV. Several pictures of San Judas Tadeo hung on the wall. Outsizing the largest picture of the saint was a portrait of a teenage girl dressed in a puffy white gown, a bouquet of red flowers in her gloved hands.

Grupo San Hipólito's padrino was a short, pudgy man with a wide smile. He asked me to call him Padrino Mike, Mike being the name he acquired during his time in the United States. He'd join me in the waiting room for an hour or so to chat. Sometimes his wife, Madrina, was there. Her name was Carmen, but she went by Madrina, the term for the female counterpart to padrino. The apartment belonged to her family, and she and Padrino Mike lived down the hall from the anexo. I tried drawing Madrina into conversation, asking questions about her family and role in running the anexo. She gave curt responses and eventually pulled away entirely, perhaps because Padrino Mike talked so much there wasn't much space for her to respond.

Padrino Mike sat on a leather armchair next to the sofa, a soda in the chair's cup holder. He was easygoing and engaging, and he answered most of my questions about the anexo, recounting his many years of being an anexado himself. But he always steered our conversation toward other matters, like the many places he'd lived in United States—California, Texas, Nevada, North Carolina—and the jobs he'd had there—day laborer, construction worker, deliveryman. It was August 2016. Padrino Mike talked about the brutal massacre at the Pulse nightclub in Orlando, Florida, where forty-nine people were killed. He talked about recent massacres in anexos, too. Twenty-eight people killed in Ciudad Juárez, six in Chihuahua. Padrino Mike called the victims at Pulse and the anexos *corderos*, lambs, a reference to their innocence. For days, he talked about the Clinton and Trump presidential race, the San Gabriel Complex Fire, climate change. *What do you think, profe?* he'd ask, never giving me a chance to answer.

My attention was split between what he was saying and the voices emanating from the other room. Laughing, yelling, wailing. They'd stop for a while, then start up again.

I visited Grupo San Hipólito for over a month and hadn't been invited to the other room. I just sat on the sofa, swallowed by its massive pillows. Padrino Mike spent less and less time with me, but he always seemed to expect my presence. "There's the *profe*!" he'd say when he entered the waiting room.

It was confusing. Had I not heard the sounds from behind the other door I would have thought that I was just paying the couple an afternoon visit. People often did. Madrina's cell phone would chime and she'd open the door to a woman carrying armfuls of food. Some smiled at me and offered me a warm tortilla or flauta. Other women glared at me or ignored me entirely. They stayed for a while, sitting with Madrina at a card table covered with a white tablecloth with crochet edges. When someone came for Padrino Mike, he met them outside. I never saw his visitors.

Sometimes I just sat on the couch and watched Madrina shuffle around in her baby-blue slippers. She listened to the radio and swept the floor. She licked her fingertips and flipped through the pages of a low-calorie cooking magazine. She sat at the table across from me and stared at her face in a compact mirror. She acted like I wasn't there.

Looking at Madrina, I thought about my parents. When did I cease to exist for them? Was it before or after they left me?

"Where I'm from, families just leave you." That's what I told Padrino Julio three years earlier, when he was interrogating me in the restaurant, trying to decide if I was capable of understanding Grupo Esperanza. Something I said must have convinced him I could, because he'd let me in to his world. But Padrino Mike hadn't. He left me in the waiting room, anxious, tired, and full of memories.

————

"Nothing is more real than nothing," Samuel Beckett writes. Sometimes the waiting room felt like the stage of a play. I watched Madrina and Padrino Mike move through their days as if they were actors while I was immobilized on the sofa.

"Why do you keep going there?" my friend Lisa asked. She couldn't understand why I spent so much time in a place where nothing happened. "It's your mother," she speculated. I shook my head no. Lisa surmised that the waiting room where nothing happened was a space for me to escape to, like the volcanic landscape had been for me years earlier. Her explanation was plausible, but I knew it wasn't the whole story.

Sometimes, while waiting, I thought about the Cathedral, where the prevailing emotion was exhaustion. I could see it in the kids that lived at the place, in the way they laid on the ground, awake but with closed eyes. Indolence and fatigue—the expressions, Emmanuel Levinas writes, of weariness of the world.

It wasn't just Kate that kept me going back to that community of castaways. It was also that there were no illusions about what one was up against. The kids had been exposed to acts of violence and neglect that disrupted the fantasy of a protected childhood. They were each other's keepers, attending to the precariousness of life together. I was welcome among them, sitting at the periphery of their bodies, careful to not come too close, but drawn in nonetheless. Was I not one of them?

There was something about the waiting room that took me back to that place and time, and my field notes from this period reflect this. *Dreamt again about the Cathedral during the summer monsoon. How permeable*

that old building was to bursts of rain and wind. A place of protection and
exposure.

————

I always brought small gifts on my visits to Grupo San Hipólito—pan
dulce, fruit, the Yakult probiotic drinks Madrina liked. Anthropologists
have written about how gifts aren't just a matter of appreciation or good
manners—they also create social bonds, assert one's power and position,
and create a sense of indebtedness. Although my intentions were innocent, I suppose I was using gifts in these ways, too. Madrina accepted
them with a quick nod and Padrino Mike happily grabbed a piece of pan
dulce as he moved between the connected rooms. Sometimes he smiled at
me and asked Madrina, "So, what did the *profe* bring today?"

To my surprise, Padrino Mike invited me into the other room on the
one day I showed up empty-handed. When I wondered about this with
my anthropology friends, they surmised that I was now indebted to Padrino Mike. But I always thought there was more to his sudden turn. To
enter the other room, I needed to be stripped of something essential to
who I was. By arriving at the anexo without my usual gifts, I could finally
be among those who had also arrived alone and with nothing.

Padrino Mike opened the door. Once I passed the threshold, a counselor rushed forward and bolted it shut.

The second room was larger than the first, but not by much. At the far
end were two vertical windows covered with large blankets depicting San
Judas Tadeo. Their fabric was so badly worn that daylight filtered into the
gloomy space.

"These are my children," Padrino Mike said, looking around at the
anexados. They sat cross-legged on the floor facing a bare wall. A few
turned their heads just slightly to catch a glimpse of me. The counselor
introduced himself to me as Pablo. He described himself as a "server of
Saint Jude" and carried a cane. Padrino Mike walked me to the windows
and pushed one of the blankets aside, revealing security bars inside and
out. I peered down to the street and was surprised to find that the windows

faced Callejón Zarco. My trips to Grupo San Hipólito always required that I travel the same confounding path, a labyrinth that seemed to take me away from the street and into the deep. I could never figure out how or at what point the path circled back to the street. I had thought that Grupo San Hipólito was protected from the outside world. I soon came to realize it was a window onto it.

Everything took place in that one room except "hygiene," which was held on the building's concrete rooftop. The rooftop was like a neighborhood in itself, with large water tanks, several small rooms, clotheslines, chairs, and dozens of plastic containers filled with herbs and vegetables. Even though the roof was uneven and smelled like stagnant water, it was generally tidy and clean. Worrisome cracks showed signs of constant repair.

The hygiene area was in the open air, with a corrugated metal roof and threadbare towels drying on a line. A steel container, not much wider than a truck tire and tall enough for three feet of water, stood in the middle. Padrino Mike explained to me that anexados either washed in the container or were sprayed down with a hose. I imagined a torrent of water assailing naked bodies but, in fact, the water pressure was hardly more than a trickle. Anexados went to the rooftop to bathe once or twice a week. Cleanliness was important, Padrino Mike said. Many of the anexados at Grupo San Hipólito had lived on the streets. Cleanliness was important in the other anexos I studied, too. More than a sign of discipline and order, it was a pathway to self-repair.

The rooftop offered an expansive view of San Hipólito Church. Its two Moorish towers glowed in the faint sunlight. A construction crane angled itself toward its badly leaning walls. Padrino Mike saw me looking toward the church.

"They go to the church. Sometimes their family finds them there and brings them to us. But many have no family. We find them there and bring them here. It has always been that way."

———

Next to the Church of San Hipólito is the first mental asylum in the Americas, San Hipólito Hospital, *la casa de las locos*. The hospitals of colonial

Mexico were the responsibility of the Catholic Church and were mainly centered in Mexico City.

San Hipólito Hospital was founded by a conquistador and ex-convict named Bernardino Álvarez in 1577. To atone for his sins, Álvarez became a servant of God and dedicated his life to caring for the sick and the poor. Among them were *plantas nuevas*, literally new plants, a reference to newly converted natives who were deemed to need instruction on the proper ways of living. Runaway slaves and petty criminals who sought asylum in the church were also brought to the hospital. The religious order of San Hipólito ran the hospital according to the Catholic ideals of discipline, care, and compassion. They committed, confined, and subjected patients to the medical treatments of the day—religious instruction, exorcism, and purging, to name a few.

The more time I spent in Group San Hipólito, the more I began to think of it as continuous with the colonial church and hospital. In fact, Group San Hipólito's counselors called each other *hermanos*, brothers, and joined the crowds each month on the twenty-eighth. They tended to the street kids, cleaning their open wounds, telling them they were wasting their lives, offering them a bite to eat. They were also rough on them. They pushed, jabbed, and insulted, eliciting tears and submission. Rescuing the kind of kids who hung out around the church meant having power over them, too. Sometimes they dragged one or two down Callejón Zarco and into Grupo San Hipólito. Toño was one of those kids.

Toño was from Gustavo A. Madero, Mexico City's northernmost borough, one of the poorest in the capital. His family lived in a neighborhood surrounded by El Tepeyac National Park and Highway 85, which leads to Ecatepec. When Toño was eight years old, his father migrated to the United States for work and, for a few years, sent remittances home to support his family. Eventually, the remittances stopped and Toño never heard from his father again.

Padrino Mike put me in touch with Toño's aunt Margi, who told me about the early years of her nephew's life. Margi was an industrious woman who sold secondhand clothing, cheap cosmetics, and whatever else she could find from her home-turned-storefront.

Margi was close to Tonō when he was a young. She and her husband were his *padrinos*, godparents, roles they took seriously not only in terms of religious guidance (Margi considered herself a devout Catholic) but also for pragmatic matters, such as helping him find odd jobs around the neighborhood to make money to pay for school supplies. When I met with Margi, she hadn't seen Toño in over two years, and she worried about him. "Is he still using *piedra*?" she asked, referring to crack cocaine. "Is he getting enough to eat? Is he suffering?"

There were several anexos in her neighborhood and she knew the kinds of things that went on in them: beatings, humiliations, deprivations. She crunched her nose up and shook her head, swearing she'd never have let Toño find himself in such a place where he needed to be annexed. He was lucky to be in Grupo San Hipólito, she said, calling it an anexo that carried out the work of God. How could it not be with a name like that? Plus, where else would he be? "On the street, with thieves?"

Margi talked as she bustled about the small house, pulling out one of the secondhand blouses she thought might suit me or a tube of lipstick that would bring out the color of my eyes. "Try this one," she'd insist, studying me as I dressed before her or held a mirror to my face. Our conversation was at turns serious and light. I watched her as she cheerfully stuffed a plastic bag full of items she intended to sell to me at the end of our meeting, her lips adding the prices like a calculator.

Margi said Toño's family had been close, but things began to fall apart when Margi's sister, Toño's mother, got involved with a man who drank excessively. When he moved into her home, she also started to drink and eventually joined him on binges that lasted for days. Sometimes they showed up at Margi's house and asked for money. "The nerve." Margi scowled. "We weren't raised to be beggars and drunks." Her relationship to her sister turned sour, and the atmosphere of Toño's house darkened. Margi remembered coming to the house early one morning and finding Toño and his younger sister, Amanda, asleep in a makeshift bed beneath the kitchen table while their mother and her boyfriend slept off a binge in the other room. The sight infuriated her.

Toño was protective of Amanda and took on the role of her provider. His earnings from odd jobs around the neighborhood were meager. Toño's friends convinced him that there was good money to be made stealing the wallets and backpacks of tourists who visited Tepeyac Hill.

Catholics from all over the world visit Gustavo A. Madero to make a pilgrimage to the enormous basilica of Our Lady of Guadalupe, which sits on Tepeyac Hill. Long before the arrival of the Spanish, the hill was a place of sanctity, with a temple to the Nahua mother goddess, Tonantzin. Like all other places of indigenous religious devotion, the shrine to Tonantzin was destroyed during the conquest. Just ten years after the fall of the capital city in 1521, the Virgin Mary is said to have appeared on the hill to a baptized indigenous man, Juan Diego Cuauhtlatoatzin. She was dark skinned and spoke in his native tongue. According to tradition, the Virgin Mary left her image, that of Our Lady of Guadalupe, on Juan Diego's *tilma*, or shawl. This miraculous event influenced the advancement of the Church's mission of conversion in Mexico.

Today, Juan Diego's *tilma* is preserved behind bulletproof glass and hangs above the main altar in the New Basilica, an ugly tent-like structure built in the '70s that sits next to the original colonial-era basilica. Pilgrims and tourists stand on one of the moving walkways that pass the *tilma*. Smaller chapels, an ex-convent, and a museum about the basilica complete the complex. More than twenty million pilgrims and tourists visit the compound each year to venerate Our Lady of Guadalupe. In the bustling plaza, vendors sell religious items, snacks, and souvenirs.

Toño made the pilgrimage to Tepeyac Hill many times as a child. Margi never imagined that he would become a *ratero*, a thief, and that the holy site would become his domain.

When I met Margi, I was living in La Romita, a small enclave tucked away in Colonia Roma. The Spanish filmmaker Luis Buñuel chose Romita as the setting for *Los olvidados*, his 1950 film about poverty, struggling families, and street children. Back when Buñuel was filming *Los olvidados*, La Romita had a reputation for being dangerous and filled with young thieves. The film captures this with scenes of boys released from and sent back to juvenile detention for crimes committed or assumed. Knives are stolen, women seduced. Boys witness murders and commit them, too. Mothers give up on their troubled kids and, at the end of the film, search them out. The film was initially slammed by critics as anti-Mexican fiction. Buñuel responded, "I've taken a slice of life as it's lived here . . . If it's hard to watch, that's not my fault."

———

The anexos I studied had a lot in common. They were all crowded, noisy, and Catholic oriented. The people stuck inside them were young, poor, and ensnared in a war not of their own making. The anexos were also filled with stories told formally during daily testimonies or casually during down times. There was often laughter, like when Sheila described the penis of one of her clients as being stuck in the shape of a question mark. The anexados gathered around to watch Spanish-dubbed American comedies on TV. *Friends* was a favorite. But Grupo San Hipólito stood out in two significant ways. It named testimony *desagüe*. And testimony filled entire days and nights.

In Spanish, *desagüe* means *drain*. In Grupo San Hipólito, desagüe named a daily ritual in which stories were dredged up and drained away from the speaking anexado and into a collective body called a community. It recalled testimonies given in other anexos, for which anexados are told to "go deep" and recount terrible events from their lives. But I soon came to understand that Grupo San Hipólito's ritual of desagüe was a different kind of testimony. In our conversations, Padrino Mike also referred to it as *confession*.

My brief experience of confession as a child did not prepare me for desagüe. The first one I witnessed left me so disoriented that I had to leave the anexo earlier than I'd planned. What I saw that day was a teenage girl forced to refer to herself in such grotesque terms it felt like I was being read a horror story. She cried during descriptions of torture, then blubbered incoherently, then started up with her descriptions again. The rest of the room was silent.

I dismissed Grupo San Hipólito as extreme, a cult, and resolved to never return. I called Padrino Rafa, who had arranged for my visit, and described to him what I saw. "If you can't take it, don't go back," he said.

But then he added that if I wanted to learn about what it's like to live in Mexico, I should suck it up and return.

A few days later, I was back at Grupo San Hipólito, sitting in the waiting room with Madrina. Her cell phone chimed and she opened the front door to a woman carrying a large stockpot. The woman owed Madrina money. Preparing meals for the anexo was how she paid her debt.

Madrina gestured for me to get up. She took her cell phone out of her jeans' pocket once more and made a call. "I'm going to open the door," she said. I held the stockpot while she unlocked the bolts on the outside of the anexo's door. When the door flew open, Madrina ordered me to put the stockpot, heavy with soup, on a table.

The anexados were in the process of assembling the room. I assumed they were gathering for a meal. Instead, one chair was placed up front, between the two blanketed windows, facing three straight rows of seven chairs each. The anexados took their seats. I saw the young woman who had so debased herself a week earlier. She wore a bright-pink T-shirt and appeared relaxed as she whispered something into the ear of the woman seated next to her. The two giggled.

That day, it was Toño upfront. It was his turn to drain.

The audience of anexados collected themselves and sat with their bodies carefully composed. Backs straight, faces forward, legs slightly parted, arms outstretched, hands on knees, fingers spread just enough so that the hands appear defenseless. The two counselors kept watch over the room like prison guards. Padrino Mike had me sit on a chair in the back of the room, facing Toño. The blankets depicting San Judas Tadeo were a backdrop to his isolation. Toño looked up toward the ceiling, then down to his hands. I wondered if he was grasping for a way to begin.

"*Me llamo mierda. Mierda me llamo.*"

"My name is shit. Shit is my name."

So began Toño's "lowering" of himself. Lowering is the first phase of draining. It begins slowly and gathers momentum and precision as the counselors command that the anexado go lower. *Bajando! Bajando!* they shout. They circle the anexado, carrying canes, threatening a lash when the anexado doesn't go low enough.

"*Soy la bala.*" I am the bullet, Toño said.

Over time, Toño's identifications became darker and more abject. Toño wasn't just the bullet; he was the bullet that ripped through his own chest. He wasn't just piss; he was the piss wetting his own pants. Bruised face, hungry child—his identifications drew on images of overt violence and misery. He offered no context to explain the staccato sentences and flashing images—not even a reference to drug addiction, the supposed reason Toño was in the anexo in the first place. Despite this lack of context, the images Toño offered corresponded to and communicated multiple forms of violence and pointed to their many dimensions.

> I am your broken arm
> I am your father's brains leaking onto the floor
> Oh, what a terrible night!
> I am my sister's bloody hole
> I am the blade that rips the skin
> I am the skin
> I am the rat that bites while you sleep
> I am the garbage you eat
> I eat the garbage
> You are the cigarette that burns my face
> I am the police that beat you.

———

When I first started sitting in on Grupo San Hipólito's draining sessions, much of what was said escaped me, either because it was spoken too fast, was in an unfamiliar vernacular, or seemed too bizarre. And sometimes I was simply unable to stomach the horrific images and purposefully blanked out. But the atmosphere of the room got beneath my skin, literally. I began developing rashes on my arms and scratched at myself at night, unable to sleep. I thought of quitting my research on Grupo San Hipólito but pressed on, sensing as I did that something important was being communicated.

Georges Didi-Huberman writes of images capable of "lifting one's thought to the level of anger, lifting one's anger to the level of work." He says that such images, especially of violence, force us to question the conditions of their existence, thereby enabling us to "open our eyes to the violence of the world inscribed in images." Over time, Toño's dystopic identifications forced me to open my eyes, stirring in me, as they did, feelings of disgust, grief, and anger. I tried not to not turn away from these feelings, but to understand their source. By carefully listening to the words spoken and absorbing the composition and intensity of the room, I began to understand that Toño was communicating traumatic personal and shared experiences, as well as wider social realities. In this sense, his confession carried with it a kind of collective political commentary—at once a condemnation and lamentation of the present.

———————

The anexado's lowering is just the beginning of a long journey downward during desagüe. It is the counselors who determine when the anexado has lowered themselves far enough to move on to the second phase. The counselors' decisions at times seemed arbitrary to me, like they wanted to hurry the process along or prolong it, delighting in humiliating and punishing those who didn't go deep enough. But I also witnessed confessions during which counselors were absorbed by the darkness of the anexado's lowering. On such occasions, they were among the audience, not above it. The counselors' seemingly contradictory reactions expressed the entanglements of violence and care within anexos.

The second phase of draining is the midpoint. It starts off looking like an interrogation, with counselors throwing questions at the anexado. Their questions don't seek to extract past offenses. There's no point, a padrino once told me, adding that every anexado has likely committed the same offenses. Instead, the second phase reveals the anexado's privately held secrets or urges. It is a confessional practice, with the counselors taking the role of the confessor, drawing things out of the anexado through a barrage of questions and insults.

At first, the questions the counselors ask are fairly benign provocations. *Do you think I'm ugly? Do you think so-and-so is stupid?*

Over time, the questions become more complicated and dangerous, touching on themes that revolve around sex, violence, and death. These questions are often directed at people and relationships within the anexo. The confessing anexado knows their responses can stir up resentments or problems among their peers, who wait and worry, knowing they might be implicated in some way. In this way, the anexado's confession potentially threatens, at the same time that it creates, the community in which they live.

At the heart of this community are experiences of violence at once individual and collective, isolating and shared. Confession helps anexados narrate their histories of violence and provides witnesses to it. But "overcoming" or "healing" from violence is not the only aim of these modes of expression. Another goal of confession and testimony in the other anexos I studied is the forging of communities to better endure the inescapable violence that characterizes the times. From Neto's testimony of the landslide to Magi's recounting of her cousin's abduction, these testimonies forged relations of empathy and mutual support. This was not always easy to discern at Grupo San Hipólito, at least not immediately.

The counselor asked Toño a question about Teri, a seventeen-year-old girl who had been picked up near the Church of San Hipólito a few days earlier. Teri had left home because of an abusive stepfather. She was high on *activo*, a solvent inhalant, when the Grupo San Hipólito brothers picked her up and brought her to the anexo.

"Do you get hard when you look at little Teri?" the counselor asked Toño. "Look at her over there. She still stinks but she's pretty, don't you think? Do you want to fuck her?"

"No," Toño answered.

"No? Do you think Martín is pretty? You are a faggot, aren't you, Toñito?"

"No."

"Why not then? Why don't you want Teri?"

"I just don't."

"But you're not a faggot?

"No."

"Were you raped, Toñito?"

"No."

"You weren't? Molested? Madrina said you were! She said you were molested and beaten every night. Fucked by your uncle every night."

"No. That didn't happen."

"No? Are you saying Madrina is lying?"

"No."

"So, you lie to me then. You lie to me."

The counselor threw a question at one of the anexados sitting in the audience. "Prieto! Did Toño just lie to me?"

"I don't know," he replied, timidly.

"You don't know? You fucking coward . . . Toñito, don't be a pussy like that pussy Prieto. Are you going to be a pussy like that?"

"No."

"That's right. But Toñito, we all know you piss your pants at night. Why do you piss your pants? Tell us."

"I don't know."

"You don't know!"

"No."

"Teri, did you know Toño pisses his pants at night? That's why he calls himself piss. He pisses his pants every night because his uncle raped him. Right, Toñito?"

"No."

"No? But he did. He did, right, Martín?"

Martín was Toño's friend. The two sat beside each other during meals and slept beside each other at night. When time permitted, they teased each other and cracked jokes. There was a spark between them that appeared romantic at times, like when their knees touched during "introspection"—an hour-long exercise during which anexados sat cross-legged on the floor, facing a wall. The counselor repeated his question about rape.

"I don't know," Martín answered nervously. "I think so."

"And what did Toño do about that, Martín?"

"I don't know. Push him off?"

"Pushed him off. Toño, have you always been so scrawny? A fucking *gusano* drowing in a bottle of your piss? What did you do to your uncle, Toñito? Anything? Anything at all?"

By this point, it was two hours into the desagüe. Although the room was warm with tired bodies, Toño shivered on his chair.

The counselor continued, his voice excited.

"You did nothing, Toño! You did nothing to the man who raped you! Who raped your sister! Your own blood!"

The counselor turned to the audience of anexados and screamed, "How many of you! How many of you! You lay at night, babies all, while your sister, your mother . . ."

The counselor launched into a deeply upsetting story of incest with a precision that could only have come from experience. He held nothing back. His rant was not that of a preacher, separating right from wrong. He knew both sides of the story, drawing emotions of pity, horror, and fear from everyone in the room. His voice trembled and he walked around, pointing at anexados like he was talking about them. Every once in a while, the other counselor on duty hit the wall with his fist and muttered obscenities. Toño winced. Teri cried. I sat frozen in my chair at the back of the room, overwhelmed by feelings of discomfort, uncertainty, and despair.

The counselor finally stopped and walked over to Toño. "Do you want to kill him Toñito? Do you want to kill the man who hurt you? Who raped you?"

"Yes," Toño answered faintly.

"Tell us, Toñito. How do you want to kill him?"

Toño thought for a while, then broke the silence. "I want to cut off his cock and make him choke on it."

———

Kate used to say she was lucky. Most of the girls she knew at the Cathedral were sexually abused by their father or another male relative. They ran away from home and found their way to the Cathedral. Kate said they gave themselves up too easily to the men who lived there. She called them sluts. I grew angry when she said that. Kate looked at me with concern and asked if my own father had abused me like that. I was relieved to tell her no. Still, we were aware of how close we were to girls "like that," girls who used sex as a means to protect themselves, or who no longer considered themselves worthy of protection.

Kate called her father a saint. She told me his addiction to heroin led to minor brushes with the law, but he'd never hurt anyone but himself. His fatal overdose had left her parentless, but she never felt abandoned by him. When she talked about her dad, she tugged at the pendant of Saint Jude. The only other thing she had of her father's was a flannel shirt that she tied around her waist or wrapped herself in on chilly evenings.

One day I reluctantly joined Kate at the Cathedral for her friend Joey's seventeenth birthday party. It was the magic hour when we arrived, and a prism of light filtered through the multicolored windows. Kids danced through it, their bodies briefly aglow with color. It was a beautiful scene, dreamy and devastating in equal measure. I was happy to see Kate laughing and talking to old friends. I accepted a beer from a girl whose name I'll never forget. "Penny, like money," she said.

The mood quickly changed when Joey started screaming and punching at the air, beating back a ghost. "Fuck you, fuck you, I hate you, I hate you," he cried. The rest of the room fell quiet, and we watched, helpless, as he paced around, his face stricken with bad memories or delusions, perhaps both. "I want to kill you!" he yelled, his words echoing in the cavernous space. A boy approached him. "Hey, hey," he said, trying to calm Joey down. But Joey wouldn't stop. He just kept screaming and darting around, repeating, "I'll kill you." The rest of the group dropped to the floor and hung their heads, not in fear but in desolation. Joey had exploded like this before, and there was nothing anyone could do but wait it out.

I thought about that incident while listening to Toño. There was nothing the anexados could do but remain in his presence, listening and watching as he answered the counselor's questions, each one leading to deeper levels of despair. And I remembered the sadness Kate felt as we walked home from the party that night. She had wanted to comfort Joey, but she knew that he was unreachable to her. I imagined that Martín felt the same way about Toño—that, if he could, he would have reached out to hold his friend and tell him it would be okay, that the pain would pass.

In the end, it was the counselor who gave Toño an out. He closed the end of the second phase of Toño's confession by asking if he ever planned to escape Grupo San Hipólito. Toño answered without hesitation.

"I plan all the time. Up on the rooftop. I see the church and I want to jump. I don't know where I'm jumping to. The church, maybe . . . Or closer. Closer. The church . . . Yeah, I'll fly the fuck out of here. I'll go over there . . ."

From the rooftop of the building where the anexo was located, the Church of San Hipólito's striking towers could be seen in the distance. Depending on the hour, the towers appeared purplish or black against Mexico City's gray sky.

During the colonial period, the Church of San Hipólito, like all churches, was a space of ecclesiastical immunity, offering asylum from secular courts to suspected criminals. Grupo San Hipólito can be understood as having taken on this role. The anexo was where criminalized and endangered life was held and protected, but never fully released from the harsh realities that surrounded it.

Toño continued to answer the counselor's question about escape.

"I think about strangling you up there. Holding your fat head under the water. Drowning you. The water is acid. José and Martín help throw you in and we watch you melt. We joke about it, you know . . . But it's me in the barrel. You drown me this time. And if the water is acid, I disappear. Dying and disappearing at the same time. How many do you know that went out like that? How many gone? Yeah, I want to get out of here. I plan it. The first couple of stairs back down, I can feel the whole thing crashing."

The counselor looked at José and Martín while Toño spoke. In their positions of passivity, they were more than exposed to Toño's suffering— they bore it with him.

A few days after Toño's confession, Martín said that watching and listening to Toño was hard. The connection between the friends was shaped both by Martin's own identification with Toño's history, and from his feelings of closeness and concern for him. "I knew the things he was saying, and it's like, *Is he going to make it?* You can't do anything, so you think, *Come on brother, it's almost over.*"

———

I wanted to believe there was something cathartic about the ritual of desagüe—that draining meant working toward some kind of clearing and the possibility of healing. But I was always left wondering if catharsis was possible given that Grupo San Hipólito forced anexados to participate in draining day after day. Draining lead to more draining. More sink, more crumble, more collapse. This is what is literally happening to Mexico City, to its ancient churches and poor neighborhoods. The Spanish extracted the water of the land of Tenochtitlan, the city buried below. Now the city buckles and sinks, and no one knows if and when it will stop.

For Padrino Mike and the counselors at Grupo San Hipólito, desagüe did more than cultivate humility or point out one's weaknesses. It provided a structure from which to feel and express the violence that had come to characterize anexados' lives. As Padrino Mike put it, "Have these kids ever had a chance to talk about their lives and the world they live in? Have they? Well, here they have to. Here they do."

If desagüe didn't lead toward catharsis, it did perform some kind of good. Though it was hard for me to fathom at first, I came to see that the narratives that were built through self-abasement, interrogation, and despair inspired a kind of mutuality attuned to the dangers of everyday life. Prompted by the counselor, Toño spoke of his plans to escape with Martín, referring to the two of them with the collective plural *we*. His talk of escape spoke to a diffuse image of shared freedom. Yet this image of freedom relied on a pervasive image of violence—dissolving in acid—a repugnant reality in the world of narco violence.

One of the most striking aspects of Toño's confession was how quickly he moved from perpetrator to victim. "But it's me in the barrel," he said, coming to terms with his own vulnerability. His reflection on escape spoke to the realities of criminal violence that limited his and his friend's life chances. "How many gone?" he had asked, speaking to the unfathomable number of dead and disappeared. By asking this question, Toño drew attention to an exclusionary political system that fights violence with more violence, especially within poor neighborhoods that are criminalized in advance. At one point in his confession, he spoke about the murder of a neighbor.

> I wasn't there
> I told them I didn't know
> The police . . .
> I cried, *Brother*!
> Stop looking, you will only find—
> When does it stop?
> I told him, *Bad idea*
> They kill anyway
> Oh god, oh god, oh god
> Fuck me and this world.

———

The afternoon of Toño's confession, another torrential rain fell from the sky and the room filled with its sound. Deep growls of thunder, flashes of lightning, sheets of rain slapping the pavement, people running through the rain-clogged street seeking shelter. Grupo San Hipólito vibrated with these sounds and bodies trembled in surprise. Other elements penetrated the room as well. Cold bursts of air pushed through the bent metal window frames. The hanging blankets gently swayed, revealing metal bars covering thin panes of cracked glass. Pools of rainwater collected below the windows and began seeping toward Toño's bare feet.

It was several hours into Toño's confession. Exhausted, Toño wept. For the most part, the counselor's questions and threats stopped. At various

points Toño got up from his chair and begged the counselors for cigarettes. Sometimes they gave him one, usually little more than a butt. Unlit
cigarette between his lips, Toño looked off into the distance.

Canto III of Dante's *Inferno* begins,

> Through me the way to sorrow's capital,
> Through me the way to everlasting pain,
> Through me the way that leads among the lost.

The canto opens upon a threshold between hell's entrance and first
circle. It is Dante's first encounter with hell. He listens to the sinners'
"words of suffering, cries of rage" and the sounds of hands slapping across
their bodies. Charon, the ferryman of souls, orders Dante to turn back,
because the living cannot cross the river. But Virgil explains that Dante's
journey is willed by God. They make their way, and at the end of the canto
Dante is overwhelmed by suffering and faints.

That afternoon, I thought about Canto III. I braced myself against
fainting.

There is no strict demarcation between the second and third stages of
desagüe, no archway that separates the living from the dead. Instead,
the third stage of draining, *los fondos bajos*, the lower depths, slowly becomes apparent as the anexado begins to construct a story with their own
body. This physical form of storytelling gradually takes precedence over
the verbal, and the body makes its existence tangible. The body begins
to speak for and against a world in which certain bodies—young, poor,
vulnerable—are disappeared or murdered.

The counselors' body language also changes, signaling the transition
into a different phase of desagüe. They are less aggressive and stop throw-

ing questions and insults at the anexado. They hang back, sitting in their chairs or leaning against the wall, sometimes with their eyes closed.

Confessing anexados rock in their chairs and hang their heads. There are bursts of aggression, with the anexado grabbing their chair and slamming it on the ground, again and again, or beating their chests with closed fists. They may pace back and forth, stare at the ceiling, scream, pull their own hair, kneel, or lie prostrate on the floor, sometimes with their face to it. It is impossible to see these acts and not think of ecstatic states.

For a long time, Toño stood behind his chair, holding its back with his hands, his head lowered, as though in private prayer. Then he sat down and held himself, bent over as though in pain. He looked up and began to speak.

> Rain
> Cold night
> *Shhhhh*

He held his face with his hands and shook his head back and forth.

> Vomit
> Garibaldi
> No!

At times, he appeared disoriented, speaking in a language that was opaque and lonely.

He took his T-shirt off and looked down at his skinny torso.

> Fucking cold
> Can't find, can't see
> Sister gone

He walked back and forth across the room, barefoot and muttering. Two hours passed before he returned to his chair, his face blotchy from crying. Some of the anexados sniffled and wiped tears from their eyes, others yawned. Toño rested his chin on his bare chest, his arms hanging at his sides. After several minutes he raised them, ever so slightly, in a gesture of surrender.

The counselor finally announced that Toño's draining was over. After a few minutes of silence, the anexados began to rearrange the room. It was dinner time. They worked in silence, placing their chairs around two long conference tables. Toño remained in his seat before the windows, his body slumped over in exhaustion.

That night, like the night before, dinner was a large pot of watery soup and tortillas. One of the anexados ladled bowls of soup out of the stockpot while another handed them out. People began to chatter in voices low and sad. Padrino Mike made a brief appearance. He instructed Martín to take a bowl of soup over to Toño, who hadn't moved, although he was free to. I sat at one of the tables and watched him, the food by his feet left untouched.

The idea that confession affords catharsis has been around since Saint Augustine's *Confessions*. And it was tempting for me to interpret Toño's confession as cathartic. But any purgation that takes place is temporary at best; desagüe is a daily practice and anexados find themselves "back on the chair," confessing again, within a matter of weeks, sometimes days. The ongoing, cylical nature of desagüe enables an intimate and evolving understanding of each other's suffering and establishes embodied connections between anexados. According to Padrino Mike, these connections lay the groundwork for anexados' healing. "First, they got to know they are not alone."

Desagüe is difficult work. It entails coercion and creativity, patience and pain. It offers insight into the way traumatic violence is conjured and manifest in ritual practices that do not promise recovery or redemption. This challenges the idea that the expression of pain must have some cathartic value. It also forces one to sit with the uncomfortable presence of violence and suffering as it unfolds through continuous narration. In the denial of catharsis, there can be found one of the facts about violence in Mexico: it continues.

Grupo San Hipólito does provide sanctuary from violence, but only partially. It is not only the anexo's use of coercion and violence that curtails its sanctuary status, but also the dangerous world the anexo is inextricably connected to. Grupo San Hipólito's confessional ritual takes place within the horizon of danger. This was evident in the way Toño imagined "the whole thing crashing," and crids that he "can't find, can't see," as if unable to find a way out of the wreckage. It was through confession that Toño revealed some of the concrete processes through which the anexo is produced—from poverty and inequality to political marginality and violence.

Desagüe communicates isolating experiences that arise from violence both interior and exterior to the anexo. It does not allow for detachment; instead, it is felt deeply in a range of forms, through telling, listening, and observing. As Simon Critchley writes, "Tragedy gives voice to an experience of agency that is partial and very often painful . . . It shows our heteronomy, our profound dependency." So, too, does confession. This intersubjective encounter is produced—rhetorically, performatively, existentially—in a manner that cannot be purged of violence, but that is born from it.

———

There was a profound moment in Toño's confession during the early part of the third phase. At that point, Toño was still relatively composed, and he stood facing his audience. After a long silence, he began to open and close his mouth as if he wanted to speak but couldn't find the words. "What is he saying? What is he saying?" asked the counselor as he scanned the room.

"He's saying he's tired!" an anexado shouted.

"He's saying, 'Enough!'" cried another.

More responses followed.

"He's saying he's thirsty!"

"No, he's saying he's pissed!"

The anexados continued to pronounce what Toño was silently voicing, becoming, in a sense, his voice. *Hungry, scared, angry, sick.* Toño shook his head, then nodded, then shook his head some more. The anexados and counselors worked hard to understand him and perhaps in doing so understood something of themselves. Their narrative practice was both interpretive and ethical; ethical in the sense that they navigated Toño's subjectivity through their shared vulnerability and experiences with violence.

After a few minutes, one of the counselors commanded that the audience be quiet. Toño kept making motions with his head.

"What are you saying, Toñito?" the counselor asked him.

After some hesitation, Toño responded. "All! All! All!"

"All what, *pendejo*?" the counselor yelled.

"All of us."

———

It was time for me to go home. The counselor unlocked the door for me. I walked into the waiting room where Madrina was on the couch watching TV. She must have seen how stricken I was because she told me to sit. I sat on the edge of the sofa, keeping my distance from her. But Madrina's considerable weight pulled me toward her body. My head came to rest on her shoulder. I didn't pull away.

6

THE EXPERIENCE

"*Donde hay mexicanos, hay anexos.*"

It was early in my research when Serenity's Padrino Francisco explained that there are anexos wherever there is a Mexican community. It was something Mañuel told me, too. *Anexos are everywhere.* But Padrino Francisco wasn't referring to anexos in Mexico City, or elsewhere in Mexico for that matter. He meant there were anexos in the United States.

We were in his office at Serenity, talking about Javi, a twenty-three-year-old anexado there. Quiet and shy, Javi avoided interaction with his peers and spent his free time sitting in a corner, sketching in a notebook. One evening, while I was helping him wash dishes, I noticed scars on the insides of his wrists. He caught me looking and dunked his hands into the grayish water, saying he'd finish the dishes on his own. The following day, I asked Padrino Francisco what brought Javi to the anexo. . He didn't have a drug problem, nor did he talk about violence at home or in his neighborhood. But he had been in Serenity for months. Padrino Francisco said that, before Serenity, Javi had been in three anexos in California—one in Riverside, two in Los Angeles. I was taken aback.

"There are anexos in California?"

Padrino Francisco nodded. "California. Texas, Pennsylvania, Illinois, Nevada. *Donde hay mexicanos, hay anexos.*"

I asked why Javi had ended up in them.

"Because he's crazy," he said.

———

Serenity held a visitation hour every Sunday, and Javi's mother Ana showed up each week without fail, always bringing Javi a new notebook and tamarind paste candies. Sometimes they sat in the building's courtyard under the watchful eye of a counselor. But Javi usually insisted that they stay in the anexo, where he felt safest. On those occasions, they sat near Padrino Francisco's office in full view of the other anexados, who looked at them with jealousy or disdain. They rarely, if ever, had visitors themselves.

I watched Ana try to engage her son in conversation. *Have you eaten today? Can I see your latest drawings? Are you sleeping?* Javi responded by nodding his head yes or shaking it no. He was morose and withdrawn and seemed to take little comfort in his mother's presence. But on the days that she was late, he looked at the door expectantly, worried that she might not come.

Ana shared updates about family members in the United States. Her brother Raúl had moved to a new house in Riverside, California. His daughter, Isabella, was about to have her quinceañera. Raúl complained to Ana that his wife was spending too much money on the occasion. Javi stared at the floor while his mother talked about the relatives with whom Javi once lived. When there was nothing more to say, Ana looked at him worriedly.

"Are you okay, *mijo*?"

Javi shrugged his shoulders.

The two sat in silence. When visitation hour was over, Ana stood up and touched Javi's face. A counselor unlocked the front door for her. After she slipped out, he quickly bolted it shut.

———

Shortly after my conversation with Padrino Francisco about Javi, a counselor called on him to give testimony. Javi walked to the front of the room, stood behind the lectern, and fixed his eyes on the wall opposite him. The first thing he said was "That's when I lived in California."

In fits and starts, Javi began to speak about his time in an anexo there. His uncle Raúl had committed Javi after a series of psychotic breakdowns. The anexo was a small house located in an industrial zone on the outskirts of Los Angeles. About half of the anexados left during the day in search of day labor, while the other half, the *enfermos*, the "sick ones," remained locked inside. One night, all the anexados were piled onto a bus with covered windows. They drove for hours. Finally, the bus stopped and the anexados were led into the dry heat of the Mojave Desert.

Javi described what he called his *experiencia* in loose fragments. There were men waiting in the desert with flashlights. In the distance, a fire. Men held hands and formed a circle around the flames. One tried to break free and run away but was dragged back and beaten. Meanwhile, a group of musicians played calming music. Dawn was on the horizon. The anexados were not permitted to sleep. The next day they practiced "four and five, four and five," a reference to the fourth and fifth steps of the twelve steps of Alcoholics Anonymous: taking moral inventories and admitting wrongs. At night, they were forced to write by candlelight. After several more hours, the anexados were given blankets and laid on the hard desert ground. Javi remembered looking up at the constellations that brightened the night sky. Coyotes howled in the distance.

———

I became aware of fourth-and-fifth-step groups in Mexico City in 2012. Padrinos and anexados often talked about belonging to a *grupo de cuarto y quinto pasos* ("fourth-and-fifth-step group") or practicing "four and five." A research assistant did some digging and found that these groups, many of which are tied to anexos, are an unofficial "sect" of Alcoholics Anonymous. Unlike traditional AA, they rigorously practice steps four and five, which encourage self-awareness and confession. They also go on retreats called *experiencias*, experiences.

Just like my unsuccessful attempts to locate scholarly articles on anexos, I couldn't find studies on these groups, just a few blog posts, most of which described them as illegal and dangerous. But the groups are well-known in the world of anexos, and many subscribe to their practices. Several of the anexos I studied advertised themselves as "4 y 5." More and more, I began noticing that moniker on storefronts throughout poor and working-class parts of the city, as well as a few places in my own middle-class neighborhood.

The movement's founder, Padrino Mario, established fourth-and-fifth-step groups in Mexico City in 1991, a time when the circumstances of poor Mexicans took a turn for the worse due to a weakening economy. Families could barely eke out a living and households would swell to accommodate relatives who'd lost work. Addictions to alcohol and drugs skyrocketed. Twelve-step programs, especially Alcoholics Anonymous, were widely available throughout the country, but their philosophy and traditions didn't align with the culture and struggles of poor people in Mexico. Not only was AA's ninety-minute format unrealistic—the working poor needed to be able to access meetings twenty-four hours a day—but the program lacked a strong spiritual element. Alcoholics, addicts, and *enfermos* didn't just need "steps" to end their addictions; they needed spiritual nourishment.

Padrino Mario distilled the twelve steps into two, focusing on what he saw as the root causes of suffering—the refusal to acknowledge one's sins and the need to confess them. It was hard, intimate work and, when performed well, it inspired interpersonal trust and reciprocity between the group's members. These bonds lessened loneliness and fear and led to healing that extended far beyond AA's focus on addiction.

The first fourth-and-fifth-step group in the United States was established in California in 1992. Its initial members were men who had experienced the hardships of being undocumented and separated from their families. At the time, anti-immigrant sentiment was brewing, culminating in California's Proposition 187. The "Save Our State" initiative sought to deny undocumented immigrants access to health care, public education, and public social services. It also required local and state agencies to report undocumented people to state and federal immigration authorities. The controversial proposition passed in 1994, but it was never initiated.

Still, it sowed lasting fear into the minds of undocumented immigrants. Use of public mental health services and primary care plummeted across the state among the undocumented.

The gap created in health care usage due to fears of deportation, ongoing anxieties related to legal status, and practical issues like work and housing, led to the spread of fourth-and-fifth-step groups across the border states. Anexos also proliferated, and many adhered to the fourth-and-fifth-step model. By 2014, my research team had identified twenty-three groups in the San Francisco Bay Area alone.

————

Grupo Amor y Servicio is an anexo in Oakland, California. It's located in a one-bedroom apartment on top of a garage that's set back from the street. There's no sign announcing its presence and its entrance is in the back of the building, shielding it from view. Its living room is crammed with a pull-out couch and twin-size bed pressed against the wall. The bedroom is sparse, with two sets of bunk beds and a folding cot. Pots and pans hang from a wall in the tiny kitchen. I sat in the living room during my visits to the anexo, across from a wall adorned with a portrait of Jesus and prints of desert landscapes.

At the time of my first visit, seven women lived there. All were undocumented, and four voluntarily committed themselves to the anexo. Another woman was committed by her family due to alcoholism, and two were committed because of debilitating depression. The madrina who ran the place was also undocumented and had established the anexo with the needs of women like herself in mind. She called her charges *ahijadas*, goddaughters.

Madrina Trini was short and energetic, with blue-black hair and deep brown eyes framed with purple liner. Whenever I saw her, she was wearing fashionable leggings and a shop's worth of jewelry. She had been a beautician back home in Chihuahua, where she'd owned her own salon and a two-bedroom cement-block house. One afternoon, she showed me a photograph of her former home. Tall sunflowers framed the perimeter and rebar sprouted off the rooftop, evidence of plans for a second story. Several cars were parked in the dusty front yard. She was proud of what she once had. But then the war came and tore Madrina Trini's house and family apart.

Chihuahua is a border state and home to Ciudad Juárez, which once had the highest homicide rate in the world, due to intercartel violence and corrupt military and police forces. The year 2008 was especially violent. Eighteen people were massacred at an anexo, fifteen teenagers were gunned down, and several journalists were killed. Mutilated and desecrated bodies were dumped in the streets, and car bombs exploded in broad daylight. By 2010, 20 percent of Ciudad Juárez's inhabitants had fled the violence for El Paso, which lies directly across the border, or to other destinations in the United States and Mexico. While the violence was most concentrated in Ciudad Juárez, it extended to other parts of the state as well, including the city of Chihuahua, where Madrina Trini lived.

Madrina Trini shuffled through photographs, landing on one she wanted me to see. It was of her salon, a small standalone building with a bright-blue sign. TRINI'S SALON DE BELLEZA. She looked at the photograph with a numbed expression.

"It was destroyed. I had to pay for protection. But there is no protection. That's why my husband came here to make money. And my son, he said I should go, too. But I had my mother and my other children. Two daughters married, thanks be to God, to good men."

She quickly flipped through the photographs, looking for an image she couldn't seem to find. Three of her goddaughters sat on the twin bed and watched us closely, while the other women made tamales in the kitchen to sell near a market that specialized in Mexican products. The anexo smelled earthy and sweet. It felt far removed from the story that Madrina Trini told.

In 2006, the year the war on narcos officially commenced, Madrina Trini's husband immigrated to Oakland on the advice of a friend. The Bay Area was booming due to its tech industry, and there were construction jobs to be had. The money he sent back home to Chihuahua was good, but much of it ended up in the hands of extortionists. Madrina Trini's daughters and their families relocated to central Mexico, where the security situation wasn't as bad as it was in the border state. They wanted their mother to join them, but she felt like everyone would be better off if she joined her husband and worked in the United States, so she too could send money home to her children.

"My husband told me it would be easy to find work here. I would have my own salon again. But there were things he didn't tell me."

Madrina Trini looked at the women sitting on the bed and shooed them away. "Go make yourself useful!" she barked. They went into the bedroom and returned with large bundles of laundry and headed downstairs. Behind the house was a backyard with a washer and dryer and a small garden that grew chilies, squash, and herbs. Tall tomato plants pushed through their wire cages and colorful pinwheels decorated the garden plot. On a few visits I found Madrina Trini there, stooped over, pulling weeds.

Madrina Trini peeked out of the curtained window onto the backyard. She was growing upset, so I tried to turn the subject to something lighter. But there was more she wanted to share. She turned and looked at me.

"Before crossing, I was raped. After I crossed, I was raped. Rape is a part of what we are told to expect. The shelters warn you. They ask about your period and count the days. It is safest to cross on your period or right after, that way you can't get pregnant. Even old ladies like me. You pay with your bodies, too. But you are never ready for it. You are never ready."

The experience of violence, including sexual assault, is common during migrant journeys. Studies indicate that one in four female migrants experiences sexual violence, although the rate is likely much higher, as women likely underreport the crime because of stigma and fear of deportation. These crimes are not only committed by smugglers. Numerous reports have documented high rates of human rights violations by border patrol agents, including shootings, beatings, and rape. The crimes increased after September 11, 2001, with the militarization of the US-Mexico border under the guise of preventing further terrorist attacks. Since 2016, there has been an uptick in violence, most likely because of anti-Mexican and anti–Central American rhetoric in which "illegal aliens" are characterized as threatening "Americans."

When Madrina Trini arrived in Oakland, she discovered that her husband lived with six other men in a small apartment, not in the single-family home he had promised her. It was no place for a woman, she said, especially after her harrowing journey. Most of the men left during the day to work, but a few hung back, and they frightened her. Her husband did, too. She described him as having been a good man back in Mexico, but something had changed once he arrived in the United States. He was no longer gentle. The Bay Area housing bubble burst, and construction jobs dwindled. Soon the six men in the apartment became nine, and they drank. The situation was intolerable for Madrina Trini.

For several weeks, she spent her days leafing through clothes at the Goodwill, rarely buying anything because she didn't have money. But she felt safe there, among women she recognized to be like herself. Eventually, she found a job as a stylist in a salon. She never told her husband she'd found work, only that she'd looked for it to no avail. The owner of the salon knew about her troubles and held on to her earnings for a small fee, "like a bank, not a *piso*," the owner said, differentiating her charge from the those of the extortionists in Mexico.

One afternoon, a young man came into the salon to post a flyer. It was for a fourth-and-fifth-step group. Madrina Trini had known of such groups in Mexico but never gone. Now lonely and afraid, she decided to go.

———

It is often said that one needs to reach a "bottom" before healing can occur. In this scenario, healing presumes an upward trajectory, a distancing of the self from the source of pain, and a growing invulnerability to it. But feminist scholars have argued that there is no bottom for women. Instead, women experience ongoing vulnerability. The philosopher Adriana Cavarero notes that the term *vulnus*, or wound, is embedded in the term *vulnerability.* She writes, "As a body, the vulnerable one remains vulnerable as long as she lives, exposed at any instant to the *vulnus.* Yet the same potential also delivers her to healing."

Madrina Trini described her anexo and the fourth-and-fifth-step group she attended as having this dual quality of vulnerability, of hurt and healing. Like her own anexo, the group was not only a place of last resort for women vulnerable to oppression, but it was also a gathering of women whose mutual vulnerability inspired interdependence and care. The testimonies delivered at the group she attended were often devastating. Women recounted migrant journeys like Madrina Trini's. They expressed fear of deportation and lamented their inability to travel home to see dying parents and children left behind. Some suffered from chronic illnesses but were afraid to seek medical help. Securing and maintaining housing was a constant struggle, especially with the downturn in jobs and rising rents. Kids suffered in school, and mothers worried about gangs and family members back in Mexico. They suffered from oppression, depression and *nervios*, nervous breakdowns. At the same time, their shared feelings of loss, grief, and worry enabled recognition and mutual support.

One summer afternoon, I visited Madrina Trini's anexo. It was June 2018, and nine women were sharing the one-bedroom apartment. When I arrived, I found them gathered in the living room for a meeting. They were between the ages of seventeen and fifty-two.

That day, it was Adela's turn to give testimony. Adela was in her midthirties and new to the anexo. She was diminuitive, with indigenous features, and she spoke in a voice that was almost a whisper. She left her native Oaxaca when she was six, crossing the border into California with her mother. They made it to Salinas, where her mother found farmwork alongside members of her community from back home. During the work day, Adela and the other young children of farmworkers played alone in a trailer. Although she was school-age, she spent her days in charge of those younger than her. So began her career as a domestic worker.

Every afternoon, a man visited the trailer, and he molested Adela. "He called me *mamita*," she said, looking down at the floor. The sound of *norteño* music drifted into the anexo, its waltz-like rhythm a soundtrack to Adela's memories.

When Adela spoke, she moved back and forth in space and time—from Salinas as a child to Seattle as a teen; from Oakland as an adult then back to Seattle, where she gave birth to a baby girl. Adela cried as she spoke of her daughter, who died from a respiratory illness when she was a few weeks old. Ximena, one of the women seated beside her, took Adela's hand. "*Lo siento mucho*," she said.

After the death of her daughter, Adela moved to Oakland with her spouse, Santiago. She found domestic work, and Santiago was hired as a dishwasher at a seafood restaurant. Every night, he brought home the one meal he was permitted as an employee. Once, she visited him at the restaurant for a staff holiday party. She remembered the large picture windows that faced the bay and the glittering lights of San Francisco. She and Santiago often talked of visiting the city, but they worked every day of the week and couldn't find the time.

In January 2018, Santiago moved to Monterey for a higher-paying job, leaving her behind in Oakland. Within a month, the texts and phone calls to her stopped. "I thought he left me for another woman," Adela said. In fact, Santiago had been swept up in an ICE raid that targeted Northern California and he was deported back to Mexico. Adela thought of joining him, but he told her to stay in Oakland to work and send money back home. He promised to return.

But the family Adela worked for relocated. She couldn't make rent on her apartment and asked her mother for help. She wired Adela one hundred dollars from Washington state. It wasn't enough to live on. Terrified and on the verge of homelessness, Adela appealed to Madrina Trini.

"I've been on my own since," Adela said.

"*Nena*, look around you. Your're not on your own anymore," Madrina Trini said.

———

Madrina Trini took her charges to the fourth-and-fifth-step group once a week. I accompanied them on one of these occasions. The group was in a run-down storefront with windows covered in white paint. Inside, folding chairs were arranged in rows that faced a lectern. Information about community resources sat on a table near the entrance, and there was a box of free clothes and shoes. Madrina Trini was the sponsor of several women in the group, and they approached her with hugs and donations of food for her anexo. They asked about her children back in Mexico, and Madrina Trini smiled while talking about a new granddaughter. Moments later, she furrowed her brow with a look of concern when a woman mentioned a massacre in Chihuahua, not far from where her family once lived.

Every chair was filled. Some of the attendees wore work uniforms, and others carried plastic shopping bags with groceries. Seated next to me was a woman with a toddler bouncing on her lap. Several children played on the floor in the back of the room. There were dolls and crayons, building blocks and books.

A coordinator named Andrés welcomed everyone to the meeting while another passed around a basket for donations. Some had nothing to give, others tossed in a dollar or two, or loose change. While the basket made its way around the room, Andrés led the group in a recitation of the Lord's Prayer. *Padre nuestro, que estás en el cielo, santificado sea tu nombre.*

There were several announcements. A new nonprofit was providing relief funds for undocumented immigrants. On weekends, a free dental care mobile clinic could be found on International Boulevard. In the back of the room was a new factsheet about workers' and tenants' rights. A few of the attendees took notes; others checked their cell phones.

Andrés announced that there was a new person in the group. I waited for the newcomer to stand and introduce themselves, but Andrés was referring to me. At his invitation, I went up to the lectern. By that point, I had studied anexos for six years but had never been to the lectern. I nervously faced the group's members. Faces looked at me encouragingly or warily. I introduced myself much the same way that I did in Mexico City, saying that I was a researcher interested in healing from addictions and "emotional illnesses." But this time I added that I was "from the community" and that I'd suffered from depression most of my life. It was a spontaneous admission. As soon as I said it, I wanted to take it back.

"Who is your sponsor?" someone shouted.

Madrina Trini stood. "I am," she said.

————

During my first visit to Mexico City in 2006, when I was pregnant with twins, I went to Mercado de Sonora, famous for its medicinal products and *brujería*. Benjamin was searching for a healer he had turned to earlier in his life, during his twenties and thirties, a woman who gave him prescient advice and allayed the pains of romantic heartbreak with her magic. It was our last day in Mexico City. The international book festival was over, and we'd visited some of the main tourist destinations. I was tired and ready to return to Los Angeles, where a nursery and an unfinished dissertation awaited me.

I followed Benjamin as he cut the way through the market's narrow aisles, passing closet-sized stalls overflowing with magic soap, holy water, horseshoes, and live frogs, which are used as offerings. The sweet scent of copal, a sacred incense known for warding off evil spirits and treating all kinds of ailments, mixed with the odors of caged animals, their desperate cries cutting through the din of the crowd. Benjamin sought blessings for our babies, due to be born in four months' time. His healer would perform a *limpia*, a ritual cleansing, paving the way for a healthy delivery.

My legs felt wooden and my belly heavy with the weight of impending motherhood. I complained that I might soon deliver the babies at the market if we didn't give up what felt like a futile search. But just as we were about to turn back, he spotted her, a small woman with long gray hair that hung around her shoulders.We pushed our way into her stall. It was so tiny and stuffed with sacred objects that the three of us could barely fit.

She remembered him. I watched as they embraced, trying to ignore the animal tails that dangled above my head. She asked him where he'd been—it had been years since she'd last seen him. He responded by pulling me in front of him, as if my presence explained his absence. She looked up at me with eyes veiled with cataracts. Her deeply lined face, which had just been smiling, turned serious. All traces of lightness and humor were gone.

"*Sufre mucho*," she said.

Her statement startled me. I touched my belly and shook my head. *No, I don't suffer.* She cupped my face with her chafed hands and nodded yes.

"*Sufre mucho de melancolía.*" I looked back at Benjamin, whose own grave expression seemed to confirm her diagnosis.

Just before we were married, Benjamin discovered what I flippantly called my "suicide box"—a wooden cigar box stuffed with expired bottles of sedatives and pain medications prescribed to me during graduate school. In the early 2000s, it was easy to get benzos and opioids, and I collected them like some people stockpile canned food in the event of a disaster. Rarely did I take the pills; just knowing they were there for me was soothing enough. But my relationship to my suicide box was a complicated one. It was a secret I needed close at hand. Sometimes, when I was alone, I emptied the contents on the bed and assessed my supply of Ativan, Norco, and Xanax. I vested each pill with the power to thwart pains I didn't yet understand. And I was always on the hunt for more—making appointments with campus psychiatrists, rummaging through friends' medicine cabinets.

The healer wanted me to join her behind the black curtain that hung inches from where we stood. On the other side was where she practiced her medicine. She would perform my *limpia* there. She took my arm and gently pulled me toward the curtain, but I pulled back. I didn't want to go. I was afraid.

A few weeks earlier I'd sat in the cream-colored office of my therapist. It was my first time undergoing psychotherapy, something I'd always disparaged in the past, just as my mother did when I encouraged her to seek help for her depression. Benjamin was a believer in therapy. At his urging, I reluctantly agreed to see someone. My biggest concern at the time was my relationship with my soon-to-be-born daughters. I worried that I would fall out of love with them, that my feelings for them would slowly diminish until I abandoned them altogether—if not physically, then emotionally. I never admitted this to anyone other than my therapist and when I did, I immediately regretted it.

"Love for your children doesn't work like that," she said, with too much confidence. "It grows."

I understood that she meant to be comforting, but I felt dismissed by her. With that one statement, my entire life experience was negated. My parents' love for me did not grow. I had evidence for this. There are no childhood photographs of me past the age of five, and at fifteen I was living on my own, scrambling to get by. I determined then and there to never see this therapist again.

Decades later, in my forties, another therapist said to me, "What your parents did to you was a crime." The statement shocked me, and I rejected it immediately. But it was true. I wasn't just "left" by my parents; they'd abandoned me. I was prepared to accept that my father had done this when he moved away with my younger siblings, leaving me at fifteen with four hundred dollars and no future in sight. But I was not prepared to accept that my mother had deserted me, too.

The healer couldn't convince me to follow her behind the curtain. There would be no *limpia* for me that day. She looked at her wall of herbs and pulled down a small bundle of laurel and instructed me to make an infusion. I held the brittle leaves in my hand and promised her I would.

———

Fourth-and-fifth-step group attendees are not considered full-fledged members until they have their *experiencia*, a three-day ritual focused on the intensive practice of moral reflection and confession, the fourth and fifth steps of the twelve steps. By all accounts, Javi's experience had been a distressing one. During his testimony, he recalled kangaroo rats scurrying around him at night, and men crying before a bonfire. It sounded surreal to me; cultish, too. But the experience was intended to facilitate "*catarsis*" by helping people heal from painful memories.

Participants are taken to a remote place, far from the realities of everyday life. In Southern California, initiates like Javi are usually taken to the desert, and in Northern California, the forest. In these wilds there is nothing to seek except truth and salvation. After the experience, members are expected to regularly attend meetings. Many undergo another experience within a year or two, both to atone for wrongdoings and to seek a release from the accumulation of pain that builds up over time. They also attend to guide and accompany new initiates in their journey.

After my first fourth-and-fifth-step meeting, Madrina Trini said it would be necessary for me to complete an experience if I wanted to continue to participate in the group. At the time, I wasn't sure how much further I wanted to pursue research and I felt professional pressure to finish up and write a book. But I was aware that I'd "discovered" a self-help movement in the United States for which there was no written documentation, at least not then. From what I could gather, the movement had grown considerably after Donald Trump was elected to office. I wanted to understand the concerns of undocumented immigrants in this increasingly hostile political climate, as well as how they cared for each other under the duress of possible deportation.

There were also personal matters that compelled me to undergo an experience. My ten-year marriage was ending, a new relationship with a woman was all-consuming, and my health was failing. An MRI had detected excessive scarring in my brain, which was suspected to be the cause and consequence of seizures. I felt increasingly vulnerable on emotional and physical levels. I wasn't sure if undergoing an experience was a bad idea or if it was precisely what I needed.

To move forward with the experience, I needed to attend seven preparatory meetings. The first of these introduced me to AA literature and the way testimonies are delivered during the ritual. Andrés warned me that the testimonies could be difficult if one wasn't prepared. I assured him that I had seen upsetting testimonies in Mexico City's anexos, but he rejected the comparison, insisting that their method of testimony was different. An individual's testimony in fourth-and-fifth-step groups unfolded over days, not hours. It spanned a lifetime of memories, not singular events. "Are you ready?" he asked. I told him I was.

Thirteen people attended the preparatory meetings, including me. Many rushed in late, apologizing for delayed busses and long work hours. Andrés tried to weed out people who weren't dedicated to the work that lay ahead. "Maybe it's not time for you," he said to a man who stumbled into the building with alcohol on his breath. But we all affirmed our commitment. And when asked why we wanted to undergo the experience, we responded alike: we wanted to be released from pain. One woman wanted to put the memory of her traumatic migrant journey behind her; an eighteen-year-old wanted to stop using drugs. A man talked about his overpowering rage, how he had suffered at the hands of his father when he was a child; and a woman cried when describing a marriage marred by domestic abuse. There were alcoholics, drug addicts, and people with crippling anxiety. And there was me.

I was prepared for Andrés to attribute my depression to my past, but I balked when he suggested that the experience would put an end to my epilepsy, an illness that I had confided to Madrina Trini earlier. "I have a neurological condition," I retorted, insisting that my seizures did not stem from emotional distress. Andrés was not deterred. When he asked if I suffered before and after my "spells," I shook my head no. Andrés looked at me knowingly and then addressed the room. "The most important element of establishing trust is honesty." His suggestion that I had lied left me angry and ashamed.

The next few meetings passed quickly. In one of them, we were introduced to the various roles of the participants in the experience. As expected, padrinos and madrinas directed the ritual. With them were *apoyos*, helpers, who continuously supervised the initiates, never leaving their sides. The helpers were shadowed by *oyentes*, listeners, who were still in the process of learning the ritual by following helpers in word and example. This hierarchy reminded me of the chain of command in anexos, where padrinos were supported by counselors, and some anexados trained to become counselors themselves. But in this case, there were no anexados. Instead, initiates were called *escribientes*.

"Writers?" I asked Andrés.

"Yes, writers."

The designation struck me. I was accustomed to thinking of writers as authors of published works lucky enough to have a broad audience of readers. Writing for oneself, or for an intimate, didn't count. My stack of journals, my unpublished poetry, even my published ethnography and academic articles didn't make me a writer. I could never call myself a writer. It seemed indecent.

When I worked at the detox clinic in New Mexico, I took a creative writing course at the local community college. The instructor was the poet Jimmy Santiago Baca. Baca's book *Black Mesa Poems* was a touchstone for me. Its descriptions of addiction and violence, family and loss, gave me a window into my mother's hidden life before my father whisked her away from New Mexico. I carried the book around with me for years and felt a special connection with Baca. Both of our families lived on 5 Points Road in Albuquerque's South Valley, a poor Chicano neighborhood southwest of the Rio Grande, the setting for many of Baca's poems.

I had high hopes for the class and was disappointed that Baca rarely showed up for it, the drive from Albuquerque to Española being too demanding. But on one of the rare evenings that he did show, I made a point of talking to him after class. I told him I wanted to be a writer. He looked at me with interest. Very quickly, the other students surrounded him. "I want to be a writer!" "Me too!" Baca's attention turned from me to the men whose lives were likely closer to his. I left that classroom thinking that I would forever be a member of the audience, never an author with one.

After the last preparatory meeting, Andrés pulled me aside. He needed to know about my role at the experience. Would I attend as an anthropologist or as an *escribiente*, a writer? Andrés listened patiently while I explained that my role as an anthropologist was to participate and to observe. My writings were based on this dual practice. But this wasn't what Andrés meant. He looked at me closely.

"To undergo an experience, the writing must come first."

———————

We departed on a Friday evening in August. Instead of a bus, we crammed into a white panel van with two rows of seating. There were nine of us— four people had left the group for unknown reasons. Before we entered the vehicle, we were patted down and searched for drugs. Our cell phones, watches and overnight bags were taken away.

Night fell quickly, and the headlights of oncoming cars lit up the faces of the group. Some people chatted while others stayed quiet with pensive looks on their faces. I sat next to a woman from Jalisco named Lupe. She was undocumented and cleaned office buildings in Palo Alto for a living. Her shift was from seven to twelve at night, when buildings were supposed to be empty. But people worked late, and when Lupe knocked on office doors to empty wastebaskets, she was often told to go away. She worried about not being able to do her job. Lupe had three children at home, and rent for her one-bedroom apartment was high. She developed *nervios*. She'd left her children behind with her sister, who'd undergone the experience six months earlier. Her sister called it life-changing but didn't provide details of the ritual, because her padrino instructed her not to. Despite the preparatory meetings, Lupe wasn't ready for what lay ahead. I felt the same way.

Someone began singing a traditional religious hymn: *Bendito, bendito, bendito sea Dios.* The song was beautiful, but I could feel myself stiffen. I was divorcing my husband and also a lesbian. No one knew this about me. Compared to the others in the group, I'd withheld details about my life because my role as an anthropologist seemed to dictate circumspection. But there was another reason I remained private: I was afraid of rejection. Not because I needed to be liked, but because I didn't want to be left.

The singing didn't last long, and for much of the trip people sat in silence. I sensed that we were driving around in circles, just like servers did during house calls in Mexico City, inducing fear and disorientation in the anexados. But in this case, we were in the van at our own will. We had invited this disorientation into our lives.

Time passed slowly and the sound of traffic died down. Eventually, the road turned bumpy. We bounced around in the dark van, laughing nervously. The van finally stopped, and for several minutes we waited inside while a flurry of activity took place around us. Finally, the door slid open, and the smell of the forest perfumed the chilly air. I stepped out and looked up toward the dark tips of redwoods pointing at an indigo sky.

Two helpers guided each initiate to a large open-air tent, where a long conference table was lit by kerosene lamps. At least a dozen initiates from another fourth-and-fifth-step group were already seated at the table and dozens more people stood around it, watching us as we approached. I was relieved to see Madrina Trini among them. She wore a flannel shirt and rain boots, prepared for whatever weather might come.

"*¡Bienvenidos, escribientes!* Welcome, writers!"

We joined the other writers at the table, each of us seated between our designated helpers. Behind us stood our listener, their hands resting on our shoulders, steadying us, or perhaps holding us down. My listener's fingers were slender and young. I turned to look at him and he looked down at me. A tattoo of a spider caught in a web spread across his neck.

A young person in recovery sat across the table from me. His hands trembled as he lifted a Styrofoam cup of coffee to his lips. I didn't know it at the time, but coffee and hot chocolate would be our main sources of sustenance for the next seventy-two hours. Inducing hunger was part of the experience. I worried that the boy's drug withdrawal would lead to dangerous symptoms. I wanted to reach across the table and tell him that I would watch over him and make sure that he was okay. All I could do was offer him a smile that I hoped conveyed the message.

An elaborate stereo system was set up beneath a second tent. *Toma mis lágrimas*, take my tears, rang the voice of a woman. Padrino Alberto stood at the head of the table. He had a square face, spiky black hair and wore a leather jacket. I'd seen him before, in videos posted on YouTube that I'd studied before the experience. One video had garnered over eight hundred thousand views. It showed him preaching into a microphone while a man strummed a guitar.

Padrino Alberto talked over the soundtrack. "*¡Escribientes!* You are here because you are in pain! *¡El dolor inmenso que se sienten!*" He paused for a long time, looking around the table, his gaze resting on each one of us. I looked at the kerosene lamp before me. Two moths danced around it.

The padrino's voice gathered momentum as he spoke about our lack of authority over our lives. He talked in a mixture of Spanish and English, describing how we writers would come face-to-face with our powerlessness during the experience, but we would never be alone. God was omnipresent. And we would always be accompanied by three people who would watch over us. Why? Because writers, or initiates, take advantage! They bring drugs, alcohol, cigarettes! They violate and assault when they begin to feel what it is to lose their power! And they will not succeed because they will always be outnumbered—not only by the three, but by *el Señor*, Jesus Christ, whose presence could be felt in the forest.

Padrino Alberto launched into his own story, describing how his life back in Mexico was ruled by drugs and violence. He carried a gun around with him because of the sense of power it gave him. "I killed three people, including my cousin!" he yelled. Whether or not this was true, the writers took notice, and Padrino Alberto seemed to grow in size. Power led to violence, he shouted at us, humility to peace. The padrinos and madrinas that stood in the background offered *amens* and deeply felt sighs.

Padrino Alberto continued talking about his fall into disgrace due to a lack of humility.

But then his wife had arranged for him to go to a hacienda, a farm. It was in the desert, and there he possessed nothing, only his own wretchedness. For six months, he was forced to practice steps four and five, beginning with memories of his childhood. A father who had migrated to the United States in search of work, leaving his wife and seven children alone in a small city in Guerrero; a neighborhood controlled by gangs; an uncle—a police officer—who abused him. Childhood, he said, is when the pain begins to build, and when we begin to seek to escape it. And the pain only gets worse. In the desert, he learned to practice the steps every day, while every night he wrote. "Then, I reached catharsis!" he cried. Now, we are on the same journey: the journey of writers.

"Self-help" culture underscores the necessity of speaking or writing about traumatic events to overcome them. To endure and prevail, the survivor must tell their story to heal and get through. But while accounts of trauma may begin with individual experience, they also betray broader social and political forces.

Padrino Alberto's testimony spoke to the realities of economic insecurity, familial separation, and neighborhood, police, and sexual violence. His story, like Toño's confession, is not only that of the survivor who speaks it, but also a witness to the world. This way of thinking about testimony contrasts with essentialist discourses that reduce the experience of trauma to the victim. Rather, testimony here becomes a way of expressing and interpreting violence on different discursive levels. It also affirms that individuals identify in multiple ways—not only as victims, but also as perpetrators, and even as healers.

———

There were small folding tables scattered throughout the campsite and each writer was led to one of them by their helpers. The tables were lit by kerosene lamps, but darkness pressed all around them, giving them a stage-like appearance. A stack of wide-ruled paper was anchored by a rock and three pens arranged in a neat row. My helpers sat next to me and my listener across. Their faces were shadowy, and the paper glared at me, empty. We held hands and bowed our heads in prayer. One of the helpers asked God to give me patience and courage, and to write in search of truth and forgiveness. Then the other helper removed a sheet from the stack and placed it in front of me. Her hands were small and shot through with blue veins.

"Write your first memory," she said, handing me a pen.

The first thing that occurred to me was sitting, knees to chest, in a coat closet.

The woman took the paper and read it aloud in a gentle voice. Then, she looked at me and asked me how old I was at the time and why I was in the closet. I started to speak but she passed the paper back to me.

"Write it down," she said.

I was four, maybe five years old. I preferred small spaces. Little rooms where I might be found.

The woman took the paper from me. "So, you were not hiding?"

"No."

"Write it down."

I was not hiding.

The helpers asked seemingly simple questions about family members and my age during certain events, such as my first Communion and menstruation. As instructed, I wrote answers to their questions. My sentences were precise and appeared as fragments loosely connected by memory. Every ten sentences or so, a helper took the paper and read my responses out loud. I stared at the listener across the table from me. The flickering light between us gave the illusion that the spider on his neck was moving.

At the first signs that I was growing tired, the listener was ordered to bring me coffee. I watched him walk off into the darkness. Somehow, my helpers and listener stayed alert. I sipped the acrid coffee, aware of the sound of someone weeping in the background. I heard rustling and turned to see pages falling from a table.

"Write," my helper said, turning my attention back to the paper.

My mother cried in her room.

I found her pills behind the books.

She left clues.

No wonder she didn't look for me.

———

A few hours into the writing session one of the padrinos began to clap, signaling that it was time to wrap up. To my surprise, dawn was breaking; we had written through the night. We returned to the clearing and, instead of rest, were forced to do jumping jacks, stretch, and run in place, our breath visible in the chilly air. The young man I'd noticed earlier whimpered, and others complained that they felt faint. I felt so, too, but I tried to keep up, remembering the anexados in Mexico City running in circles around the perimeters of their little rooms.

A madrina shouted at us. Her voice was loud and shrill, and she zigzagged through our bodies while calling them gifts from God that we abused with alcohol and drugs. Other people abused our bodies without remorse, she said. She named the perpetrators: spouses, employers, drug dealers, criminals, and abortionists. Our duty was to protect our bodies and the lives of innocents who depended upon them. And for this we needed to be strong and accept the authority of God. She singled out the women in the group and asked who had had an abortion. When no one responded she called us liars and murderers of the innocent—no better than Padrino Alberto once was, back when he killed his cousin.

The way she talked about abortion angered me, and I struggled to stay silent. I looked to Madrina Trini for help, remembering her stories about rape during dangerous migrant journeys. How many girls and women crossed over into this country and sought out abortions, or had wanted to but were too afraid because they were undocumented? Little did I know then that the Supreme Court would overturn *Roe v. Wade* in 2022, making it impossible for millions more women in the United States to get an abortion.

I was relieved when Padrino Alberto stepped in, turning our attention to the male writers. He singled out a heavy man and demanded that he run faster. The writer bounced up and down, panting. Padrino Alberto said his weight was as an impediment to work and the ability to contribute to the needs of his family. It was a sign of selfishness, and an insult to those living in hunger. The padrino accused him of taking from others to stuff himself. Then, he turned to the young man. His addiction was not merely the sign of moral failing, Padrino Alberto said, but abuse of his family, from whom he stole to satisfy his urges. Both men were accused of being thieves and ordered to kneel and admit before God the nature of their wrongs.

"I am selfish. A thief."

"I abuse my body. A thief."

After our morning exercise, we washed our hands and faces in a bucket of cold water. Then we were instructed to sit on the ground. It was cool and damp. Our helpers brought us coffee and a cinnamon roll, our only food until evening. Then they doled out medications. I was among the *enfermos*, the sick ones, who held out their hands and swallowed pills for epilepsy and depression.

In the afternoon, each writer was led by their helpers and listener on a silent walk around the campsite. The ground was slippery with dark green needles and the trees were alive with birds—thrushes, humming-birds, jays. The woman from Jalisco passed me, her arms spread out by her sides, balancing herself as if on a high wire.

———————

When night fell, the writers returned to their tables, new stacks of paper waiting for us. The empty paper stared at me, its blue lines blurred due to the darkness and lack of sleep. I held the hands of my helpers. They bowed their heads and asked God to give me strength to be vulnerable and hold nothing back. The first prompt that night was to write about my most distressing memories. I thought for a while and began to write.

Kate and I grabbed a ride to Santa Fe.

I brought a baguette and Kate a block of cheese that she stole from the health food store on Central Avenue.

We had a picnic in the plaza and talked about the places we wanted to travel to. Cities in Europe where we imagined living one day. I wore my hair in a pixie cut and pegged my jeans with safety pins, just like Kate did. We were seventeen and in love.

She encouraged me to make amends with my mother.

"Get over yourself" was one of her favorite lines.

It was hot in Santa Fe, and we took refuge in a bookstore.

I walked away quickly when Kate slipped a travel book about France in her jeans.

By that time, I had discovered confessional poetry and hid myself in the poetry section.

We had an old record player.

I was holding a book by Anne Sexton, staring at the black-and-white photo of her on the cover, thinking her beautiful. It was a paperback but still too expensive for me to buy, too thick for Kate to steal.

I heard my name. My father's voice.

Two years passed since he left me.

He stood a careful distance.

I glanced at him quickly when he held out his hand.

He didn't want my hand, he wanted to see the book I was holding.
He leafed through the pages.
He landed on a poem.

> *Come friend,*
> *I have an old story to tell you—*

I turned to look at my father. He was looking at the poem.
I waited for him to look at me.
He walked away, taking the book with him.
I turned to the wall of books. Dizzy.
Then my father came back.
He came back!
He handed me a paper bag.
Did we touch?
We never touched.
I didn't open the bag for days.
I cried in Kate's arms.
She finally opened it one morning.

> *For Angela.*
> *Love,*
> *Ares (Dad)*

———

I wrote pages and pages of memories—ages fifteen, forty-two, seventeen, twelve—time not chronological but a mysterious mix. Why this memory and not another? Why father and not mother? Occasionally, the helpers brought me coffee, or took the pen and rubbed my sore hand. I wept and they told me to keep writing. When the fog turned icy, my listener brought me a blanket and placed it around my shoulders. The moisture in the air caused the blue ink to bleed, forming bruises across the paper.

At times, I became aware of the sounds around me—sniffling, words of encouragement, the occasional reprimand. The young man vomited behind a tree and complained he was freezing. When I walked to the bathroom, accompanied again by my helpers, I caught a glimpse of his paper. The only word I could make out was *stop*.

I wondered about the content of the other writers' pages. What memories were being awakened?

Padrino Alberto clapped, calling us to the tent, where we were offered hot chocolate and coffee. "Drink," Madrina Trini said to me. I took a cup of hot chocolate from her and remembered the instant cocoa my mother made during the cold Maine winters. An aura of light gathered behind my eyes. I worried I might seize.

Before daybreak, we were back at our tables. Padrino Alberto walked through the forest, stopping at each table, telling us that we needed to remain vulnerable to our memories.

My brother and I collected bottles and cans from our neighbors.

Five cents apiece.

We pooled our earnings and bought candy from the gas station.

The sweetness of youth.

We put on plays in the hallway that separated the living room from the dining room.

Back then we had both rooms.

Mother sat on a wood chair in her blue bathrobe, her unkempt hair framing her face.

———

I remembered reading somewhere that Kafka had a hard time finishing his stories because they caused him such anguish. He'd often begin a story and abandon it, because if he didn't let go, he would never be able to come back to the world. "Do I live now in another world?" he asked in one of his diaries. "Do I dare say it?" For Kafka, to write was to abandon the self and surrender to the work.

The shadowy atmosphere of the woods, the helper evoking and recording my memories, the listener's constant gaze upon me, all of it led to a feeling of surrender of the self to the work at hand. My world became one of writing: recollection, reflection, purgation. The ritual of writing was tragedy. Realized in an aesthetic form not usually associated with tragedy (not theatre, film, or philosophy), the *experiencia*'s nocturnal writing practices provided a space where the brokenness of the world could be lamented and shared.

"Tragedy gives voice to what suffers in us and in others, and how we might become cognizant of that suffering," Simon Critchley writes. It stirs emotions, especially fear and pity, and these emotions become the grounds for what Aristotle called *catharsis*. Though Aristotle never defines it directly, catharsis is often understood as a ritualistic process of purification, one that requires a stage. I began to see the tables in the woods as small stages where individual tragedies were being performed and observed.

At one point, Madrina Trini walked over to our table and took a page from the pile held by one of the helpers. She stood above me, appearing as a gleaming face emerging from the darkness. I watched her lips move as she silently read my text. She met my gaze when she was finished. "Go on," she said, as she handed the paper back to me.

———

In the 1930s, the French writer Georges Bataille started a secret community and journal called *Acéphale*, headless. *Acéphale* was both a protest against Nazism and fascism and a celebration of creativity in the face of political disaster. The community that it envisaged was related to an ecstatic practice that called for an entirely different way of being. Like wrenching crying or violent laughter, writing was among the "limit experiences" that could rupture the individual as they existed in normal, everyday life.

There was an element of *Acéphale* during the *experiencia*'s nocturnal writing practices. Among the forms of violence that marked the time were the atrocious acts against undocumented immigrants: hostile rhetoric, ICE raids, rape, families separated, kids in cages. These violences were partly what fueled anexos, fourth-and-fifth-step groups, and the journey to the forest.

Meanwhile, we writers, seated at our wobbly tables, were pushed to an absolute limit. Deprived of sleep, our minds were saturated with painful memories. Deprived of food, our stomachs growled with hunger. The mental and physical elements of our individual deprivations amplified a sense of vulnerability and singularity. Yet we were never alone, not with our helpers and listeners by our sides, reading aloud and listening to our words, ready to respond to our individual needs.

Writing during the experience became a kind of ecstatic activity, an "inner experience," to use Bataille's term, that emerged from personal pain. Ecstasy involves the loss of the sense of oneself. While not all ecstasies are religious in origin, there were elements of religiosity during the *experiencia*'s writing ritual: prayers, hand-holding, religious hymns. But the dislocation of the self was accomplished primarily through the practice of writing, and the gradual dissipation of the boundaries between writer, helpers, and listener. Disrupting the self from its normal routines and forming bonds between self and other are the preconditions of alleviating suffering and transformation.

Looking over the text I produced over the course of two nights, I can sense the breakdown that gradually overtook me. It isn't just what I wrote—*spider on his table-neck, our heart bleeds fast*—it's my handwriting and its unraveling to the point that I can only make out certain recurring refrains: *hand spasm, blurry girl, recollect the collection*. My breakdown, which was simultaneously my healing, was produced by and expressed in the shared experience of writing.

On the final evening of the experience, before the last writing session, I sat next to one of Madrina Trini's goddaughters. She looked to be in her sixties, older than Madrina Trini, but with a playful demeanor that made her seem younger than her age. She spoke with an accent that carried the melody of an indigenous tongue foreign to me. "This forest reminds me of home," she said, looking at the soaring redwoods. We were quiet for a while, heavy with fatigue. Then she took my hand. Her palms were smooth as silk, and she said that the trees were strong. I looked up, unable to hold back the tears that gathered in my tired eyes.

The previous evening I'd noticed how, during the writing practice, she spoke her memories to her listener, who transcribed them on paper for her. It was an arrangement so distinct from loneliness. I imagined her voice was a sonority resounding among the gathering trees, her concert hall. What brought this woman to the forest? She must have sensed my question because she turned to me and said, "I am finally writing my story."

————

"As it so often happens with gentleness," Anne Dufourmantelle writes, "there is a double gift that appears: the one who offers it and the one who receives it are both brought together." I received this gift of togetherness through the gesture of a fellow writer taking my hand in the forest, and through the practice of writing itself. The helpers' conjuring of memory and recitation of my words. The listener's steady gaze upon me, a witness to my grief. What characterized the experience was the reciprocal communication between writer, helper, listener. To be a writer meant being together—exhausted, hungry, dizzy, encouraging, ecstatic, receptive, grieving, hurting, gentle.

Nearly three days after I entered the forest, I returned to my apartment in Oakland. The scent of pine and sweat clung to my body, and my hair was sticky with sap. I felt shattered, but not in the sense of broken. Light gathered behind my eyes. An opening.

7

THE GRAY ZONE

I saw Hortencia again in 2018. Four years had passed since our first meeting, when she described to me Daniel's planned abduction and delivery to an anexo. He had stayed there for three months, long enough for Hortencia to hope that he'd return home clean and stay out of harm's way. And he did—at least for a while. He avoided the troublemakers in the neighborhood with whom he had bought and sold drugs. He was less volatile and more communicative. He even shared meals with Hortencia, both sitting in front of the television watching their favorite shows. Hortencia described the few months after his return from the anexo as *tranquilo*, calm.

Her apartment was dark and warm when I arrived, and heavy with the scent of perfumed votive candles lit in the corner of the room. The image of Santo Niño de Atocha, the Child Saint of Atocha, was affixed to one of them. It glowed brightly, a long column of light, its wick nearly expired.

The candle was for Daniel, whom Hortencia hadn't seen or talked to in over a week. "I don't know where he is," she said in a worried tone. "I don't know if he's okay . . . To tell you the truth, I don't like to think about it." But it was obvious to me that she could think of little else.

Her body showed the signs of stress. She was thin, even frail looking, with dark, wet eyes. But she didn't cry. She held herself up straight, her long ponytail trailing down her back like a schoolgirl's. She appeared old and young at once, and her voice wavered with uncertainty, one moment sounding strong and firm, the next hesitant and unsure.

Life was harder than it was four years ago. Daniel was using and sell-ing drugs again. It was a deadly combination, as it left him exposed to the combined dangers of addiction and violence. Hortencia told me she'd prefer him to do drugs or sell them, but not both. She reasoned he'd be safer that way. If he was just using drugs, she could get him help to stop. If he was just selling them, he'd be more careful. "If I knew we'd end right back here, I'd have kept him inside," she said, referring to the last anexo she had committed him to. She regretted having to release him. It was something she had been forced to do, as she could no longer afford the anexo's monthly fee.

She had lost her job cleaning rooms at a hotel. It was one of many being remodeled to better reflect the tastes of international tourists. Colo-nial nostalgia, bohemian-chic. The hotel was a block from the Zócalo and a twenty-minute walk from Hortencia's home. She worked there for over a decade, pushing a cart from room to room, just as I had decades earlier, when I was a maid in Albuquerque. We both knew what it was like to collect rumpled sheets and damp towels and to leave a room as if no one had ever been there.

―――――――

In the 1990s, the Centro's reputation for crime kept tourists away. Locals who used to stroll through the neighborhood and shop were also fearful of venturing there. It wasn't just the growth of the drug trade that led to a growing sense of insecurity. More broadly, between 1995 and 1998, Mex-ico City's crime rate tripled.

Scholars have unambiguously shown how Mexico's "illiberal democ-racy" was intimately intertwined with criminality and violence. Under the seventy-year reign of the PRI, several major drug cartels coexisted in relative peace, with corrupt state security and judicial systems protecting the drug trafficking industry. This system of protection during the period of pax mafiosa began to crumble as Mexico transformed from author-itarian rule to democracy. The redefinition of power, shifting alliances, and new democratic policies meant uncertainty about state protection for criminal groups. This uncertainty led to the destabilization of cartels and the proliferation of intercartel wars across states with drug trafficking routes. Large-scale criminal organizations grew and smaller gangs multiplied, which dramatically reshaped life for millions of citizens across Mexico.

Cuauhtémoc Cárdenas was Mexico City's first democratically elected mayor. Cárdenas was a founder of the Party of the Democratic Revolution (PRD), a break-off faction of the PRI. After taking office in 1997, Cárdenas vowed to establish a "secure and just city," beginning with an overhaul of the corrupt and inadequate police force. But the police remained loyal to the PRI and opposed his reforms. When Cárdenas left office in 2000, it was widely acknowledged that the government lacked control over the police force and that most crimes in Mexico City involved them.

Cárdenas's electoral successor, Andrés Manuel López Obrador of the PRD, also sought to reform the local police force and secure the city. In 2002, López Obrador, along with a group of private-sector individuals, most notably the business magnate Carlos Slim, hired Rudy Giuliani to design a plan for new police practices and security measures to address Mexico City's crime problems. For $4.3 million, Guiliani and his team of consultants surveyed the capitol in a fleet of armored cars, accompanied by military officers and hundreds of bodyguards. Six months later, Guiliani Partners delivered a set of recommendations about how to reverse the problems of violence and insecurity in Mexico City.

The proposal was built around the ostensibly successful "zero-tolerance" framework that Guiliani had applied as mayor of New York City. This strategy included restrictions on free movement and policing of public behavior. The proliferation of citations for "civic crimes" would target the survival strategies of the urban poor—from kids performing magic tricks for weary drivers to squeegee men washing car windows. There were recommendations for enforcing anti-graffiti and anti-noise crimes, traffic crimes, and police bribery crimes, although the police wouldn't penalized for accepting them. Guiliani's report all but avoided police corruption and impunity, instead relying upon police and surveillance technologies for resolving the growing problem of crime.

Critics of the proposal argued that Guiliani's policies did not amount to serious crime fighting but was instead designed to foster downtown real estate development. In fact, the same year Guiliani surveilled Mexico City, Carlos Slim founded a nonprofit organization dedicated to "rescuing" the Centro through private investment. Money, especially Slim's, poured into the area and financed infrastructural upgrades, building preservation, and renovations, much of it to promote international tourism. Like in other global cities, the securitization and "upgrading" of the Centro accelerated its gentrification. Streets were cleared of merchants, and new hotels, restaurants, and cafés opened, some of them in renovated vecindades. These changes occurred in tandem with the displacement of low-income people living in the surrounding areas, including Hortencia's neighborhood. But in Tepito, there were no large private investments to explain the rising rents, evictions, and zero-tolerance policing strategies. Hortencia's neighborhood hadn't changed, except in one way: it had grown more insecure.

According to the 2022 National Survey on Victimization and Perception of Public Safety, insecurity ranked as the first concern among people aged eighteen and over in the country. The same survey found that 53 percent of people in Mexico City felt unsafe in their own neighborhood. Over the years the survey has been conducted, one of the long-standing concerns has been repression at the hands of police.

The year 2018 saw a record number of international visitors to Mexico, despite the country's homicide rate, the highest ever in Mexico (though 2019 surpassed it). López Obrador took presidential office that December after having won a landslide victory. He promised an end to criminal violence, and to the corruption, impunity, and economic inequality that fueled it. But his "Hugs, Not Bullets" (*Abrazos, No Balazos*) program, a set of policies that emphasized an approach to violent crime that minimized the police's role in security, was largely met with ridicule. Citizens wanted an end to military involvement in the fight against cartels, but López Obrador's long-term security policies—school scholarships, stipends, and more drug treatment—didn't address their immediate concern: safety.

That summer, crimes of all sorts spiked in Mexico City. In June, body parts were strewn across one of the city's main thoroughfares, along with a message to rival criminal groups: *Empezó la limpia* (The cleaning begins). That same month, an American tourist was killed when gunmen on motorcycles opened fire. And on September 14, gunmen disguised as mariachi musicians shot people gathered in Plaza Garibaldi, a downtown spot popular with locals and tourists alike. Five were killed and several wounded. The belief that Mexico City was safe from the narco violence raging in other parts of the country was revealed to be untrue.

But the predominant response to criminal violence in the capitol by government officials was to deny its existence in the city. *No hay narcos en la ciudad* (there are no narcos in the city) was one of the oft-repeated statements made by officials. Incidences of narco violence were dismissed as isolated events and Mexico City was depicted as safe from the dangers that exist beyond its supposed walls. *La ciudad está blindada* (the city is armored). Such characterizations followed high-profile massacres, disappearances, and gruesome discoveries. They were meant to appease anxious investors and tourists, and to reassure a frightened and exhausted electorate.

Hortencia worried about the uptick in violence in her neighborhood. It wasn't just the spectacular violence that gripped the media that concerned her, or the "generalized violence" that accompanied organized crime and continued militarization. It was what was happening in her own vecindad. Police were performing raids there. In their searches for drugs or pirated goods, they broke everything in their way—windows, doors, furniture. They were rough on residents but rarely arrested anyone, even when they confiscated drugs. Rumors circulated that the police were not, in fact, cracking down on drug dealing. Nor were they acting on behalf of corrupt bosses who had a stake in the drug trade. Rather, the police actions responded to the economic interests of real estate developers who for years have wanted to enter the neighborhood and evict people from it. "They want us to disappear," Hortencia said. Her statement about disappearance forged a historical continuity across decades, indeed centuries, of violent displacements—from the Spanish colonists' destruction of Tenochtitlan to Porfirio Diaz's "beautification" efforts in the Centro, to the *guerra sucia*'s destructive tactics.

Weeks before my visit in 2018, Hortencia's front door had been busted down by police. She was still shaken when she described returning from work to find it hanging precariously in its frame. "I was afraid to enter, not knowing who or what I'd find." Neighbors helped her repair the damage, and she even installed an additional lock, which was more symbolic than anything else. But Hortencia's anxiety worsened. Following the break-in, she left the house only when necessary. Not only did she need to be there in case Daniel returned, she said, but she wanted to protect the only home she'd ever really had.

But protecting her home meant having to leave it. Hortencia's days were now spent working in the sundries section at a location of Sanborns, a chain restaurant and department store owned by Slim. Three nights a week, she attended classes at a secretarial school, where she was learning to type and file in hopes of landing an office job. A friend who lived in the same vecindad worked as an office assistant and was earning enough to save money toward the goal of moving to a safer neighborhood. Hortencia had no plans to move, but she wanted a stable, better-paying job, and what she called "dignified work."

Dignity was a quality Hortencia often evoked. She distinguished between those who had it and those who didn't, and she tried to associate only with those who did. She said that her friend and neighbor Lupe lost her dignity when a disreputable man moved in with her. When Lupe showed up at her door crying after a fight with her boyfriend, Hortencia took her in. "I told her she was living an undignified life."

As far as I could tell, Hortencia hadn't been romantically involved with anyone in years. Most men, she said, didn't treat women with dignity. Her husband, Rey, had been different. He treated women with respect, and she taught Daniel to do the same. She instilled in her son proper manners and punished him when he used vulgar language. He had been a good child, polite and well-behaved. She showed me photos that corroborated her story. There was Daniel dressed in a school uniform. There he was riding on his father's shoulders, his small hands covering his father's eyes. Things changed during his teenage years, after Rey died. His first stint in an anexo was when he was fifteen years old, as a punishment for stealing money from Anselma. It wasn't just the fact of him stealing that so upset Hortencia—it was that he stole from his grandmother. "She's a mother to me," Hortencia said. She looked around the living room. "This is still her house. It's my job to keep it safe."

Though Daniel was an adult now, Hortencia still felt the need to protect him. She said she'd commit him to an anexo again, if only she could find him. The times when he was locked away in an anexo were quieter, less anxiety inducing. Yes, she worried about him while he was inside. Was he eating enough? Was he getting into fights? Was he being abused? But having the ability to locate him outweighed such concerns. What worried her most was not knowing where he was.

She intimated that Rey's family's business may have created tensions between Rey's family and another. It was unclear to me whether that put Daniel at risk, but the thought of it bothered Hortencia. More than once she confided that, were Rey still alive, she'd have insisted that he also find "dignified work."

Hortencia talked to neighbors and made phone calls to try to locate Daniel. She enlisted her in-laws for help. Though she had little faith in the authorities, she even reported his disappearance to them. "I made a report," she said.

———

In 2017, Mexico passed the General Law on Disappearances, in large part because of the advocacy of families of the disappeared. The law created mechanisms at the state and federal levels to improve search, identification, and investigation processes for disappearances. It also mandated the creation of a citizens' council to keep the public involved. But progress has been limited. Local search commissions and state prosecutors' offices are weak and underfunded, and coordination between them is irregular. Investigations are anomalous, and between only 2 and 6 percent of all disappearance cases in Mexico result in prosecutions.

In recent years, family collectives have sprung up across the country to search for their relatives. The National Disappeared Persons Search

Brigade, composed of relatives and volunteers, uses shovels and picks in their searches for clandestine graves and human remains. Hasta Encontrarles CDMX is a search collective in Mexico City. Every day, its Facebook page posts pictures of people who have disappeared, many of them girls and young women. A recent update to one case reads: *Gracias por compartir la foto de mi amiga. Su mamá ya la encontró, desafortunadamente sin vida. En paz descanse.* (Thank you for sharing the photo of my friend. Her mother found her, unfortunately not alive. Rest in peace.)

As of 2022, more than one hundred thousand people have disappeared in Mexico, although the number is likely much higher since many disappearances are unreported, partly because of fears of reprisal. The context of these disappearances have evolved since the *guerra sucia*. Most victims are not linked to political dissidence, nor are they linked to criminal organizations, as official discourse maintains. They are vulnerable migrants and women, the poor and marginalized, journalists and social activists who report on and organize against violence. Extensive documentation shows that the disappearances are committed by organized crime groups and state agents, who are often one in the same.

Hortencia was terrified that Daniel had been disappeared. At night, she laid on the couch, the living room aglow from the muted TV, her constant companion. Anselma brought Hortencia relaxants to calm her nerves, but Hortencia refrained from taking the pills, afraid, as she was, of missing a phone call from Daniel or from someone who might know his whereabouts.

"Can I do anything?" I asked her.

Hortencia shook her head. There was nothing to do but wait.

———

In *The Drowned and the Saved*, the writer and Holocaust survivor Primo Levi asks the reader to consider morally ambiguous groups during World War II, especially Jewish prisoners in camps who compromised and collaborated with oppressors because they were ordered to or because in exchange they received preferential treatment. Levi insists that one cannot pass easy judgement on these prisoners who were fighting to survive, for they occupy a "gray zone" of culpability. "We tend to simplify history," Levi writes. "But the pattern within which events are ordered is not always identifiable in a single unequivocal fashion."

In the anexos, my eyes had been opened to a gray zone of violence. These little rooms were envisioned as places of sanctuary by padrinos, parents, and sometimes anexados. At the same time, they occupied a crucial position along a continuum of violence, especially since many of their practices—kidnappings, physical discipline, verbal abuse, forced confessions—were shaped by the war that existed beyond their walls. My experience in the forest took place within the gray zone, too. The deprivations, fear, and uncertainty that formed the basis of the ritual was matched by the tenderness and care of my helpers, who always stayed by my side, coaxing painful memories to the surface. For much of the time, I didn't know if I was being harassed or helped.

The mothers I spoke with were wrestling with this moral ambiguity. They maintained that the anexo kept their children safe from violence. They also knew that the anexo subjected them to it. There was no simplification, no final assurance. Would their child return home "damaged or deranged," as one mother put it, or "full of resentments," as another said? Hortencia shared both worries. She agonized over how long she should keep Daniel in the anexo. Three months? Six months? A year? Would he worsen and grow angrier with time? Meanwhile, in conversations with me, anexados voiced feelings of betrayal, anger, and hurt about being committed to an anexo by their mothers. But sometimes they expressed appreciation for their mothers' sacrifices. They, too, were torn.

―――――――

Right before COVID-19 hit Mexico in March 2020, Serenity housed forty-three anexados, more than double the number from when I first visited. It was hard to imagine. Back then, anexados already complained of being "packed in like sardines." Serenity's population had swelled. And according to Padrino Francisco, more people were voluntarily committing themselves to escape the insecurity and violence in their neighborhoods. When I asked him how the self-committed paid the anexo's monthly fee, he answered vaguely, "They work."

More than half of Mexican workers are in the unwaged "informal" sector. One feature of Mexico's vast informal economy is that it's difficult to differentiate between an offer of help or employment and the delivery of a threat. To do so requires a nuanced understanding of the prevailing system of social organization. And even then there's a persistent ambiguity, for it is often through coercion and violence that the system of "reciprocity" is maintained. (This is far from being a Mexican phenomenon, as it's seen in virtually every part of the world.) An intricate system of extortion and protection extends throughout Mexico City, affecting merchants in the working-class areas of the Centro and restaurant and bar owners in the upscale neighborhoods of Colonia Roma, La Condesa, and Polanco. It also ensnares padrinos in the poorest boroughs, who must pay a weekly *derecho de piso* ("right to work" fee) to criminal organizations, which are often tied to state actors, to continue to operate their anexos.

I saw the willful bartering by mothers to secure an anexo's help with a child or a spouse. I was aware, at least peripherally, of the coercion and violence that accompanied anexos' fee-for-service structure. In addition to weekly or monthly fees, many of the women I talked to reported having to supply the anexo with clothes, food, medicines, and labor for their relative's treatment. Meanwhile, those "abandoned" by their relatives had to take on more than their share of chores. I heard whispers about other ways they earned their keep, namely telephone extortions.

Once, while hanging out in Padrino Francisco's office, I noticed a cardboard box filled with old cell phones. It didn't occur to me then that they might be anything more than the confiscated personal property of anexados. But upon reflection, I realized that the phones may have been used more in the manner of weapons.

Ninety-three percent of crimes registered as extortion in Mexico are carried out by telephone. Telephone extortionists use psychological tactics to scare and confuse their victims. They may identify as a member of a cartel and demand protection money to prevent a kidnapping or murder of a loved one. Or they may pretend to be a relative who has been kidnapped and held for ransom. Mexican law enforcement declares that calls purporting danger or personal harm are empty threats. But the calls sound real, and the context in which they are made is all too credible.

One afternoon my friend Sandra's mother received such a call. On the other end of the line was the sound of a woman screaming and pleading for her help. "Mamá, Mamá, please help me, Mamá!" A male voice cut in, telling Sandra's mother that she needed to deposit thousands of pesos in a bank account if she wanted to see her daughter again. "They knew my name. They knew where I lived. I was terrified," she said. Sandra's mother hung up and called her daughter. Thankfully, she answered and was safe.

It was difficult to think that Serenity might be a call center for extortions, because it challenged my view that the anexo was a refuge from crime. Given how social institutions operate in Mexico today, and the overall context of widespread violence and impunity, it would not have been that surprising if Serenity was extorting people. Still, I tried to convince myself otherwise, recalling how Padrino Francisco complained bitterly about the bribes that he was forced to pay to remain in operation. How could he then inflict the same demands on other people under the threat of violence?

The cell phones may have been the property of anexados. They could have been mere objects, perhaps stolen, to be sold on the street. And they could have been used for extortion. The cell phones presented a profound ambiguity that made me feel uneasy. They were part of the disquieting gray zone in which victims, trying to survive in a system of violence, could also be perpetrators.

———

There was a knock at Hortencia's door. During my previous visits, Hortencia kept the door to her apartment open, allowing neighbors to stop in as they walked by. But now the door was locked shut.

"¡Voy!" Hortencia yelled as she leaped up off the couch.

I turned to see a neighbor standing in the doorframe. She held a cutting from a pothos plant, its fragile, vein-like roots hanging from her hand. "Stick it in water and it will keep growing," she said as she moved into the apartment to fetch a glass. She was younger than us, maybe twenty-five years old, and she carried herself with enviable confidence. She placed the small plant by the window, then turned toward me. "I'm Alicia," she said.

Alicia asked Hortencia for an update about Daniel. Eight days had passed since Hortencia last heard from him. She called his cell throughout the day, but it cut off before the first ring. "He probably lost it," Alicia said, sounding upbeat. She tried to lighten the atmosphere by talking about neighborhood gossip. Someone was cheating on their girlfriend. Someone else was in prison. She nibbled on the crackers Hortencia laid out and laughed at things I didn't understand. Then she got up, stood behind Hortencia, wrapped her arms around Hortencia's shoulders, and addressed me.

"Is your mother alive?"

"Yes."

"You should call her."

———

Just before a trip to Mexico City in 2018, I traveled home to New Mexico. My mother had had surgery to remove a malignant tumor from her neck. She'd been unwell for months prior to the cancer diagnosis. For years I tried to coax her into seeing doctors for depression, mania, extreme weight loss, but she'd always refused. Her aversion to health care and medicine felt like a judgment, especially given how dependent I was on doctors for the treatment of my own condition. When I tried to talk with her about my own illness she drifted off or changed the subject. Eventually, I stopped talking about it altogether.

I was called into the recovery room where my mother lay on a narrow hospital bed, the steel rails enclosing her like a baby. She looked vulnerable and old under the garish light, her thin body barely rumpling the blanket that was tucked in tight around her. I sat by her bedside and watched her stir awake. When she saw me, she started to cry. "It hurts."

A nurse instructed me on how to drain the blood from the catheter that sprung from her neck like a spigot. Then my mother was released into my care. When we got to her house, I helped her change clothes and get into bed. Her room smelled strongly of cigarettes. "Don't go," she said. Her eyes looked panicky. I promised I would stay.

I sat on the reading chair beside her bed. A folding table cluttered with books stood next to it. Tolstoy's *War and Peace*, Steinbeck's *The Grapes of Wrath*, Pema Chödrön's *When Things Fall Apart*. My mother had taken a few classes at a community college, although never with any intention of pursuing a degree. But she was learned. Written on a piece of paper were a column of definitions for unfamiliar words she'd come across during her reading. *Symbiosis* was one of them.

The kitchen was nearly empty of food, but I found dried lentils and made soup. A stack of unpaid bills lay on the kitchen counter. I sat at the table and wrote out some checks, knowing my mother would discover that the bills were taken care of but would never speak of it. That was how it was between us, she increasingly dependent and avoidant, I reluctant to share news about my life. I was divorcing my husband of ten years and embroiled in a desperate, long-distance relationship with a woman. Once, on an evening drive along Highway 1 in California, I told my then lover, "I finally understand women who leave their children." My statement shocked me, and I immediately took it back. "But I would never leave my daughters," I added.

When my mother woke up from her nap, I emptied the catheter of her blood. It was thick and glistening.

"How many days can you stay?" she asked.

"Just five." I needed to get back to my daughters.

My mother reached for my hand. I sat on the side of the bed and held it for a very long time.

———

A Mexican colleague recommended I move every week or so because I worked in increasingly insecure environments. Anyone could follow me out of an anexo and back to my apartment, where I could be harmed. I thought she was overreacting, but Padrino Francisco thought it was a good idea, too. Things were very "hot," he said. In fact, May 2018 proved to be the deadliest month since the war began. Padrino Francisco suggested that it might be time to wrap up my study. Besides, he said, what else did I need to know?

I left my apartment in Colonia Roma and moved to the Hilton Mexico City Reforma hotel, where I had stayed at the very start of my research. Tall windows overlooked the Alameda Central, the oldest park in the Americas. In the mornings, I strolled along its symmetrical pathways and in the afternoons, I sat on a bench under the violet canopies of jacarandas, listening to the spray of fountains. The atmosphere was light and peaceful, and the war felt a long way off.

For two weeks, I shuttled between the hotel and Grupo San Hipólito, passing by the Church of San Hipólito and crowds of devotees of San Judas Tadeo along the way. Madrina always opened the door with a stern expression and gestured for me to sit in what I had come to think of as the waiting room. But the real waiting room was where the anexados lived, and it was more crowded than ever. In May 2018, thirty-four anexados shared the space. Their faces had changed since 2016, but the stories they told were largely the same. They recounted lost relatives and friends, run-ins with gangs and the police, drug using and selling, wretchedness and grief. At mealtimes, they laughed at each other and themselves, remembered things that had happened, and anticipated things that might.

One anexado was named Dulce. She was nineteen and had been confined in Grupo San Hipólito just short of a month when we met. One afternoon, she joined me in the waiting room, which was a rare occasion because anexados were not usually permitted there. We sat at opposite ends of the bulky sofa and looked at each other. Her cheeks were dimpled and gave the impression of cheerfulness, just like her name—*sweet*—did.

It was Dulce's last day at the anexo, and she was waiting for her mother to pick her up and escort her home. Her stay had been short compared to most, and she was glad for it. She was tired of the smells, of the food, of sleeping on the floor. But she wasn't excited about going home because it was hard for her to be there. She bit at her nails and called herself *atascada*, stuck.

"When you're stuck it's easy to get hurt."

I looked to Madrina, thinking she might respond to Dulce in some way, maybe even comfort her. Instead, she sat at the table and punched messages into a cell phone.

"I have family in Washington," Dulce said. "I would like to go there, you know? Or maybe Chicago . . . Where do you live? . . . Well, if I stay here, I'll probably just end up in a place like I'm in now."

I thought it would be difficult for Dulce to talk in Madrina's presence, but she seemed emboldened by the fact that she was leaving. She imagined life outside the anexo and looked forward to walking around the city and seeing her friends. Before her mother committed her (for reasons she didn't explain), she had just started seeing a guy. She wondered if they would pick things up again. She hoped so.

Dulce stared at her hands. "But even if I'm feeling good out there, you know, I'll know someone inside here is telling their story and—oh! I don't want to think about it anymore! But you can't forget . . . They make it so you can't forget."

"The *grupo*?"

Dulce didn't respond.

"What time is it?" she asked after a long silence. She was growing anxious.

I took out my cell phone to read the time. Dulce spotted the image of my daughters on the screen and grabbed the phone from my hands. The girls were nine years old. One leaned into the arms of the other while they sat together in a cardboard box, huge grins on their faces. Dulce handed the phone back to me. "They look like you," she said.

The next day, I learned that Dulce's mother never showed up.

———

I was preparing to leave for California when I received news from Hortencia via WhatsApp. "He's back!" She didn't explain where Daniel had been, nor did she give details about his return. I invited them to dinner the next evening and we agreed to meet at my hotel.

I waited for them in the lobby, suddenly embarrassed by its ostentatiously high ceilings and sleek lines. Well-heeled travelers passed through the glass entryway, while security personnel discreetly monitored the comings and goings of guests. I worried they might question Hortencia and Daniel or, worse, refuse them entry.

That summer, the film *La camarista*, *The Chambermaid*, was released. Directed by Lila Avilés, the film follows Eve, a young housekeeper (*camarista*) as she is dispatched from room to room at the posh Hotel Presidente Intercontinental, located along the Paseo de la Reforma in Mexico City. The grind of service work is set against the hotel's hypermodernist design. Eve holds babies, pushes elevator buttons, replenishes toiletries. Meanwhile, she aspires to get her GED, spend more time with her son, and work her way up to the forty-second floor, where the penthouses are located. Yet there is a sense of resignation and melancholy that courses through the film. Glimpses of Mexico City, drained of color by smog, are visible from the hotel's expansive windows. Eve is often seen standing before them, gazing outward.

The final scene shows Eve traveling down the passenger elevator, not the service one. Back to the camera, she passes through the hotel lobby, which hums with voices and the sound of heels clinking against the polished floors. She looks side to side, as if taking in the scene for the first time. Then she exits the hotel's guarded front doors and steps onto the street.

Hortencia arrived alone at the hotel. She was dressed in a plaid buttondown shirt tucked into jeans, and her long hair fell smoothly around her flushed face. Her smile did not disguise her upset.

"What happened?" I asked once we'd exited the hotel.

We crossed Avenida Juárez and walked along the edge of the Alameda Central. The air was cool and the park full of people. Hortencia headed east toward the Zócalo. It had been a long time since we'd walked together and I'd forgotten how fast and determinedly she moved, how she expertly cut through crowds. I had a hard time keeping pace with her and suggested we enter the park and find a place to sit and talk. She shook her head no and charged ahead.

The Torre Latinoamericana rose above us. When it opened in 1956, it was the tallest building in the city at forty-four stories and housed an insurance company. I remembered crowding onto its observation deck with Benjamin and our daughters, how the girls clung to my legs as we looked down onto the Zócalo, Plaza Garibaldi, and toward the mountains that appeared to stand at the city's limits. Benjamin took a photo of me standing against the steel caging, the city spread below me, a great geometric expanse. I recited to him lines from T. S. Eliot's *The Waste Land*: "Unreal City / Under the brown fog of a winter noon . . ."

I followed Hortencia into the Zócalo, just as I had years earlier, when we walked to the Metropolitan Cathedral. Groups of protestors gathered along the edges of the great square. Among them were demonstrators commemorating the upcoming fiftieth anniversary of the Tlatelolco massacre. Signs announced FUE EL ESTADO (it was the state), the now-iconic phrase first pronounced on October 22, 2014, during a mass protest after the disappearance of forty-three students from the Raúl Isidro Burgos Rural Teachers' College in Iguala, Guerrero.

Hortencia pushed forward.

I asked her where Daniel was.

She pinched her lips together, as if holding back an answer. We walked a few blocks north of the Cathedral to the Plaza de Santo Domingo. Hortencia stopped at the dry fountain that anchored the square. Rising from its center was a statue of Josefa Ortiz de Domínguez, an insurgent who fought for Mexico's independence from Spain. I sat beside Hortencia along the fountain's edge. Young families and laughing groups of teenagers strolled past us.

"Daniel played here as a little boy," she said, breaking her silence.

In fits and starts, she talked about what had happened that morning—how she made herself coffee, scrambled an egg, and ate quietly while Daniel slept. She urged Daniel to get up from the sofa before she left for work and asked him to join her on an evening excursion to meet me. He looked at her with hatred and said he had no interest in meeting me, nor in spending time with her, as she had destroyed his life by committing him, again and again, to hellholes, to prisons, to anexos. Hortencia told me he'd said it all before.

"How did you respond?" I asked.

"I told him I would do it again."

Just then, a young man with a face painted like a clown entered the plaza. He wore everyday clothes and carried a bouquet of colorful balloons. One of them bore the smiling face of Dora the Explorer, the adventurous Latina character from the Nickelodeon cartoon. Another had an image of Mickey Mouse. The clown passed through the plaza with a sense of urgency, balloons trailing behind him.

I looked up to the darkening sky and remembered a conversation I'd had about belief decades earlier. I was sixteen at the time. During the day I cleaned rooms at the motels along Albuquerque's Central Avenue, and in the evening I worked as a dishwasher at a restaurant about a mile away from my mother's house. We were estranged then, my mother and I, though I'm not sure she was aware of it. She was busy with my baby brother and settling into a new marriage and home. It was when I lived at the Mother Road Hostel; I rarely visited her and, to my recollection, she never visited me.

Juan worked beside me at the restaurant, cutting vegetables and assembling plates. He had a family in Mexico and spoke of them often—his young son, a soccer fanatic; his older daughter, smart and with dreams of college. It had been five years since he'd seen them. He planned to leave Albuquerque and return to Mexico, where he would build a house in his mother's village. He could feel the presence of God there.

I asked him how he knew if God was present. He said he didn't know, but he believed. Every day he committed himself to this belief, even if he did not know.

Hortencia looked at me with an expression of sadness. "I believe I am doing the right thing," she said. "What other choice do I have?"

———

"There is magnificent risk in belief," writes Anne Dufourmantelle. Belief is not easy. It is animated by ambiguity, a fundamental reality that undermines the possibility of moral certainty or absolutes. Simone de Beauvoir writes of ambiguity that it is a "genuine condition of our life from which we must draw our strength to live and our reason for acting." From this perspective, ambiguity is the ground of ethical action that recognizes our own limits when grappling with the complexity of the world.

Throughout my fieldwork, mothers talked about their belief that they were doing the right thing in sending their kids to anexos. *Yo creo, yo creo*, I believe, I believe, was a common refrain during conversations. Their belief was conditioned by the harsh realities in which they lived. In belief, they found ways of survival and sustenance, but always in the face of ambiguity.

In 2021, I gave grand rounds in Harvard's psychiatry department. My talk focused on the implications of anexos for rethinking a universal standard for ethical addiction treatment. One of the attendees posed a question I regularly receive when I deliver talks to physicians: Do anexos work? Because the question usually seeks to know whether anexos help people kick alcohol and drug addiction for good, I proceeded to respond in the usual manner—reminding the audience that the issue of drug addiction is secondary to the question of safety from violence. In this regard, anexos "work" but are unavoidably flawed, for the world in which they exist is saturated with violence. But on this occasion, the attendee was getting at something else. She rephrased the question. "Do anexos help mothers who commit their children to them?"

My initial response came easily: yes. I was thinking about Hortencia and all the mothers I knew who'd turned to anexos to keep their children, and sometimes themselves, safe from harm. But my answer to her question was also insufficient, because there is no guarantee that the help anexos offer will be absolute or lasting, or that the cost for securing it will be bearable. In this sense, anexos are variably horrid and hopeful. They are also the grounds for an ethics of care that cannot be known or measured in advance.

After a brief pause, I revised my response to the question about the help that anexos offer mothers. "Sometimes and in some ways," I said. "Yes, sometimes anexos help."

———————

The Church of Santo Domingo faced the plaza. The front facade of the baroque temple is built from tezontle, a reddish volcanic stone, and cantera rosa. I watched as the stones faded from pink to gray with the setting sun. The air turned chilly and damp. It would rain soon. I suggested that Hortencia and I find a nearby restaurant or café, but she shook her head no. She wanted to sit awhile longer.

"I have a gift for you," Hortencia said, breaking a long silence. She rummaged around in her purse and pulled out a laminated prayer card. It showed Santo Niño de Atocha. "Protector of prisoners and travelers," Hortencia said.

I stared at the image of the Divine Child and thought of the votive candle alight in Hortencia's home. Was Daniel the prisoner and I the traveler? I turned the card over and began to read the prayer.

Cast your merciful look upon my troubled heart. Take from me all affliction and despair.

Hortencia stood and looked around the plaza. It was time to go, which meant heading in opposite directions on República de Brasil.

"*Cuídate,*" Hortencia said as we hugged each other goodbye.

"*Cuídate,*" I repeated as she turned and walked away.

———————

President López Obrador's security strategy—demilitarization, job creation, and educational opportunities—has not been borne out. Since taking office, he's strengthened the armed forces and expanded their reach. In 2019, López Obrador created a national guard, a supposedly civilian-controlled police force that he said would take soldiers off the streets. But the national guard is commanded by a former military officer, and former soldiers compose most of its ranks. "The National Guard is the Army in a different uniform," writes Esteban Illades in a scathing article in *The Washington Post.*

In April 2021, the United Nations Committee on Enforced Disappearances released a report that expressed grave concern about Mexico's militarized focus on security and the risk it posed for human rights. It named the Mexican military and the national guard as among the most frequently cited in disciplinary hearings for human rights violations by the Mexican government's National Human Rights Commission. Further extending the military's power was López Obrador's allocation of $10 billion to the armed forces in 2022. The National Guard received an additional $2.5 billion.

La violencia continues, and so does the narrative that the capital is immune from it. During a press conference in May 2022, Mexico City mayor Claudia Sheinbaum declared that the capital was one of the safest cities in the world, with homicide rates lower than New York, New Orleans, and Los Angeles. She attributed the reduction of crime to new security measures implemented during her administration. Immediately following her announcement, major publications, including *Proceso* and *Reforma*, refuted Sheinbaum's claim and questioned the veracity of government statistics. New numbers were presented that showed increases in extortion rates and homicide. Sheinbaum pushed back, suggesting that the refutation of her advances against crime revealed pervasive sexism.

Whether the critiques were sexist or not, life in poor and working-class communities across Mexico grew more precarious, ensuring the continued proliferation of anexos. In November 2019, Padrino Francisco established another anexo, Serenity II. Within weeks of opening, Serenity II housed seventeen anexados, most of them under the age of twenty-five. The youngest was Nati, a sixteen-year-old girl with Down syndrome who hailed from Morelia, the capital of war-torn Michoacán. Before she was committed to the anexo, Nati was kidnapped and held for ransom for two days while her parents scraped together enough money to secure her release. Like other stories I heard, Nati's parents thought it safer for their daughter to take up residence with a relative in Mexico City. When that relative couldn't care for her any longer, she committed her to Serenity II.

Padrino Francisco assured me that Nati was treated well. But given the kinds of behavior I witnessed at anexos—harassment, insults, punishments, beatings—I worried about her. I hoped there was someone looking after her—someone like Sheila, who protected Catorce from the harassment of their peers. Or Omar, who inspired gentleness in his fellow anexados.

"Who looks after Nati?" I asked Padrino Francisco.

"We all do," he said.

Shortly after the opening of Serenity II, COVID-19 hit Mexico. There were more than 2.4 million cases of the disease reported in June 2021, making Mexico a global hot spot." Tests, vaccines, and face masks were scarce, especially in poor areas. Padrino Francisco reported that no one wore face masks in his anexos and that everyone had the disease. "Lockdown" was nothing new. "We're used to it," he joked. But things did change. Many anexados were kicked out of Padrino Francisco's two anexos because their out-of-work families could no longer afford the monthly fee. The number of anexados at Serenity II dwindled from seventeen to six.

Some studies found a significant decrease in crime during lockdown, which may explain the narrative heralded by Mayor Sheinbaum. This may partly be due to reductions in mobility, which likely made reporting crimes, already low to begin with, more difficult or unlikely. But other studies showed that while "conventional" crimes like burglary and vehicle theft went down, COVID had no effect on violent crimes related to kidnappings and homicides. "Drug lords don't stay at home," a study in the *Journal of Criminal Justice* concluded.

The fear of contagion receded as vaccines became more widely available. Restaurants reopened, kids went back to in-person schooling, and international travel to Mexico rose. But so did signs that *la violencia* was ramping up to pre-COVID levels. In June 2022, gunmen assassinated two Jesuit priests inside a church in the northern state of Chihuahua, prompting Pope Francis to exclaim on Twitter, "How many killings there are in Mexico!" In August 2022, drug cartels and gangs went on violent rampages in four states, shutting down roads, businesses, and schools. In September, a report from the nongovernmental organization Global Witness named Mexico the deadliest country for environmental and land defense activists, with fifty-four activists killed in 2021 alone. According to the Mexican Commission for the Defense and Promotion of Human Rights, 45,000 people fled their homes due to violence in 2021.

Many officials say that the violence was exacerbated by President López Obrador's anticrime strategy. But the president has consistently downplayed the violence or blamed it on previous administrations. "All this is the rotten fruit of a policy of corruption, of impunity, which has been implemented since the time of Felipe Calderón," he said when asked about the murders of the priests.

"Not much has changed," Padrino Mike told me when we spoke by phone in September 2022. The confessions delivered at Grupo San Hipólito attested to this. One given by a thirteen-year-old boy recounted the murder of a beloved grandfather in the state of Jalisco. Another described a neighborhood terrorized by local gangs. But there were moments of levity, too. Padrino Mike talked about a new anexado who knew a few magic tricks. "It's a real circus," Padrino Mike laughed.

I asked him about Toño, the anexado who, during his confession, imagined "the whole thing crashing." Padrino Mike called Toño a "truth sayer." But no one at the anexo knew his whereabouts. Like so many young men and women, he seemed to vanish after leaving the anexo.

As we were about to hang up, Padrino Mike said he had bad news. Madrina had *cáncer de mama*, breast cancer. Chemo was hard, but she was strong. She'd pull through. The women in the building who prepared foods for the anexados also brought her soup and herbal remedies. She was never alone.

A long silence opened between us. I imagined Madrina on the sofa in what I thought of as the waiting room. Padrino Mike must pass her by dozens of times a day as he walked to and from the room where the anexados lived. Was he tender? Did he caress her hand or kiss her brow? Did she let him? The news of Madrina's cancer reminded me that all the challenges of everyday life, including sickness, existed in anexos, too. Life went on in these little rooms.

I promised Padrino Mike I'd call Madrina, but I didn't—at least not right away. Instead, I called my mother. The phone rang five or six times before I finally hung up. But before the familiar feeling of disconnection sank in, my telephone rang. It was my mother, out of breath from pulling the weeds that dotted her desert acre. "Sorry," she said. "Sorry I missed your call."

EPILOGUE

·

There are five dormant volcanoes within ten miles of my mother's house. Kate and I used to visit them on weekends, exploring their cones and dark basalt rocks. We'd scurry up a boulder, smoke a joint, and look down on the Rio Grande Valley. Sun setting behind us, we'd talk about the places we planned to live. Paris, New York, San Francisco. The volcanic landscape was the backdrop of our dreams.

In the fall of 2022, on a return trip to New Mexico, I visited the volcanoes once more. It was a chilly weekday afternoon, and I was alone in the field. I walked the trail toward the lower slopes of Black Volcano, following the fingerlike flows of ossified lava that radiated out from it. The surrounding landscape, a mix of desert grasses and sagebrush, shimmered gold in the sun.

I found a rock and sat, looking down onto Albuquerque's sprawl. Edging closer to the volcanoes were low-cost tract houses and trailers, neigborhoods populated by the city's growing Mexican population. A few days before my visit home, sixty undocumented immigrants, mostly from Mexico, were found locked up in a trailer home not far from my mother's house. Three weeks earlier, fifty immigrants, many of them young children, were rescued from a one-bedroom apartment where they were being held for ransom. Some recounted being trafficked for labor; others said they left Mexico because of *la violencia*. When asked by a reporter if she'd make the dangerous migrant journey again, one woman answered,

"I don't know. It seems that there is no safe place for me. Not there, not here."

How many undocumented migrants might be held captive in my hometown? How many anexos, like Madrina Trini's Grupo Amor y Servicio, sought to keep them safe?

Mexico is suffering a profound humanitarian crisis perpetuated by the United States with military aid and illegally trafficked guns. The war in Mexico reaches deep into the United States, where it is characterized by drug seizures, overdose statistics, and refugees fleeing unremitting violence. The spread of anexos in the United States keeps pace with the worsening conditions in Mexico. Anexos dot a perilous landscape that spans both sides of the Rio Grande.

I sat in the lava field waiting for dusk, trying to push these thoughts out of my mind. I wanted to see the sun cast shadows across the volcano's angular rock, and the amber-colored light glisten across the city. I wanted to watch the moon, nearly full, make its way from behind the Sandia Mountains. The slight chill turned cold, but I waited for signs of life that could not be extinguished.

———

More than a decade has passed since I first ventured to Mexico to study the City of Health. My research there was supposed to relieve my childhood ache and the sense of powerlessness that accompanied years of caring for addicts in a setting of poverty. But the hypermodern campus and the promise of technocrats to improve Mexico's widening health inequalities were never realized. It wasn't just real estate disputes and the challenges posed by the volcanic landscape that got in the way. It was the violence that had taken over Mexico, a profound crisis that has stymied the present and future of the country, with no end in sight.

In the shadow of the fantasy of Health City are countless little rooms where people care for each other in ways that correspond to the reality of Mexico. Rooms like Serenity, Casa Dolorosa, and Grupo San Hipólito. These rooms couldn't be more different from the ideals of Health City.

They're not sleek, spacious, or investment driven. Their practices of care do not correspond to the dictates of money or professional ethics, but to the experiential proximity of Mexico's most marginalized citizens. And while Health City remains a work of imagination, anexos proliferate in neighborhoods of intensifying violence, the inhabitants of which carry the burdens of their own protection and survival. These rooms embody these burdens in their harsh material conditions, in therapeutic practices, and in testimony.

The growing and changing population of anexos makes visible the reality of Mexico's present. Rather than providing a way out, anexos foreground this reality, while challenging the way it is normally understood. They represent not just violence and despair, but also care and hope. In so doing, anexos do not deflect ambiguities of life. Instead, anexos draw our attention to them, if only we open our eyes.

———

In April 2023, I returned to Mexico City with my sixteen-year-old daughters. On the plane ride south, they chatted about the things they wanted to do over our weeklong visit. First thing: visit Parque España, where they had played as young children.

Our Airbnb was only a few blocks from the park, so we headed over there after dropping our luggage off. Outdoor cafés bustled and neighborhood boutiques beckoned, but the girls were singularly focused. When we approached the park, their pace hastened with excitement. I watched as they made their way to their favorite play structure, a spider climber whose shape recalled Cuicuilco's circular pyramid. They scrambled up the ropes, their flushed faces turned toward me with wide smiles.

My attention was split between watching the girls and trading text messages with Hortencia. We were trying to firm up plans to meet, but her work schedule made fixing a place and time difficult. Finally, she suggested meeting at the Metropolitan Cathedral on Friday, telling me she'd be by the Altar of Forgiveness, where Christ hovers over his devotees. But on the morning we were to meet, she texted that she had to work and couldn't make it. I wondered if what she said was true. A few hours later she texted again and said she could see me Thursday afternoon.

We decided to meet at San Hipólito Church, which Hortencia called "an equal distance between us." I arrived there first and stood near the main entrance, where vendors sold statues and scapulary medals of San Judas Tadeo. I bought a twelve-inch figure of the saint, thinking I'd give it to my mother, whose own collection of *santos* lined her fireplace mantel.

Hortencia was late and I nervous; nearly five years had passed since I'd last seen her and I wasn't sure what condition I'd find her in. I was relieved when I spotted her walking brusquely toward me, dressed in a flowery blouse and jeans. She gave me a stiff embrace, stepped back, and looked around. "I haven't been here in years," she said.

We walked to Toks, a nearby chain restaurant with mostly Mexican food. As soon as we were seated, Hortencia announced that she wasn't hungry and asked for coffee. I ordered enough food for both of us, anticipating that she would eat once it arrived, but it sat untouched on the table.

"Anselma died two years ago," Hortencia said, breaking a silence that had spread between us. "It was a sickness," she added, not specifying its kind. I waited for Hortencia to say more but she didn't. I knew how much Anselma meant to her. She was her guardian, her mother, her friend. She'd given her the gift of home.

Hortencia told me that Anselma's siblings wanted to sell the apartment where Hortencia had lived since she was sixteen years old. I asked her what she was going to do. She shook her head; she didn't know. She had a few options, but none of them were very good. Her older sisters were scattered across the city and had large families of their own. A neighbor offered to rent her an apartment in her vecindad, but it was too expensive. Her in-laws in Jiutepec had an extra room, but she was angry at them for putting her in the position of having to move, especially now.

"I'm a grandmother," Hortencia announced.

She pulled out her phone and showed me a picture of her granddaughter, Luna. She was chubby and cute, with short black hair and dimples. I scrolled through the photos, moving back in time, from toddler to newborn. One photo showed Luna in Daniel's arms. Luna was reaching up to touch his face, her hand frozen in midair. Father and daughter gazed at each other with curiosity.

I handed the phone back to Hortencia.

"She lives with me," Hortencia said with a heavy sigh.

"And Daniel? The mother?" I asked. She shook her head no.

"She calls *me mamá*," Hortencia said, tapping her chest.

For the next hour, Hortencia described having to work less to care for her granddaughter. When she did work, she had to pay a neighbor to watch Luna. Money was tight and she was exhausted, but she called Luna a blessing.

I thought about how hard Hortencia had worked to keep Daniel safe in anexos. All those years taking on extra shifts at restaurants and hotels to pay the anexo's fees, and her constant worry about whether she was doing the right thing. I wondered if her efforts had made a difference. Hortencia must have sensed my question because she looked at me and said, "I haven't given up. But everything I do now is for Luna."

That evening, I suggested to my daughters that we return to Parque España one last time before heading home to San Francisco. I craved seeing them running wild on the playground, innocent of worry. But they were tired and wanted a movie instead—not at a theater, but in *la cama de mamá*. They had used that phrase, mama's bed, when they were little. "Let's sleep in *la cama de mamá*," they'd say. I hadn't realized how much I missed hearing them say it until that moment.

We settled on my bed, me in the middle, and scrolled through the offerings on Netflix. The girls couldn't agree on anything, but I didn't care. All that mattered was that their bodies were turned toward me, safe and at ease.

RECOMMENDED READING

Malcolm Lowry's *Under the Volcano* (Perennial Classics) is a touchstone for this book, as are Lowry's letters to his editor, compiled in *Sursum Corda! The Collected Letters of Malcolm Lowry* (Jonathan Cape). For a fascinating biography of Lowry, see Gordon Bowker, *Pursued by Furies: A Life of Malcolm Lowry* (St. Martin's Press).

Before it fizzled, there was much fanfare about Mexico City's Campus Biometrópolis, the so-called City of Health. The United Nations' *Shanghai Manual: A Guide for Sustainable Urban Development in the 21st Century* characterizes the megaproject as "a clear example of how science and technology can be used to trigger new economic activities directly linked to the information economy." Ghostly representations of Foster + Partners' master plan can be found online. For work on the politics of megaprojects, see Bent Flyvbjerg, Nils Bruzelius, and Werner Rothengatter's *Megaprojects and Risk: An Anatomy of Ambition* (Cambridge University Press); Glen David Kuecker and Alejandro Puga, eds., *Mapping the Megalopolis: Order and Disorder in Mexico City* (Lexington Books); and Felicity D. Scott, *Architecture or Techno-Utopia: Politics After Modernism* (MIT Press). On the political and social implications of Mexico's University City, see Carlos Lazo, "Piedra sobre Piedra," in *Pensamiento y destino de la ciudad universitaria de México* (M. A. Porrúa). Mario Pani and Enrique del Moral's *La construcción de la Ciudad Universitaria del Pedregal* (Universidad Nacional Autónoma de México) offers a rich history of University City's creation.

Readers interested in contemporary and historical portraits of Mexico's capital might turn to the following: Nick Caistor, *Mexico City: A Cultural and Literary Companion* (Interlink Books); Vera S. Candiani, *Dreaming of Dry Land: Environmental Transformation in Colonial Mexico City* (Stanford University Press); Cornelius Conover, *Pious Imperialism: Spanish Rule and the Cult of Saints in Mexico City* (University of New Mexico Press); Diane E. Davis, *Urban Leviathan: Mexico City in the Twentieth Century* (Temple University Press); David William Foster, *Mexico City in Contemporary Mexican Cinema* (University of Texas Press); Rubén Gallo, ed., *The Mexico City Reader* (University of Wisconsin Press); Ben A. Gerlofs, *Monstrous Politics: Geography, Rights, and the Urban Revolution in Mexico City* (Vanderbilt University Press); Francisco Goldman, *The Interior Circuit: A Mexico City Chronicle* (Grove Press); Matthew C. Gutmann, *The Meanings of Macho: Being a Man in Mexico City* (University of California Press); Alicia Hernández Chávez, *Mexico: A Brief History* (University of California Press); Daniel Hernandez, *Down and Delirious in Mexico City: The Aztec Metropolis in the Twenty-First Century* (Scribner); Jonathan Kandell, *La Capital: The Biography of Mexico City* (Random House); Michael Johns, *The City of Mexico in the Age of Diaz* (University of Texas Press); Oscar Lewis, *The Children of Sánchez: Autobiography of a Mexican Family* (Random House); David Lida, *First Stop in the New World: Mexico City, the Capital of the 21st Century* (Riverhead Books); Enrique Espinosa López, *Ciudad de México: Compendio cronológico de su desarollo urbano, 1521–2000* (Instituto Politécnico Nacional); Rubén Martínez, *The Other Side: Notes from the New L.A., Mexico City, and Beyond* (Vintage Books); Pablo Piccato, *City of Suspects: Crime in Mexico City, 1900–1931* (Duke University Press); Mauricio Tenorio-Trillo, *I Speak of the City: Mexico City at the Turn of the Twentieth Century* (University of Chicago Press); Matthew Vitz, *A City on a Lake: Urban Political Ecology and the Growth of Mexico City* (Duke University Press); and Peter M. Ward, *Mexico City: The Production and Reproduction of an Urban Environment* (G. K. Hall).

The North American Free Trade Agreement went into effect on January 1, 1994, with promises of economic growth and better employment opportunities for Mexicans. Scholars have since shown that NAFTA led to deepening poverty and inequality in Mexico, especially for the agricultural sector. See Emmanuel Alvarado, "Poverty and Inequality in Mexico after NAFTA: Challenges, Setbacks and Implications" (*Estudios fronterizos* 9, no. 17); James M. Cypher and Raúl Delgado Wise, *Mexico's Economic Dilemma: The Developmental Failure of Neoliberalism* (Rowman & Littlefield Publishers); Gerardo Esquivel, *Desigualdad extrema en México: Concentración del poder económico y político* (Oxfam-Mexico); Gerardo Esquivel, "The Dynamics of Income Inequality in Mexico since NAFTA" (*Economía* 12, no. 1); Patricia Fernández-Kelly and Douglas S. Massey, "Borders for Whom? The Role of NAFTA in Mexico-U.S. Migration" (*The Annals of the American Academy of Political and Social Science* 610); Alyshia Gálvez, *Eating NAFTA: Trade, Food Policies, and the Destruction of Mexico* (University of California Press); Bill Ong Hing, *Ethical Borders: NAFTA, Globalization, and Mexican Migration* (Temple University Press); Asa Cristina Laurell, "Three Decades of Neoliberalism in Mexico: The Destruction of Society" (*International Journal of Health Services* 45, no. 2); Gerardo Otero, "Neoliberal Globalization, NAFTA, and Migration: Mexico's Loss of Food and Labor Sovereignty" (*Journal of Poverty* 15, no. 4); Pablo Ruiz Nápoles, "Neoliberal Reforms and NAFTA in Mexico" (*Economía UNAM* 14, no. 41); Elizabeth F. S. Roberts, "What Gets Inside: Violent Entanglements and Toxic Boundaries in Mexico City" (*Cultural Anthropology* 32, no. 4); Kathleen Staudt, "How NAFTA Has Changed Mexico" (*Current History* 117, no. 796); Lilia Domínguez-Villalobos and Flor Brown-Grossman, "Trade Liberalization and Gender Wage Inequality in Mexico" (*Feminist Economics* 16, no. 4); Sidney Weintraub, ed., *NAFTA's Impact on North America: The First Decade* (CSIS Press); Mark Weisbrot et al., "Did NAFTA Help Mexico? An Update After 23 Years" (*Mexican Law Review* 11, no. 1); and Albert Berry, ed., *Poverty, Economic Reform, and Income Distribution in Latin America* (Lynne Rienner Publishers). For work on how NAFTA facilitated the growth of the drug economy and, by extension, drug-related violence, see Alfredo Carlos, "Mexico 'Under Siege': Drug Cartels or U.S. Imperialism?" (*Latin American Perspectives* 41, no. 2) and Eduardo Hidalgo, Erik Hornung and Pablo Selaya, "NAFTA and Drug-Related Violence in Mexico" (CESifo Working Paper no. 9981).

Mexico's maquiladora industry expanded with the passage of NAFTA. The following readings offer critical perspectives on maquiladoras: Mary-Kay Bachour, "Disrupting the Myth of Maquila Disposability: Sites of Reproduction and Resistance in Juárez" (*Women's Studies International Forum* 48); David Bacon, *The Children of NAFTA: Labor Wars on the U.S./Mexico Border* (University of California Press); Altha J. Cravey, *Women and Work in Mexico's Maquiladoras* (Rowman & Littlefield); María Patricia Fernández-Kelly, *For We Are Sold, I and My People: Women and Industry in Mexico's Frontier* (State University of New York Press); Rosa-Linda Fregoso and Cynthia Bejarano, eds., *Terrorizing Women: Femicide in the Américas* (Duke University Press); Norma Iglesias Prieto, *Beautiful Flowers of the Maquiladora: Life Histories of Women Workers in Tijuana* (University of Texas Press, Institute of Latin American Studies); David Tittensor and Fethi Mansouri, "The Feminisation of Migration? A Critical Overview," in *The Politics of Women and Migration in the Global South* (Palgrave Pivot London); Carolyn Tuttle, *Mexican Women in American Factories: Free Trade and Exploitation on the Border* (University of Texas Press); and Devon G. Peña, *The Terror of the Machine: Technology, Work, Gender, and Ecology on the U.S.-Mexico Border* (CMAS Books). For analyses of the relationship between maquiladoras and the murder of women in Ciudad Juárez, see Alicia Gaspar de Alba, ed., with Georgina Guzmán, *Making a Killing: Femicide, Free Trade, and La Frontera* (University of Texas Press); Julia Estela Monárrez Fragoso, *Trauma de una injusticia: Feminicidio sexual sistémico en Ciudad Juárez* (Colegio de la Frontera Norte / M. A. Porrúa); Mariana Berlanga Gayón, "El color del feminicidio: De los asesinatos de mujeres a la violencia generalizada" (*El Cotidiano* 29, no. 184); Sergio González Rodríguez, *The Femicide Machine* (Semiotext[e]); and Melissa W. Wright, "The Dialectics of Still Life: Murder, Women, and Maquiladoras (*Public Culture* 11, no. 3). Lorenzo Vigas's fictional film *La Caja* (The Box), set in Chihuahua, links the proliferation of maquiladoras, the brutal reality faced by the female workforce, and the disappearance of women. Lourdes Portillo's *Señorita Extraviada* (Missing Young Woman) is a documentary film that examines the disappearance and murder of more than 350 young women in Juárez, many of whom worked in maquiladoras.

Scholarly and journalistic books on Mexico's narco war are a vast and growing group. Readers looking for an overview of Mexico's drug trade might try a few of Luis Astorga's books, including *El siglo de las drogas: El narcotráfico, del Porfiriato al nuevo milenio* (Plaza y Janés); *Drogas sin fronteras* (Grijalbo); *Mitología del "narcotraficante" en México* (UNAM / Plaza y Valdés). Works by other authors include Carmen Boullosa and Mike Wallace, *A Narco History: How the United States and Mexico Jointly Created the "Mexican Drug War"* (OR Books); Isaac Campos, *Home Grown: Marijuana and the Origins of Mexico's War on Drugs* (University of North Carolina Press); Francisco Cruz, *El cártel de Juárez* (Planeta); Froylán Enciso, *Nuestra historia narcótica: Pasajes para (re)legalizar las drogas en México* (Debate); Paul Gootenberg, *The Oxford Handbook of Global Drug History* (Oxford University Press); Ioan Grillo, *El Narco: Inside Mexico's Criminal Insurgency* (Bloomsbury); Anabel Hernández, *Narcoland: The Mexican Drug Lords and Their Godfathers* (Verso); Wil G. Pansters and Benjamin T. Smith, eds., *Histories of Drug Trafficking in Twentieth-Century Mexico* (University of New Mexico Press); Matthew R. Pembleton and Daniel Weimer, "US Foreign Relations and the New Drug History" (*Social History of Alcohol and Drugs* 33, no. 1); David A. Shirk, *The Drug War in Mexico: Confronting a Shared Threat* (Council on Foreign Relations / Center for Preventive Action); Benjamin T. Smith, *The Dope: The Real History of the Mexican Drug Trade* (W. W. Norton); Aileen Teague, "The War on Drugs in Mexico," in *The War on Drugs*, ed. David Farber (New York University Press); Guillermo Valdés Castellanos, *Historia del narcotráfico en México* (Aguilar); and Deborah J. Yashar, *Homicidal Ecologies: Illicit Economies and Complicit States in Latin America* (Cambridge University Press).

Works that help to understand the causes and consequences of drug-related violence in Mexico include José Antonio Aguilar, "Las bases sociales del crimen organizado y de la violencia en México" (*Centro de Investigación y Estudios en Seguridad*); Rubén Aguilar and Jorge G. Castañeda, *El Narco: La guerra fallida* (Punto de Lectura); Peter Andreas, "Drugs and War: What is the Relationship?" (*Annual Review of Political Science* 22); Luis Astorga and David A. Shirk, "Drug Trafficking Organizations and Counter-Drug Strategies in the U.S.-Mexican Context (UC San Diego, Center for U.S.-Mexican

Studies); Laura H. Atuesta and Alejandro Madrazo Lajous, eds., *Las vio-lencias: En busca de la política pública detrás de la guerra contra las drogas* (Centro de Investigación y Docencia Económicas); Lydia Cacho and Ana-bel Hernández, among others, in *The Sorrows of Mexico: An Indictment of Their Country's Failings by Seven Exceptional Writers* (Quercus); Guadalupe Correa-Cabrera, *Los Zetas Inc.: Criminal Corporations, Energy, and Civil War in Mexico* (University of Texas Press); Viridiana Rios Contreras, "The Role of Drug-Related Violence and Extortion in Promoting Mexican Migra-tion: Unexpected Consequences of a Drug War" (*Latin American Research Review* 49, no. 3); David T. Courtwright, "Drug Wars, Drug Violence, and Drug Addiction in the Americas" (*Criminal Justice Ethics* 42, no. 1); Me-lissa Dell, "Trafficking Networks and the Mexican Drug War" (*American Economic Review* 105, no. 6); Arindrajit Dube, Oeindrila Dube, and Omar García-Ponce, "Cross-Border Spillover: US Gun Laws and Violence in Mex-ico" (*American Political Science Review* 107, no. 3); Jessica Wax-Edwards, "Collateral Damage: Necropolitical Lives in the Mexican Drug War" in *War in Film*, ed. Frank Jacob (Büchner-Verlag); Ted Enamorado et al., "Income Inequality and Violent Crime: Evidence from Mexico's Drug War" (*Journal of Development Economics* 120); Gustavo Fondevila and Miguel Quintana-Navarrete, "War Hypotheses: Drug Trafficking, Sovereignty and the Armed Forces in Mexico" (*Bulletin of Latin American Research* 34, no. 4); Nilda M. Garcia, *Mexico's Drug War and Criminal Networks: The Dark Side of Social Media* (Routledge); John Gibler, *To Die in Mexico: Dispatches from Inside the Drug War* (City Lights); Ioan Grillo, *Blood Gun Money: How America Arms Gangs and Cartels* (Bloomsbury); Joel Salvador Herrera, "Cultivating Violence: Trade Liberalization, Illicit Labor, and the Mexican Drug Trade" (*Latin American Politics and Society* 61, no. 3); Edward Hunt, "Staying the Course in Mexico: The Role of the US in the Drug War, 2006–present" (*Third World Quarterly* 40, no. 6); Claudio Lomnitz, "The Ethos and Telos of Mi-choacán's Knights Templar" (*Representations* 147, no. 1); Beatriz Magaloni et al., "Living in Fear: The Dynamics of Extortion in Mexico's Drug War" (*Comparative Political Studies* 53, no. 7); Angélica Durán-Martínez, *The Poli-tics of Drug Violence: Criminals, Cops, and Politicians in Columbia and Mex-ico* (Oxford University Press); Jorge Fernández Menéndez, *El otro poder: Las redes del narcotráfico, la política y la violencia en México* (Aguilar); Rolando Ochoa, *Intimate Crimes: Kidnapping, Gangs, and Trust in Mexico City* (Oxford University Press); Dawn Paley, *Drug War Capitalism* (AK Press); Guillermo Trejo and Sandra Ley, *Votes, Drugs, and Violence: The Political Logic of Criminal Wars in Mexico* (Cambridge University Press); Pablo Piccato, *Historia mínima de la violencia en México* (El Colegio de México AC); Ricardo Ravelo, *Herencia maldita: El reto de Calderón y el nuevo mapa del narcotráfico* (Grijalbo); Viridiana Rios, "How Government Coordination Controlled Organized Crime: The Case of Mexico's Cocaine Markets (*Journal of Conflict Resolution* 59, no. 8), and "The Role of Drug-Related Violence and Extortion in Promoting Mexican Migration: Unexpected Consequences of a Drug War" (*Latin American Research Review* 49, no. 3); David Shirk and Joel Wallman, "Understanding Mexico's Drug Violence" (*Journal of Conflict Resolution* 59, no. 8); Jeremy Slack, *Deported to Death: How Drug Violence Is Changing Migration on the US-Mexico Border* (University of California Press); Aileen Teague, "Mexico's Dirty War on Drugs: Source Control and Dissidence in Drug Enforcement" (*The Social History of Alcohol and Drugs* 33, no. 1); María Celia Toro, *Mexico's "War" on Drugs: Causes and Consequences* (Lynne Rienner Publishers); Guillermo Trejo and Sandra Ley, "Why Did Drug Cartels Go to War in Mexico? Subnational Party Alternation, the Breakdown of Criminal Protection, and the Onset of Large-Scale Violence" (*Comparative Political Studies* 51, no. 7); Teun Voeten, *Mexican Drug Violence: Hybrid Warfare, Predatory Capitalism and the Logic of Cruelty* (Xlibris); and Peter Watt and Roberto Zepeda, *Drug War Mexico: Politics, Neoliberalism and Violence in the New Narcoeconomy* (Zed Books).

Books on Mexico's democracy and its future in the wake of the transition from the Institutional Revolutionary Party (PRI) include Roger Bartra, *La sombra del futuro: Reflexiones sobre la transición mexicana* (Fondo de Cultura Económica); Kathleen Bruhn, *Taking on Goliath: The Emergence of a New Left Party and the Struggle for Democracy in Mexico* (Penn State University Press); Héctor Aguilar Camín and Jorge G. Castañeda, *Un futuro para México* (Santillana Ediciones Generales); Roderic Ai Camp, *Politics in Mexico: The Decline of Authoritarianism* (Oxford University Press) and *Politics* in Mexico: Democratic Consolidation or Decline? (Oxford University Press); Miguel Ángel Centeno, Democracy within Reason: Technocratic Revolution in Mexico (Penn State University Press); Judith Gentlemen, ed., Mexican Politics in Transition (Routledge); Jorge I. Domínguez et al., eds., Mexico's Evolving Democracy: A Comparative Study of the 2012 Elections (Johns Hopkins University Press); Claudio A. Holzner, "The Poverty of Democracy: Neoliberal Reforms and Political Participation of the Poor in Mexico" (Latin American Politics and Society 49, no. 2); Guillermo Hurtado, México sin sentido (Siglo Veintiuno Editores); María Inclán, The Zapatista Movement and Mexico's Democratic Transition: Mobilization, Success, and Survival (Oxford University Press); Joy K. Langston, Democratization and Authoritarian Party Survival: Mexico's PRI (Oxford University Press); Gerardo Otero, ed., Mexico in Transition: Neoliberal Globalism, the State and Civil Society (Zed Books); Dolores Trevizo, Rural Protest and the Making of Democracy in Mexico, 1968–2000 (Penn State University Press); Andrew Selee and Jacqueline Peschard, eds., Mexico's Democratic Challenges: Politics, Government, and Society (Woodrow Wilson Center Press); Jo Tuckman, Mexico: Democracy Interrupted (Yale University Press); Joseph S. Tulchin and Andrew D. Selee, eds., Mexico's Politics and Society in Transition (Lynne Rienner Publishers); José Luis Velasco, Insurgency, Authoritarianism, and Drug Trafficking in Mexico's "Democratization" (Routledge); Louise E. Walker, Waking from the Dream: Mexico's Middle Classes after 1968 (Stanford University Press); and Gareth Williams, The Mexican Exception: Sovereignty, Police, and Democracy (Palgrave Macmillan).

The drug trade and drug-related violence have become important themes in Mexican literature. These books tell stories of migration, violence, and the precariousness of life: Roberto Bolaño, 2666 (Farrar, Straus and Giroux); Yuri Herrera, Kingdom Cons (And Other Stories); Élmer Mendoza, Balas de plata (Tusquets Editores); Emiliano Monge, Las tierras arrasadas (Random House); Antonio Ortuño, La fila india (Oceano de México); Victor Hugo Rascón Banda, Contrabando (Planeta); Carlos Velázquez, La biblia vaquera (Sexto Piso); Juan Pablo Villalobos, Down the Rabbit Hole (Farrar, Straus and Giroux); and Heriberto Yépez, Al otro lado (Planeta).

The poet, essayist, novelist, and founder of *el Moviemiento por la Paz con Justicia y Dignidad* (Movement for Peace with Justice and Dignity) Javier Sicilia has written profound works on violence following the murder of his son in 2011, including *El deshabitado* (Grijalbo). María Rivera's haunting poem "Los muertos" names those killed in the drug war and has become a symbol of resistance to violence. English translations of the poem can be found online. In *Antígona González* (Les Figues Press), poet Sara Uribe draws on the myth of Antigone to draw attention to Mexico's disappeared. For scholarly analyses on the political and aesthetic implications of Mexican literary engagements with violence, especially as it relates to drug-related violence, see Hermann Herlinghaus, *Violence without Guilt: Ethical Narratives from the Global South* (Palgrave Macmillan) and *Narcoepics: A Global Aesthetics of Sobriety* (Bloomsbury Academic); Raúl Diego Rivera Hernández, *Narratives of Vulnerability in Mexico's War on Drugs* (Palgrave Macmillan); Fernando Escalante Gonzalbo, *El crimen como realidad y representación: Contribución para una historia del presente* (Colegio de México); and Oswaldo Zavala, *Drug Cartels Do Not Exist: Narco-Trafficking and Culture in the US and Mexico* (Vanderbilt University Press).

The mass kidnapping and disappearance of forty-three students from the Raúl Isidro Burgos Rural Teachers' College in Iguala, Guerrero, in 2014 led to outrage and protests in Mexico and abroad. Works on the social and political significance of these events include Carlos Martín Beristain, *El tiempo de Ayotzinapa* (Editorial Foca); John Gibler, *Una historia oral de la infamia: Los ataques contra los normalistas de Ayotzinapa* (Grijalbo/Sur+); Anabel Hernández, *A Massacre in Mexico: The True Story Behind the Missing Forty-Three Students* (Verso); Tommaso Gravante, "Forced Disappearance as a Collective Cultural Trauma in the Ayotzinapa Movement" (*Latin American Perspectives* 47, no. 6); and José Manuel Valenzuela,ed., *Juvenicidio: Ayotzinapa y las vidas precarias en América Latina y España* (NED Ediciones). Scholarship and nongovernmental reports on disappearance in Mexico include Dawn Marie Paley, "Cold War, Neoliberal War, and Disappearance: Observations from Mexico" (*Latin American Perspectives* 48, no. 1); Amnesty International, *Confronting a Nightmare: Disappearances in Mexico*; Sylvia Karl, "Rehumanizing the Disappeared: Spaces of Memory in Mexico and the Liminality of Transitional Justice" (*American Quarterly* 66, no. 3); Paola Marín and Gastón Alzate, eds. *Cartografías críticas, volumen I: Prácticas políticas y poéticas que piensan la pérdida y la desaparición forzada* (Ediciones KARPA); Francisco Ferrándiz and Antonius C. G. M. Robben, eds., *Necropolitics: Mass Graves and Exhumations in the Age of Human Rights* (University of Pennsylvania Press); Silvana Mandolessi and Katia Olalde, eds., *Disappearances in Mexico: From the "Dirty War" to the "War on Drugs"* (Routledge); Federico Mastrogiovanni, *Ni vivos ni muertos: La desaparición forzada en México como estrategia de terror* (Grijalbo); Sergio González Rodríguez, *Los 43 de Iguala, México: Verdad y reto de los estudiantes desaparecidos* (Editorial Anagrama); Alejandro Vélez Salas, *Narrativas interdisciplinarias sobre desaparición de personas en México* (Comisión Nacional de los Derechos Humanos México); Marcela Turati and Daniela Rea, eds., *Entre las cenizas: Historias de vida en tiempos de muerte* (Sur+); Human Rights Watch, *Mexico's Disappeared: The Enduring Cost of a Crisis Ignored*; Open Society Justice Initiative, *Undeniable Atrocities: Confronting Crimes Against Humanity in Mexico*.

For reading on Mexico's *guerra sucia*, see Alexandra Délano Alonso and Benjamin Nienass, "The Struggle for Memory and Justice in Mexico" (*Current History* 121, no. 832); Sergio Quezada Aguayo, *1968: Los archivos de la violencia* (Grijalbo); Alberto Ulloa Bornemann, *Surviving Mexico's Dirty War: A Political Prisoner's Memoir* (Temple University Press); Fernando Herrera Calderón and Adela Cedillo, *Challenging Authoritarianism in Mexico: Revolutionary Struggles and the Dirty War, 1964–1982* (Routledge); Elaine Carey, *Plaza of Sacrifices: Gender, Power, and Terror in 1968 Mexico* (University of New Mexico Press); Susana Draper, *1968 Mexico: Constellations of Freedom and Democracy* (Duke University Press); George F. Flaherty, *Hotel Mexico: Dwelling on the '68 Movement* (University of California Press); Raúl Álvarez Garín, *La estela de Tlatelolco: Una reconstrucción histórica del Movimiento estudiantil de 68* (Grijalbo); Claudio Lomnitz, ed., *1968–2018: Historia colectiva de medio siglo* (Universidad Nacional Autónoma de México); Silvana Mandolessi and Katia Olalde Rico, eds. *Disappearances in Mexico: From the "Dirty War" to the "War on Drugs"* (Routledge); Carlos Monsiváis, *El 68: La tradición de la resistencia* (Ediciones Era); Carlos Montemayor, *La violencia de estado en México: Antes y después de 1968* (Grijalbo); Jacinto Rodríguez Munguía, *1968: Todos los culpables* (Debate); Wil G. Pansters,ed., *Violence, Coercion, and State-Making in Twentieth-Century Mexico: The Other Half of the Centaur* (Stanford University Press); Jaime M. Pensado, *Rebel Mexico: Student Unrest and Authoritarian Political Culture During the Long Sixties* (Stanford University Press); Jaime M. Pensado and Enrique C. Ochoa, editors, *México Beyond 1968: Revolutionaries, Radicals, and Repression During the Global Sixties and Subversive Seventies* (University of Arizona Press); Elena Poniatowska's *La noche de Tlatelolco: Testimonios de historia oral* (Ediciones Era) and *Massacre in Mexico* (University of Missouri Press); Paco Ignacio Taibo II, *'68: The Mexican Autumn of the Tlatelolco Massacre* (Seven Stories Press); Álvaro Vázquez Mantecón, ed., *Memorial del 68* (Universidad Nacional Autónoma de México); and Daniela Rea, *Nadie les pidió perdón: Historias de impunidad y resistencia* (Ediciones Urano).

The following works and interviews offer accounts of the 1985 earthquake in Mexico City: Daniel Cazés, ed., *Volver a nacer: Memorial del '85* (La Jornada); Diane E. Davis, "Reverberations: Mexico City's 1985 Earthquake and the Transformation of the Capital," in *The Resilient City: How Modern Cities Recover from Disaster*, ed. Lawrence J. Vale and Thomas J. Campanella (Oxford University Press); Ramón de la Fuente and Michael Vale, "The Mental Health Consequences of the 1985 Earthquakes in Mexico" (*International Journal of Mental Health* 19, no. 2); Martha Fernández, *Ciudad rota: La ciudad de México después del sismo* (Universidad Nacional Autónoma de México / Instituto de Investigaciones Estéticas); Carlos Monsiváis, *"No sin nosotros": Los días del terremoto, 1985–2005* (Ediciones Era); Eugenia Allier Montaño, "Memorias imbricadas: Terremotos en México, 1985 y 2017" (*Revista Mexicana de Sociología* 80); Elena Poniatowska, *Nothing, Nobody: The Voices of the Mexico City Earthquake* (Temple University Press).

This work contributes to a growing body of anthropological scholarship on coercive addiction treatment centers across the globe: Kevin Lewis O'Neill, *Hunted: Predation and Pentecostalism in Guatemala* (University of Chicago

Press); Anna Pagano et al., "Sociopolitical Contexts for Addiction Recovery: Anexos in U.S. Latino Communities" (*International Journal of Drug Policy* 37); Eugene Raikhel, *Governing Habits: Treating Alcoholism in the Post-Soviet Clinic* (Cornell University Press); and Claudia Rafful et al., "'Somebody Is Gonna Be Hurt': Involuntary Drug Treatment in Mexico" (*Medical Anthropology* 39, no. 2). There are numerous reports and opinion pieces that emphasize the illicit and dangerous nature of anexos and other coercive drug treatment centers in Latin America. Among these are Ralf Jürgens and Joanne Csete, "In the Name of Treatment: Ending Abuses in Compulsory Drug Detention Centers" (*Addiction* 107, no. 4); International Drug Policy Consortium, "Compulsory Rehabilitation in Latin America: An Unethical, Inhumane and Ineffective Practice"; and Open Society Foundations, *Treated with Cruelty: Abuses in the Name of Drug Rehabilitation*. Stanley Brandes's seminal work *Staying Sober in Mexico City* (University of Texas Press) is a key reference for the culture of alcoholism in Mexico.

The philosophical work of Jean-Luc Nancy has been a vital resource for my thinking about the kinds of relations that develop within anexos, particularly *The Sense of the World* (University of Minnesota Press), *Listening* (Fordham University Press), *Being Singular Plural* (Stanford University Press), and *The Inoperative Community* (University of Minnesota Press). Other philosophical texts that guide this book's analytical currents include Gaston Bachelard, *The Poetics of Space* (Beacon Press); Roland Barthes, *How to Live Together: Novelistic Simulations of Some Everyday Spaces* (Columbia University Press); Maurice Blanchot, *The Unavowable Community* (Station Hill Press) and *The Writing of the Disaster* (University of Nebraska Press); Simone de Beauvoir, *The Ethics of Ambiguity* (Open Road Media); Judith Butler, *Precarious Life: The Powers of Mourning and Violence* (Verso) and *Giving an Account of Oneself* (Fordham University Press); Adriana Cavarero, *Relating Narratives: Storytelling and Selfhood* (Routledge); Anne Dufourmantelle, *Power of Gentleness: Meditations on the Risk of Living* (Fordham University Press); Georges Didi-Huberman, *Survival of the Fireflies* (University of Minnesota Press); and Primo Levi, *The Drowned and the Saved* (Simon & Schuster). Cristina Rivera Garza's *Grieving: Dispatches from a Wounded Country* (Feminist Press) and

The Restless Dead: Necrowriting and Disappropriation (Vanderbilt University Press) are inspirations and ethical guides for my own writing.

Ethnographies on precarious social worlds that have helped shaped some of the analytic currents of this book include Anne Allison, *Precarious Japan* (Duke University Press); Javier Auyero, *Patients of the State: The Politics of Waiting in Argentina* (Duke University Press); João Biehl, *Vita: Life in a Zone of Social Abandonment* (University of California Press); Veena Das, *Affliction: Health, Disease, Poverty* (Fordham University Press); Robert Desjarlais, *Shelter Blues: Sanity and Selfhood among the Homeless* (University of Pennsylvania Press); Didier Fassin, *Prison Worlds: An Ethnography of the Carceral Condition* (Polity); Clara Han, *Life in Debt: Times of Care and Violence in Neoliberal Chile* (University of California Press); Michael Jackson, *Lifeworlds: Essays in Existential Anthropology* (University of Chicago Press); Shahram Khosravi, *Precarious Lives: Waiting and Hope in Iran* (University of Pennsylvania Press); Julie Livingston, *Improvising Medicine: An African Oncology Ward in an Emerging Cancer Epidemic* (Duke University Press); Elizabeth A. Povinelli, *Economies of Abandonment: Social Belonging and Endurance in Late Liberalism* (Duke University Press); and Lisa Stevenson, *Life Beside Itself: Imagining Care in the Canadian Arctic* (University of California Press). Similarly, the field of feminist care ethics has inspired and influenced my thinking around care as a practice and politics. See Carol Gillian, *In a Different Voice: Psychological Theory and Women's Development* (Harvard University Press); Virginia Held, ed., *Justice and Care: Essential Readings in Feminist Ethics* (Routledge); Eva Feder Kittay, *Love's Labor: Essays on Women, Equality, and Dependency* (Routledge); Eva Feder Kittay and Ellen K. Feder, eds., *The Subject of Care: Feminist Perspectives on Dependency* (Rowman and Littlefield); Audre Lorde, *A Burst of Light: And Other Essays* (Ixia Press); Joan C. Tronto, *Moral Boundaries: A Political Argument for an Ethic of Care* (Routledge).

Visual artists offer another perspective from which to comprehend the toll that violence has taken on Mexico and its citizens. A selection of artists whose work powerfully evokes violence and bears witness to its victims include Herman Aguirre, Francis Alÿs, Edgardo Aragón, Miguel A. Aragón,

Rigoberto A. Gonzalez, Teresa Margolles, Luz María Sánchez, and Marcela Rico. For work on art's ability to express and create new social and political realities, see Arthur C. Danto, *The Transfiguration of the Commonplace: A Philosophy of Art* (Harvard University Press); Jacques Rancière, *Dissensus: On Politics and Aesthetics* (Bloomsbury Academic); Gianni Vattimo, *Art's Claim to Truth* (Columbia University Press); and Santiago Zabala, *Why Only Art Can Save Us: Aesthetics and Absence of Emergency* (Columbia University Press). Martín Ramírez's motifs and narrative elements have influenced the way that I understand experiences of confinement and creativity. For work on Ramírez, see Víctor M. Espinosa, *Martín Ramírez: Framing His Life and Art* (University of Texas Press).

Some of the ideas and interlocutors presented in this book appear in the following publications: "Serenity: Violence, Inequality, and Recovery on the Edge of Mexico City" (*Medical Anthropology Quarterly* 29, no. 4); "Heaven" in *Unfinished: The Anthropology of Becoming*, ed. João Biehl and Peter Locke (Duke University Press); and "The Confessional Community: Narratives of Violence and Survival in Mexico City's Anexos" (*American Ethnologist*, forthcoming).

ACKNOWLEDGMENTS

I am forever grateful to the people in this book who shared something of their lives with me. I owe a debt of gratitude to Eric Chinski for finding me and believing in this book, to everyone at Farrar, Straus and Giroux, particularly Tara Sharma, and to Amy Medeiros for copyediting. I thank Rubén Martínez for his encouragement and guidance. For their support at different stages of research and writing of this book, I thank Carlos Zamudio, Mónica Martínez, Brian Anderson, Keith Humphreys, João Biehl, Tanya Luhrmann, Anne-christine d'Adesky, and Isela Aguilar. I am indebted to Elizabeth Roberts and Sandra Rozental for their careful and generous reading of early drafts. Thank you, dear friends, Tali Bray and Jaime Santos. And Ruby and Lucía . . . I thank you for everything.

INDEX

TK [allow 14 pages]